5 24
STAND PRICE
7 00
D1029456

Typography 21
The Annual of the TypeDirectorsClub

Adult dosage
The consumption of this book should be ... with precautionary measures. Our recommendation is a sporadic food with rousing interest.

Can be viewed 2-4 times daily by a person ... If symptoms persist consult your doctor.

Typography 21
The Annual of the TypeDirectorsClub

TDC 46+ P.001

QUALITY ASSURED

CONTENTS: The highest quality typographical work.

Information: The design of this product is intended to aid navigation of the work within.
Crafted with pride.

TypeDirectorsClub Acknowledgements

TDC 46+ P.004

First published in 2000 in the United States by HBI, an imprint of HarperCollins Publishers, Inc.
10 East 53rd Street
New York, NY 10022-5299

Distributed in the U.S. and Canada by Watson-Guptill Publications
770 Broadway
New York, NY 10003-9595
ISBN 0-8230-5555-8

Distributed throughout the rest of the world by HarperCollins International
10 East 53rd Street
New York, NY 10022-5299
Fax: 212-207-7654

ISBN 0-06-019892-3

The Library of Congress has cataloged this serial title as follows:
Typography
{Type Directors Club (U.S.)}
Typography: The Annual of the Type Directors Club.
New York:HBI
2000

Annual.

Typography (New York, NY)
1. Printing, Practical–Periodicals.
2. Graphic arts–periodicals.
3. Type Directors Club (U.S.)

Printed in Hong Kong by Everbest Printing Co. Ltd. through Four Colour Imports, Ltd., Louisville, Kentucky
Color Origination: Classicscan Pte Ltd (Singapore)
Paper: 128gsm Korean Matt Art

Acknowledgments
The Type Directors Club gratefully acknowledges the following for their support and contributions to the success of TDC46 and TDC² 2000:

Design & A/W: ATTIK
Aporva Baxi, Simon Dixon, Paul Driver, John O'Callaghan, David Rothblatt, Michael Spoljaric

Exhibition Facilities:
The Aronson Galleries, Parsons School of Design
Judging Facilities: School of Visual Arts
Chairpersons and Judges' Photos: Fran Collins

TDC46 Competition (call for entries):

Design: ATTIK. Paul Driver

Printer: The Hennegan Press
Paper: Fox River Paper Co.

TDC² 2000 Competition (call for entries):
Design: Linda Florio Design
Printer: Printing Methods, Inc.
Prepress: A to A Graphic Services, Inc.
Paper: Potlatch 70# Mountie Matte

The principal typeface used in the composition of TYPOGRAPHY 21 Akzidenz Grotesk BE.

Contents

TDC 46+ P.005

003 002 001 OPEN

FOLLOW RECOMMENDED INSTITUTIONAL PROCEDURE.

MULTIPLE USE. 

when a word crosses the line, it becomes invincible

00 Susan Cotler-Block

TypeDirectorsClub
Chairman's Statement

TDC 46+ P.006

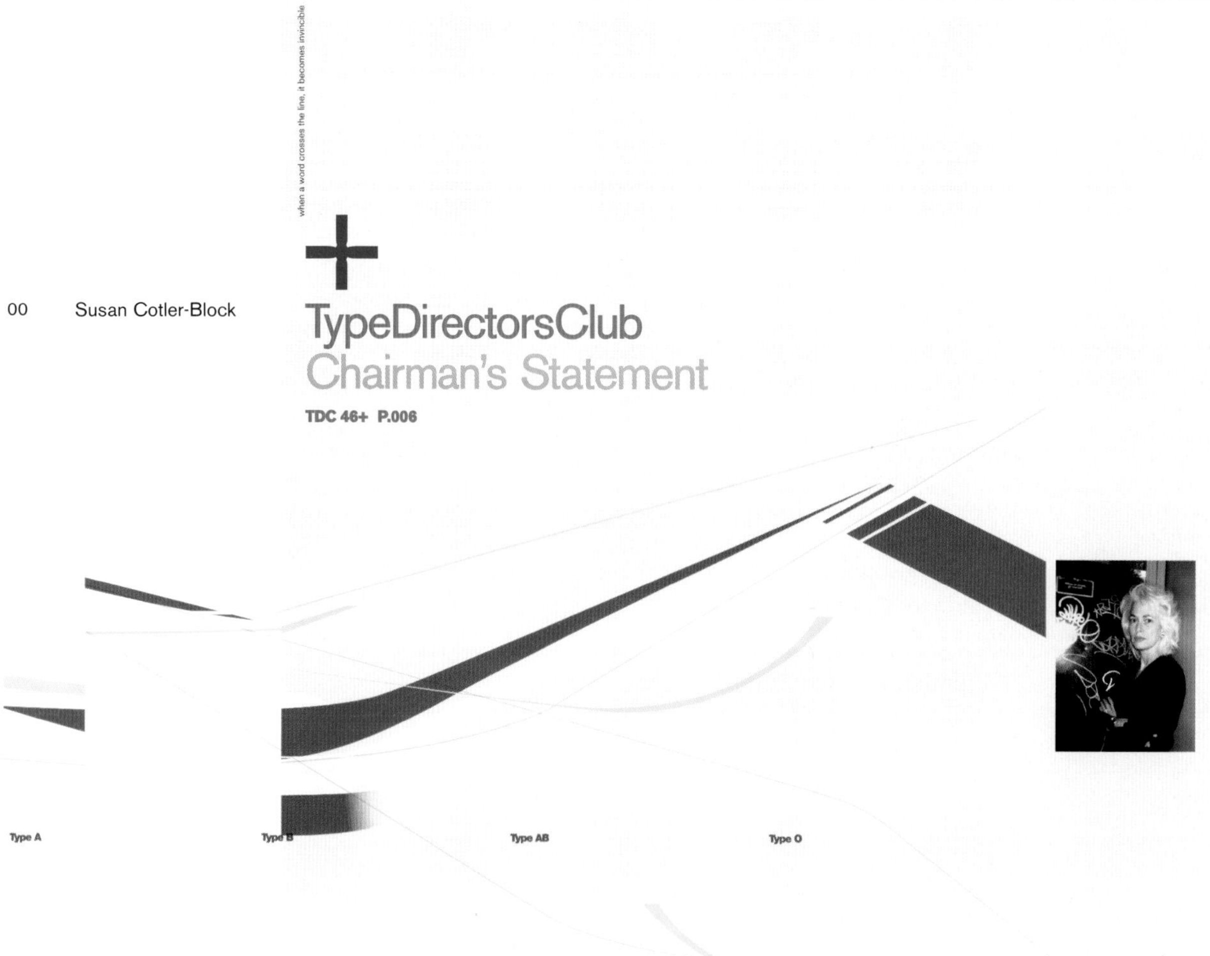

Type A

Type B

Type AB

Type O

To judge the 3,346 entries (from 33 countries) for TDC 46 and choose the winners for this competition, I selected a diverse team of judges whose work, for me, represents the standard by which typographic excellence should be measured. The judges were Bridget DeSocio, David Ellis, Chip Kidd, Lana Rigsby, Ina Saltz, James Sommerville and Anthony Vagnoni. I want to thank them all. The entrants for their entries, ATTIK for the design of the call, invitations, posters, certificates and annual, and the judges for throwing themselves into the task at hand, and though it was a daunting task, managing to maintain their high level of enthusiasm throughout a grueling two days of judging. The outcome seen here is a wondrous panorama, which chronicles the best of the best typographic design produced in the last year of the 20th century. These winning entries mark the end of an incredible era. Looking back on the 20th century, we see some amazing technological advances. My 89 year-old mother-in-law, who was born long before the invention of television, is so busy these days emailing everyone she knows, that she hardly has the time anymore, to spend on spinning wool (she no longer dyes her own), and knitting baby booties. She has essentially traded in her spinning wheel and knitting needles for her laptop! It truly is a "Brave New World". As we enter the new millennium, we do so with all the excitement and trepidation that is always created by a journey into the unknown. And, as an educator, I can only hope that this superb collection of typographic excellence will inspire the growth of future generations of designers, well into the 21st century.

Susan Cotler-Block is Chair of the Advertising Design Department (which includes Graphic and Packaging Design) at the Fashion Institute of Technology. She joined the faculty in 1977. Susan counts amongst her many accomplishments, the design of the current course in Publication Design (Magazine Editorial/Layout) in the BFA Program of the Advertising Design Department, and chairing the Advertising Design Department's Academic Standards Committee. Also, as a member of the Advertising Design Department's Curriculum Committee, Susan has been instrumental in shaping the AD/BFA program, by pioneering interdisciplinary assignments between the Photography, Illustration, and Advertising Design departments, adding Typography to the curriculum of the Foundation Year of the AD/AAS Degree program, and adding Web Design to the curriculum of the AD/BFA Degree Programs. Susan is currently adding an Evening/Weekend AD/BFA Degree program to FIT's many offerings. This program is scheduled to begin Fall 2000, and will afford working people the opportunity for higher education in the field of Graphic Design. A graduate of the School of Visual Arts, and the recipient of a full tuition scholarship from the School Art League, Susan has provided art direction for such organizations as Family Communications, Sterling Publications, Avon, MacFadden Bartell, Book-of-the-Month Club, the New York Health and Racquet Club, Hearst Publishing, Watson-Guptill, Ziff Davis, the Pablo Picasso Society, and the Erté Society. Susan is also the principal of Circle, Square and Triangle Graphic Designs, Inc., a niche advertising agency, specializing in print media. Currently, Susan is a member of the Board of Directors of the Type Directors Club and Chair of their Scholarship Committee. She is also a member of the New York Art Directors Club, the Society of Publication Designers, the Society of Illustrators, and the American Institute of Graphic Arts. Susan consistently introduces her students to the benefits of professional club membership through student attendance at speaker lectures and seminars. "Bringing student and industry together early on in the academic process, through professional societies and clubs, benefits everyone." In addition, Susan is a Fine Artist and has had her paintings shown in New York and London.

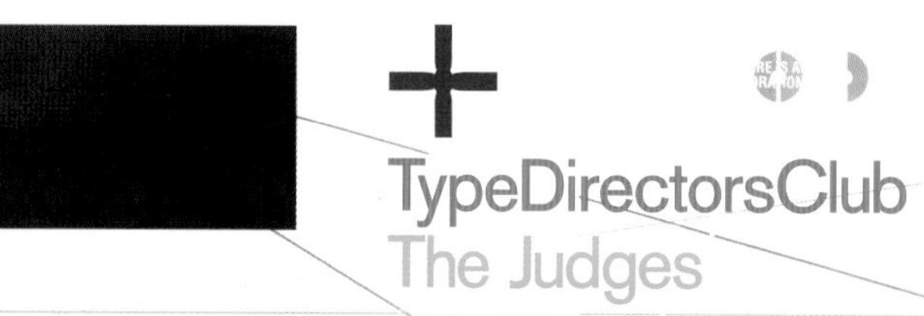

TypeDirectorsClub
The Judges

TDC 46+ P.008

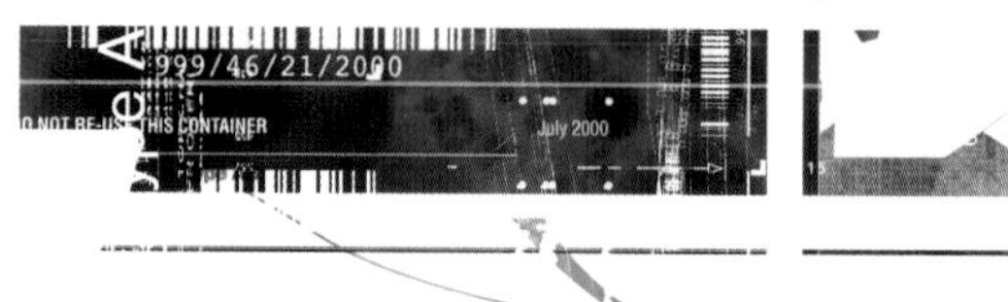

62599F-21-2000

OBJECTIVITY GUARANTEED

SECTION CONTAINS: 7 Judges' Biographies and Sample Work.

Judges: Bridget DeSocio David Ellis Chip Kidd Lana Rigsby
Ina Saltz James Sommerville Anthony Vagnoni

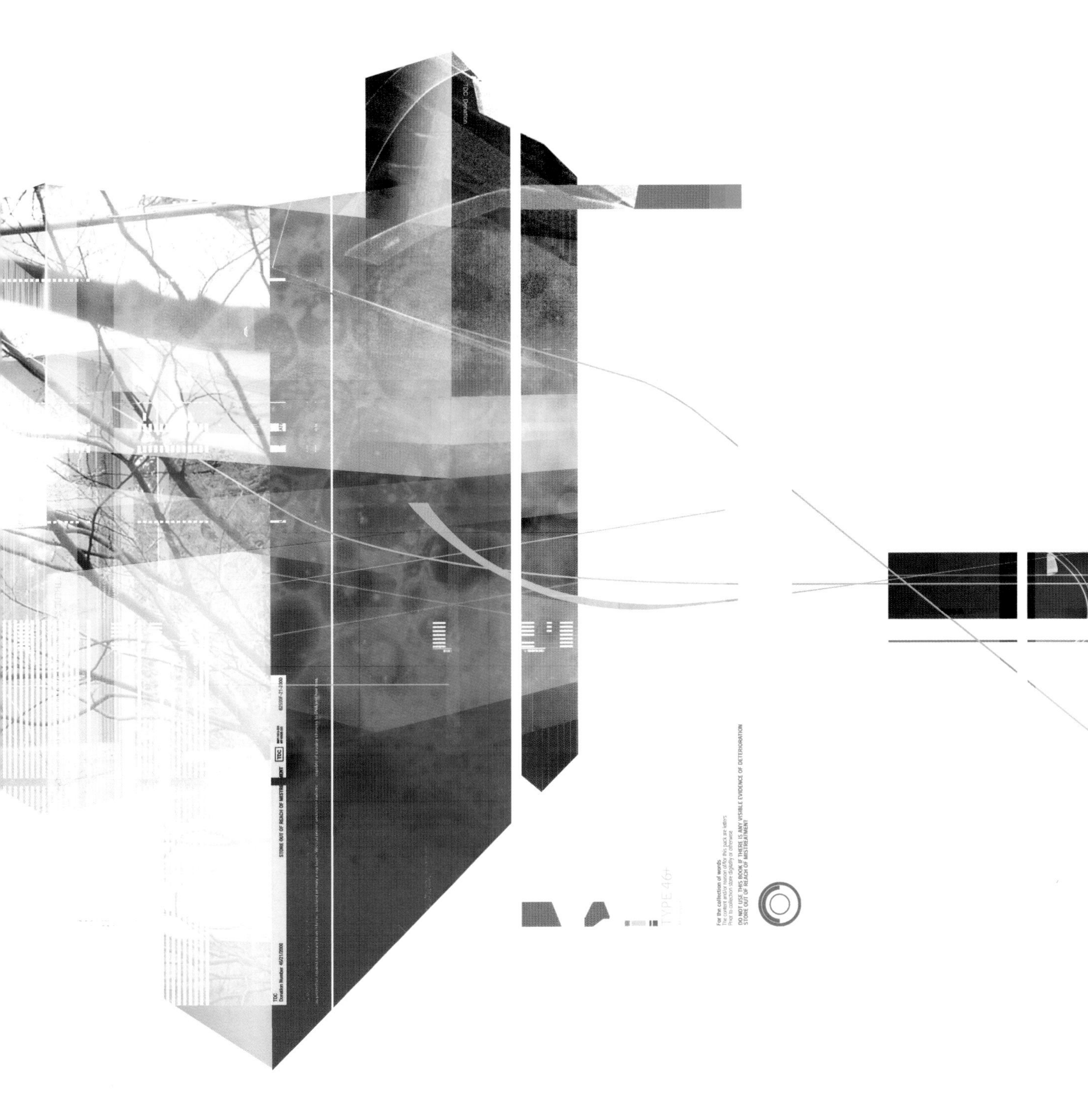

#	Name	Company / Location
J.01	Bridget DeSocio	Socio X New York
J.02	David Ellis	Why Not Associates London
J.03	Chip Kidd	Chip Kidd Design New York

\# Name Company Location

Art Director of Extremes has a passion for the visual culture in all its varied forms from *PAPER Magazine* to *Town & Country* or Cone Denim to Vera Wang. More than simply a graphic designer, Bridget's interest in the meaning of the signs and symbols that surround us makes her a cultural critic extraordinaire. DeSocio bills herself not as a graphic designer, which she is by trade, but as a semiologist, motivating desire, studying the commercial why. Fueled by social purpose, DeSocio is a designer manqué. Her clients are paying her as much for her Toffler instincts as for her trademark tech-with-taste work. "We get approached by people who want to take a new look at the classics as well as a classic look at the new." Socio X, the three-year-old design firm in New York, founded by Bridget DeSocio, boasts an impressive client roster, which includes cultural icons such as Kodak, Palm Pilot, Vera Wang, Cone Denim, Pantone, *PAPER Magazine*, *Town & Country* Magazine, Saks Fifth Avenue, David Byrne, Island Records, Rizzoli and Hermés. In just a short time Socio X has gained international attention and praise from design industry institutions such as The New York Art Directors Club, Type Directors Club, Society of Publication Designers, *Communication Arts Magazine* and *Print Magazine*. *ID Magazine* and *Graphis Magazine* have both ranked the firm among the top ten in the design field. Her work has been exhibited by the Cooper-Hewitt Museum, and twice included in the New York Art Directors Club's YOUNG GUNS exhibition. She has been an influence to sub-culture kids, skate culture and gen Xers for over ten years as a result of her on-going relationship as Creative Director of New York City's *PAPER Magazine* (consistently known for its ever-changing logo, which has never appeared the same twice).

David Ellis set up Why Not Associates with Andrew Altmann after graduation from the Royal College of Art in 1987. Since then they have lectured in England, Germany, France, Holland, Switzerland, Japan, America, and Australia. They have designed exhibition material for various clients including the ICA, the Foreign and Commonwealth Office, Pompidou Centre, Royal Academy of Arts, Natural History Museum, and the DTI, and have designed postage stamps and booklets for the Royal Mail. Why Not Associates directed television and film titles including a ppb [what's that? "paid political broadcast," maybe?] for the Labour Party shortly before the last election. They produced two-, three-, & four-dimensional work for clients including Antony Gormley, the Barbican Centre, One Telecom, Branson Coates, Virgin Records, Chiat/Day, Adidas, BBC, Bellsouth, Branson Coates Architecture, British Telecom, Channel 4, the Design Museum, the Green Party, *Shots* magazine, Hull City Council, the ICA, Internos Books, Kobe Fashion Museum, Lancaster City Council, Midland Bank, the Next Directory, Oilily, the Royal Academy of Arts, Renault, Smirnoff, *Time* magazine, *Upper and lowercase* magazine, and Weiden & Kennedy. David Ellis has fathered several children. [Or does he mean that why not, collectively, have fathered several children? Originally it was just "Fathered several children," which is completely ambiguous. You'll have to ask him. If it's they, collectively, then say, "Why Not Associates have..." and begin the next sentence, "David Ellis is currently designing:..."] He is currently designing: a 300-metre typographic pavement of bird literature in Morecambe, a book for architect Nigel Coates, Euro 2000 films for Nike, and an e-commerce issue of *Time* magazine.

A graphic designer and writer in New York City. His book jacket designs for Alfred A. Knopf (where he has worked for over thirteen years) have helped spawn a revolution in the art of American book packaging. His work has been featured in *Vanity Fair*, The Graphic Edge (by Rick Poyner), *Eye*, *Print* (cover story), *Entertainment Weekly*, *The New Republic*, *Time*, *The New York Times*, *Graphis*, *New York* and *ID* magazine. The latter chose him as part of its first *ID* 40 group of the nation's top designers and has awarded him "Best of Category, Packaging" twice. In 1997, he received the International Center of Photography's award for Use of Photography in Graphic Design, and he is a regular contributor of visual commentary to the Op-Ed page of *The New York Times*. In 1998, he was made a member of the Alliance Graphique Internationale (AGI). His designs have been described as "monstrously ugly" (John Updike), "apparently obvious" (William Boyd), "faithful flat-earth rendering" (Don DeLillo), "surprisingly elegant" (A.S. Mehta), "a distinguished parochial comic balding Episcopal priest" (Allan Gurganus), "two colors plus a sash" (Martin Amis), and "not a piece of hype. My book was lucky." (Robert Hughes). Mr. Kidd has also written about graphic design and popular culture for *Vogue*, *The New York Observer*, *Entertainment Weekly*, *Details*, *2WICE*, *The New York Post*, *ID* and *Print*. He has authored Batman Collected (Bulfinch, 1996), in which he attempts to rid himself of his inner demons. To no avail—he is co-author and designer of the subsequent Batman Animated (HarperCollins, Fall 1998).

J.01 J.02 J.03

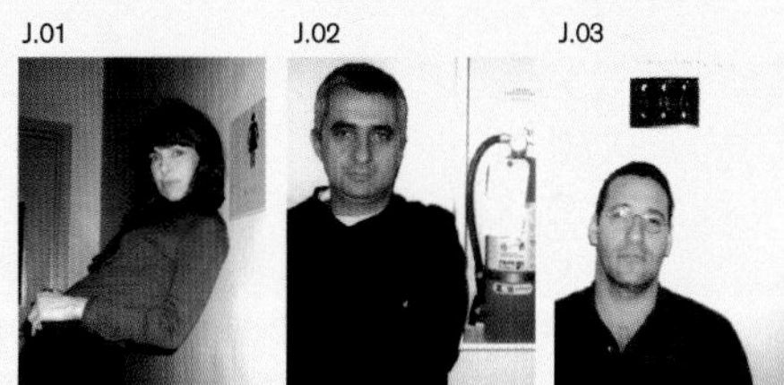

#	Name	Company / Location
J.04	Lana Rigsby	Rigsby Design Texas
J.05	Ina Saltz	Golf Magazine New York
J.06	James Sommerville	ATTIK Huddersfield
J.07	Anthony Vagnoni	Young & Rubicam New York

Name Company
Location

Lana Rigsby is principal of Rigsby Design, a Texas-based firm known for creating engaging, intelligent communications for a diversity of organizations. Her firm's work includes branding, corporate identity, and web site development for such companies as Dell Computers, Weyerhaeuser, Mohawk Paper Mills, American Oncology Resources, and the Earth Technology Corporation. Rigsby has edited and designed three comprehensive volumes on annual-report design: Graphis International Annual Reports volumes 5, 6, and 7. She co-chaired the AIGA's 1998 business conference, Brandesign. Her work has been consistently recognized in the most respected national and international design forums, including Communication Arts, Graphis, the New York Art Directors Club, the AIGA, and the Type Directors Club; it is included in the Cooper-Hewitt National Design Museum's exhibition "Mixing Messages: Graphic Design in Contemporary Culture." Lana has lectured on design throughout the U.S., and serves as a national director for the American Institute of Graphic Arts.

Ina Saltz is the Design Director of Golf Magazine which has a circulation of 1.5 million. Ina has previously art-directed Time magazine's International Edition, Worth, Golf for Women, Worldbusiness, PC Tech Journal, High School Sports, and Home Video magazines; she has been a consulting art director at Business Week and The New York Times Magazine; her redesign projects include the Dow Jones Investment and the Hamilton Alumni Review. Ina was one of the first art directors to work on a computer, in 1981, where she created animated graphics as part of Time Inc.'s Teletext Project, a precursor of the World Wide Web. She is a member of the design faculty of the Stanford Professional Publishing Course and a member of the board of the Type Directors Club as well as of the Society of Publication Designers. Ina graduated from the Cooper Union for the Advancement of Science and Art in New York City, where she studied painting and calligraphy. She is on the Alumni Council at Cooper Union, and she completed several terms on its Executive Board.

James Sommerville [Hon DLitt], co-founder of ATTIK, was born and raised in the North of England in Huddersfield, West Yorkshire. After graduating from Batley Art and Film School, he opened a graphic design studio at age 19 in his grandma's attic bedroom, with college friend Simon Needham. Since then, James has been a major force in positioning ATTIK as one of the world's most innovative group of people, now with further offices in London, New York, San Francisco and Sydney. In his drive to push new avenues of business and creativity, James developed creative solutions for local, regional and national brands, established himself as a commercial director and filmed a short documentary–Negative Forces, Witchcraft and Idolatry. As well as continuing to direct, James now takes on the global role of overseeing the development of ATTIK's strategic brand and business positioning throughout all five offices. Recently, James sat on the panel of the 'Labour Government Internet Inquiry' and has been requested by HRH The Prince of Wales Trust to become an advisor to The Princes' Youth Business Trust. James and ATTIK have also been awarded the BACC Transatlantic Entrepreneurial Business Award 2000 for their outstanding contributions to strengthening the vital economic relationship between the UK and US. This year, the University of Huddersfield presented James with the Degree of Honorary Doctor of Letters to formally recognize an 'outstanding global creative business success'.

Anthony Vagnoni is the publicity director for creative work at Young & Rubicam Inc. In this role he is responsible for raising the profile of the creative work of the various Y&R companies. Prior to joining Y&R in January of 2000, he was an editor at large for *Advertising Age*, where he covered a wide range of issues and trends that affected advertising and marketing. He joined *Ad Age* in September of 1997 from Creativity magazine, *Ad Age's* glossy publication devoted to examining the best new creative work in print and broadcast advertising. Anthony joined Creativity in 1990 as managing editor, and was named editor the following year. A native of Washington, D.C., Anthony graduated from New York University with a Bachelor of Fine Arts degree in film and television. He lives a pastoral life in the Jersey suburbs with his two young daughters.

J.04 J.05 J.06 J.07

J.01 Bridget DeSocio
J.02 David Ellis
J.03 Chip Kidd

+

TypeDirectorsClub
Judges' Work

TDC 46+ P.014

J.01

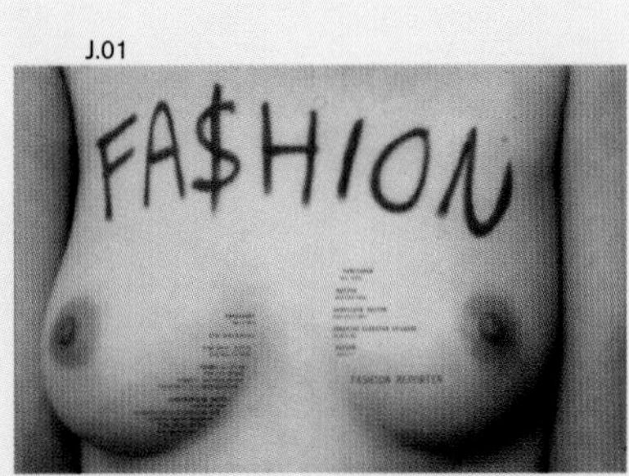

J.02

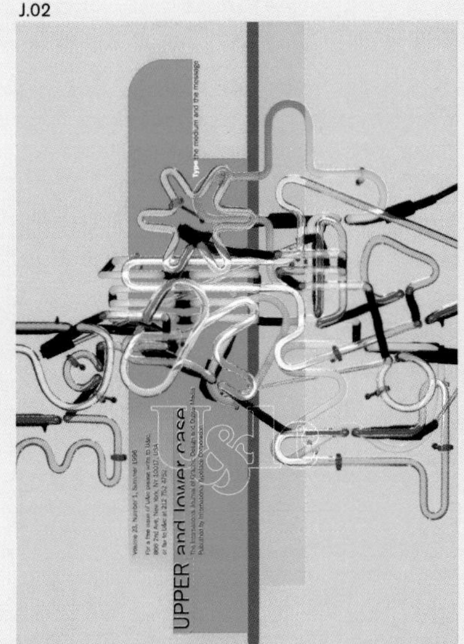

J.03

MULTIPLE VIEWING RECOMMENDED.

J.04	Lana Rigsby
J.05	Ina Saltz
J.06	James Sommerville
J.07	Anthony Vagnoni

+
TypeDirectorsClub
Judges' Work

J.04

J.05

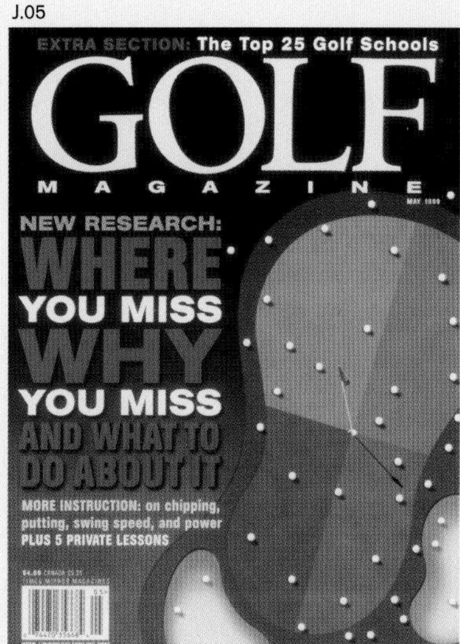

J.06

J.07

TypeDirectorsClub
The Judges' Choices and Designers' Statements

TDC 46+ P.018

QUALITY ASSURED

SECTION CONTAINS: 7 Judges' Choices, Work and Statements.

Judges Choices: Bridget DeSocio/Bill Cahan David Ellis/Antje Hedde Chip Kidd/B.J. Krivanek Lana Rigsby/Design: M/W Ina Saltz/Werner Schneider James Sommerville/Jennifer Sterling Anthony Vagnoni/Bill Douglas

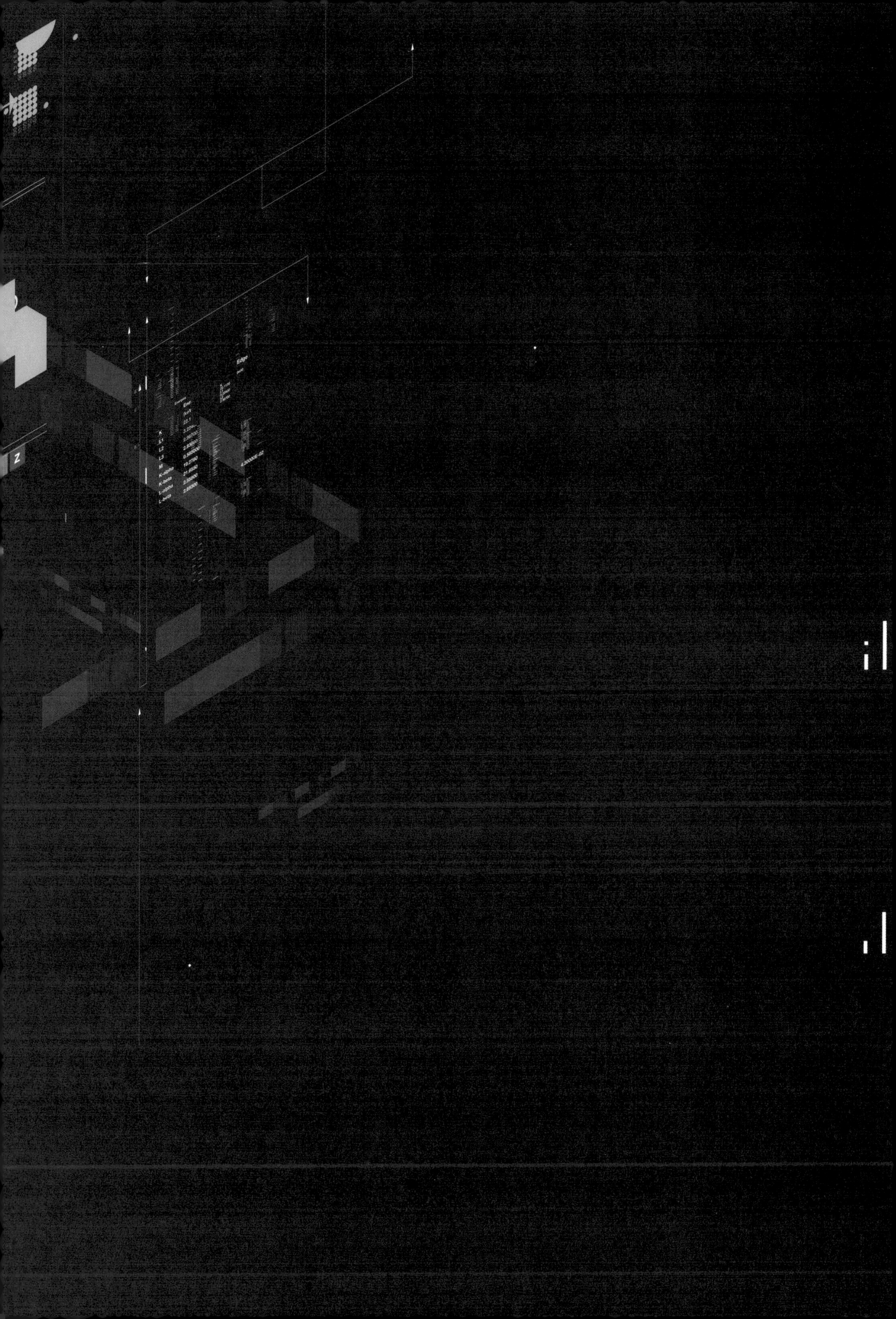

Annual Report

Design_Bob Dinetz,
San Francisco, California
Art Direction_Bill Cahan

Creative Direction_Bill Cahan
Copywriters_Thom Elkjer and
Bob Dinetz
Design Office_Cahan & Associates
Client_General Magic

Principal Type_Akzidenz Grotesk

Dimensions_5½ x 7½ in. (14 x 19.1 cm)

J.01 Bridget DeSocio

D.01.5 Bill Cahan

Name

AUDIOVISUAL and MULTILINGUAL. If talk is type in the auditory realm. This piece's plain and simple use of words streaming across the mouths of multi-culti heads all aligned on a fold out format ~50 feet long says so much about what type means deeply. It means sound in the mouth and it means language to the eye and it means interaction. Today it ALSO means global communication in a non-language-specific way. This piece is not about fonts, nor is it about surface materials, e.g., paper, printing inks, or spot varnishes. It is about a world-wide commonality, intuitive communication, speech enabling technology and a non-linguistic-dependent interface. I am not implying that typography is passé or that intuitive computing via speech enabling technology is what is NOW, I am merely saying that a great piece is intuitively made and formed from a direct, languageless approach to design. You should understand the content without having to search for the subtext... A great piece of typography works without language, just as computing will eventually work without a keyboard.

Though General Magic has unique technologies and interesting products, what seemed most compelling was simply the idea of your own voice being the next interface with the digital environment. Ironically, people have always tried to control their televisions, cars and computers by speaking to them. Now, General Magic wants to make the human voice the logical replacement for the graphical user interface (GUI). We made a case for voice as the most natural way to communicate throughout the world. Rather than confine the message to a narrow application or product, it was this broad idea that would be associated with General Magic.

Book

Design_Antje Hedde, London, England
Lettering_Antje Hedde
Art Direction_Antje Hedde

Creative Direction_Kurt Georg Dieckert and Stefan Schmidt
Photography_Julian Broad, Colin Gray, Mischa Haller, Martin Parr and Terry Richardson
Agency_Springer & Jacoby International, London
Client_DaimlerChrysler AG

Principal Type_Various

Dimensions_5 15/16 x 8 1/4 in. (15 x 21 cm)

J.02 David Ellis

D.02.5 Antje Hedde

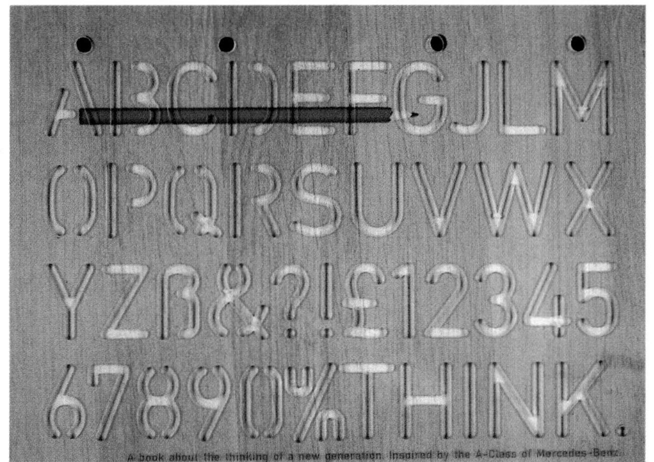

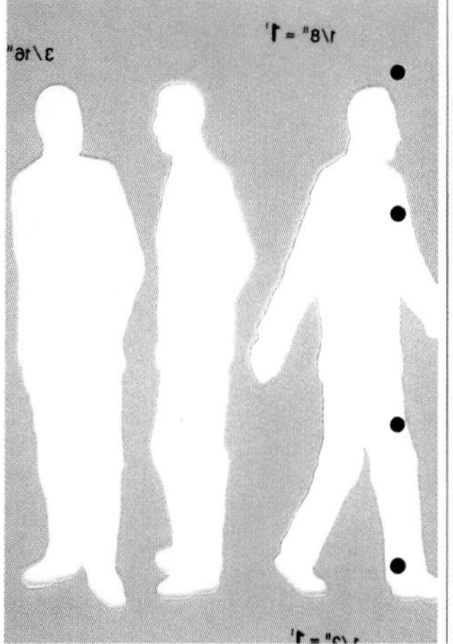

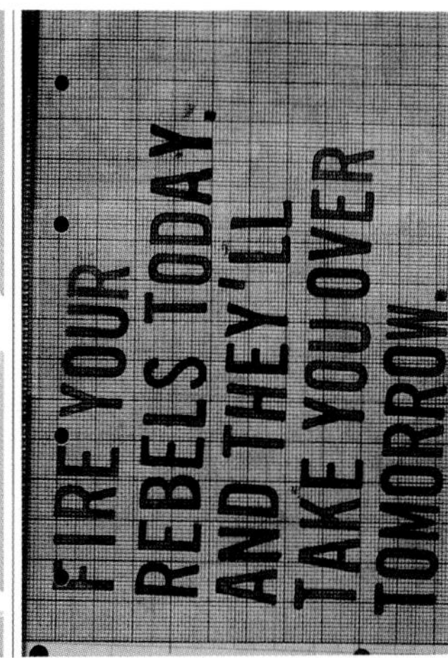

Every year there is a lot of great work entered for the Type Directors Club awards, and this year is no exception. However, within all that excellence there are occasional pieces that really make me excited. And what they have in common is that they have broken out of their market definitions. This takes balls. There are many examples of thought-provoking, cutting-edge new design on show this year, but not many of them are for such a mainstream blue-chip company as Mercedes-Benz. Hats off to Antje Hedde at Springer & Jacoby for the book to mark the launch of the Mercedes A-class. Not many people would even attempt to produce such an arresting design for this kind of client. Most designers would assume that contemporary design, utilitarian binding techniques, edgy typography, and oblique imagery would be outside the realm acceptable to Mercedes-Benz. For me, this book is a million times more adventurous and exciting than any style magazine or music CD package you care to mention. Top notch.

Our lives are guided by so many rules that external pressures constrict our way of thinking. But who's to say that a room should have four walls, that a bicycle should have two wheels, that a Mercedes should always look like a Mercedes? This is exactly the reason why the founders of the car built the A-class. It is the result of a new thinking generation. Whilst the A-class was being developed, S&J also had to devise a new method of communication, which meant breaking with convention and has resulted in the production of this book, showing the thoughts of a new generation. These thoughts are presented typographically with items taken from a sub-culture which the new generation come into contact within everyday life. The use of grey as a background colour on the right page is still a link to Mercedes-Benz CI. This book has been written and designed for those who do not want to be part of the mainstream.

Design_ Community Architexts, Chicago, Illinois
Art Direction_B.J. Krivanek

Outdoor Environment

Photography_ Edward Lines, Jr.
Witnesses and Writers_ Halyna Boyko-Hrushetsky, Ivan Kolomayets, Lydia Kurylak, Lena Schrebetz-Skyba, and Sinovi Turkalo
Program Director_ Jennifer Van Winkle
Design Assistant_ Cynthia Perkin
Researcher_ Karla Roberts

Principal Type_ Futura Heavy and Matrix Bold

Funders_ Chicago Department of Cultural Affairs, Gaylord & Dorothy Donnelley Foundation, and Illinois Arts Council

J.03 Chip Kidd

D.03.5 B.J. Krivanek

In the interest of full disclosure, I have to say: for me it was a toss-up between two outstanding entries. The commercial for Tide detergent by Imaginary Forces (which I assume is elsewhere in this tome–check it out) is truly astonishing on more than one level: it's not only technically masterful in a way I've never before seen; it's original, ground-breaking work commissioned by, of all people, Proctor and Gamble (!). Just picturing what the agency must have gone through to get it approved makes me want to weep openly, and at the same time gives me a vicarious sense of hope. The other submission that I kept returning to is called "Witnesses," a project out of California State University that explored the experiences of local Ukrainian village survivors of the 1932–33 Ukrainian famine, and compared them to those of today's suburban Chicago schoolchildren. Statements were taken from both parties, typeset (handsome, bold, blocky Futura–readable on any surface), and projected onto buildings that faced each other across a campus street. The result was a conversation that spanned space and time as dramatically as it spanned generations, and all on a scale that was truly impossible to ignore. Ultimately, I had to cast a blind eye to Form and base my decision on Content. That is: I ignored what the typography of both looked like and let their words speak to me. That is after all, what type is for. After that it was easy–"Learn from History" vs. "Buy more Tide." No contest.

This multi-disciplinary site activation involved the projection of large-scale texts onto two buildings which face each other across Chicago Avenue. These dynamic, historic billboards suggest a dialogue between factions in the Ukrainian Village community–elderly survivors of the 1932-33 Ukrainian Famine (Us) and outsiders such as Soviet officials and recent Latino immigrants (Them) represented by the voices of Soviet propaganda and local Chicago schoolchildren. This site work explored the commodification of land, crops, labor, real estate, and history itself, while drawing parallels between the historic genocide and the contentious survival of urban children. The texts incorporated into this site activation were created and collected during outreach workshops conducted at the Ukrainian Cultural Center and Ellen Mitchell Public School in the Ukrainian Village.

Catalog

Design_Allison Williams, Mats Hakansson, Yael Eisele, Abby Clawson, and J.P. Williams, New York, New York
Art Direction_Allison Williams

Photography_Gentl + Hyers and Geof Kern
Studio_Design: M/W
Client_Takashimaya New York

Principal Type_Helvetica Neue

Dimensions_9 x 9 in. (22.9 x 22.9 cm)

J.04 Lana Rigsby

D.04.5 M/W

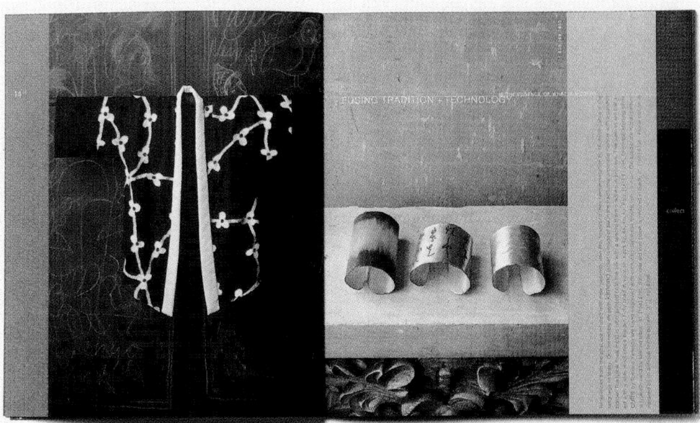

Takashimaya's most recent holiday book by Design: M/W embodies all the values that make this firm's work so deliciously special. There's no Big Idea, just lots of small ideas that are honestly conceived and lovingly, immaculately executed–that combine to create a piece that radiates purity and authenticity. At first glance, this small book is simple, clean, classic. But on closer inspection, there's a lot going on: subtle variations in typography that give emphasis to words and ideas; patterns and textures that add emotional shadings; photographic treatments that give each page a unique point of interest. All of this is managed within the sparest palette of color and typefaces. As I turned this book over and over, discovering something new each time, I kept thinking it met Albert Einstein's definition of essentiality: "things should be as simple as possible. But no simpler."

Takashimaya New York is a retail store selling unique merchandise created by artisans throughout the world. This holiday mailer, the sixth in the series created by M/W, builds upon the monochromatic palette of colors and myriad textures throughout the store. The mailer is divided into three sections: "crave" (food related), "covet" (jewelry and accessories), and "collect" (decorative home). The photography and layouts in each section reflect the subject matter; crave/food is warm and calm, covet/jewelry is eclectic, and collect/home is shot in natural surroundings in a landscape format.

Cards

Design_Werner Schneider, Bad Laasphe, Germany

Calligraphy_Werner Schneider

Principal Type_Schneider-Antiqua

Dimensions_8¼ x 11$^{11}/_{16}$ in. (21 x 29.7 cm)

J.05 Ina Saltz

D.05.5 Werner Schneider

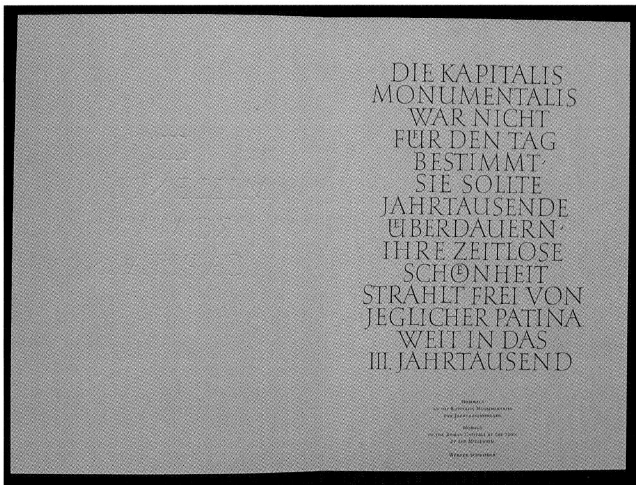

After reviewing thousands and thousands of wonderful (and some not-so-wonderful) entries, there were so many clever possibilities. I especially admired the fabulously overworked and eyeball-jarring Japanese posters, some with fluorescent velvets and rubberized flocking; I also loved the self-ironic Fifties-era packaging with their winking posterpaint silkscreen effects...but when the time came to choose one piece, this serenely classical work of exquisitely hand lettered Roman majescules sang out to me from amidst the cacophony. Werner Schneider's masterful touch is something to be treasured forever...after all, these shapes were written out directly and fluidly with wet ink filling a broad-edged dip pen, not chosen from a pre-existing drawn font. Each letter is a unique original; each required the full attention and focus of its maker at the exact moment of its making. Schneider's piece is designed with a modern sensibility yet with an understanding of the rich history of Roman capitals from the era of classical antiquity. The quiet dignity of his presentation enhances the meaning of the text (a paean to the immutability of traditional forms); yet upon close inspection, one can detect a playfulness about the baseline and the inset characters. The power of Schneider's artwork does not depend on gimmickry, loud color, gigantic size, or attention-grabbing imagery. In the simplest of terms, blind embossing and black and white, its surpassing beauty is undeniable. Let us never forget the debt of gratitude that all typography owes its predecessor, lettering done utterly by hand.

Speaking of myself, refined forms have been my best teacher for my work as a type designer, above all Roman Capitals. Looking at the inscription on the Trajan Column awakens in me again and again a strong aesthetic feeling and fills me with a sense of deep respect. These nearly perfect forms and their qualities could not be improved upon during the 2000 years of their existence. In my reverence (admiration) for the form qualities of the Roman Caps I always try to give new expressions to these shapes. For the understanding of form writing and drawing are the most important prerequisites. Only proficiency here guarantees a solid foundation for computerized type. For the embossed letterforms I already have design concept as a typeface. Translation of the text from the inner side: "The Roman Capitals were not intended for the day. They were to last the centuries. Their timeless beauty shines free from any patina far into the third millennium."

J.06 James Sommerville

D.06.5 Jennifer Sterling

Brochure

Design_Jennifer Sterling and Venus D'Amore, San Francisco, California
Art Direction_Jennifer Sterling
Creative Direction_Jennifer Sterling

Photography_John Casado
Design Office_Jennifer Sterling Design
Client_Consolidated Papers

Principal Type_OCRB, Frutiger, Futura Medium, and Not Caslon

Dimensions_9 x 12 in. (22.9 x 30.5 cm)

Name

There was some excellent work in and amongst the masses, and several pieces that interested me for different reasons. In fact, when I started to search for a single piece of work to be chosen as "my favorite" it was both interesting and fun–recycled and spat back out as difficult. To top that, I had to write a 250 word statement. I haven't written one of those since juvenile court in the early 80's. At this moment in my life, I've gone full circle in many ways and I am biased towards what I studied at school–print design. This is most likely due to the dot-com, convergent world we now live in. A world where traditional approaches to typography are being molested and "bashed out" via high powered machines that sometimes go so fast they don't remind the designer of basic fundamentals of good type–balance, structure, composition and [the sometimes never seen these days] attention to detail. The piece I finally chose, from Jennifer Sterling, had all of those elements and more. The brochure shows genuine experimentation of typography, coupled with a classic appreciation of what good type still stands for. The text and visual timeline of each spread creates focus, leading my eye through the brochure. I knew where I was, what I should look at and in what order–which is the basis of all successful communication. From a visual point of view, the full-page photography was interesting and didn't detract from the written word, but instead created visual layers and a good hierarchy of information.
Does she want a job at ATTIK?

When Consolidated Paper came to me to design their upcoming paper brochure there were few restrictions. It had to be 9 x 12" in form, and it must contain the copy provided. The copy is a wonderful narrative written on the subject of time. Originally written for the Smithsonian, it wraps the facts of time. One year (i.e. "the year of confusion") was actually 15 months long, or when the people of the time went to sleep one day only to awaken on a day that was 11 days later according to the calendar. The other restriction was that it contain absolutely no sex, drugs or religion. It was a bit difficult to discard the religion issue. After all A.D. and B.C. are not random acronyms. So I put the religion issue right up front. It is after all, how we mark time, so to discard it is more than silly it would be conceptually irresponsible. I felt the copy was wonderful yet I was hesitant to design a historical piece. The market was designers and too many of these historical pieces just get tossed. So, how to do a futuristic piece, particularly with the issue of clothes? Who knows what would be in style in 2020? We've all done the 60's, the 70's, the 80's, and the repetition happens so quickly, I imagine soon we'll all be doing tues @ 1:30. So I dressed the models in materials that relate to paper; Saran wrap, aluminum foil, rubber matting under carpets and hired John Casado to shoot it. The purpose of using these materials was to show materials that an uncoated sheet would be unable to accurately produce on press. A photo time line runs along the bottom indicating the shots you would see if it was filmed. The type runs horizontally to depict a standard calendar format, and numerous typographic dates from the story are pulled out and used as design elements.

Magazine

Design_Bill Douglas,
Toronto, Canada
Studio_The Bang

Client_Coupe

Principal Type_Trade Gothic,
Times New Roman, and Helvetica

Dimensions_9⅝ x 11½ in. (24.5 x 29.2 cm)

J.07 Anthony Vagnoni

D.07.5 Bill Douglas

Buried on the contents page of this issue of Coupe is the following observation: "We've been busy the final decade of the last thousand years huffing and puffing on the spiritual equivalent of some piece of shit stationary bicycle-slash-walking machine we purchased on a late-night infomercial while stuffing ourselves with low-fat baked Cheetos, madly pedaling, watching Springer with the headphones on while speed-reading The Celestine Prophecy." This single, ambulatory sentence summed up what I liked most about Coupe. A somewhat precious mix of art, photography, poetry, and attitude, Coupe defies conventions about the publishing business: quarterlies like this aren't supposed to exist in an age of global media consolidation. One would expect to find Coupe existing quietly as an obscure web site, yet here it is anyway, largely devoid of advertising and defiant in its anti-commercial stance. From a design standpoint, Coupe blithely ignores current trends in its ramrod use of a single font–in this issue it's Trade Gothic, seen in a relatively limited number of variations. The effect unifies the book, and makes each editorial segment merge with the one that follows. On top of that, it's immensely readable. Content here doesn't suffer from design prerogatives that value style over clarity. Overall, I was impressed by just how clear a view of itself Coupe seems to have. That they managed to maintain this at a time when publications around the world fell all over themselves chronicling the most over-hyped event of the last hundred years–the millennium!–speaks volumes to their cocky self-assurance.

Coupe is both a commentary on, and a reaction to the information age we live in. Featured on the cover of Coupe 2 is a 220 word text block set a la legal fine print describing in detail what awaits the reader on the inside. "Yes, we've added great new departments such as our sassy *"Who's Hot, Who's Not,"* where we tell you who's hot and who's not; and you'll love our new section called *"What's Hot, What's Not"*, where we tell you what's hot and what's not...In this issue we take an in-depth look at America's newest sweetheart, Britney Spears (pg. 147)". There is no Britney Spears interview. There isn't even a page 147. Instead, featured is the work of artists, photographers, and writers, printed using five colours on two different paper stocks and weights, melted down and melded together to create a singular work in which the past and future collide head-on.

Typography 21
The Annual of Typography
2121
TypeDirectorsClub
Selected Entries
TDC 46+ P.035

Design_Joe Scorsone and Alice Drueding
Jenkintown, Pennsylvania
Art Direction_Joe Scorsone

Design Office_Scorsone/Drueding

Principal Type_Monoline Script, Schwere, and Franklin Gothic Extra Condensed

Dimensions_30 11/16 x 22 13/16 in. (78 x 58 cm)

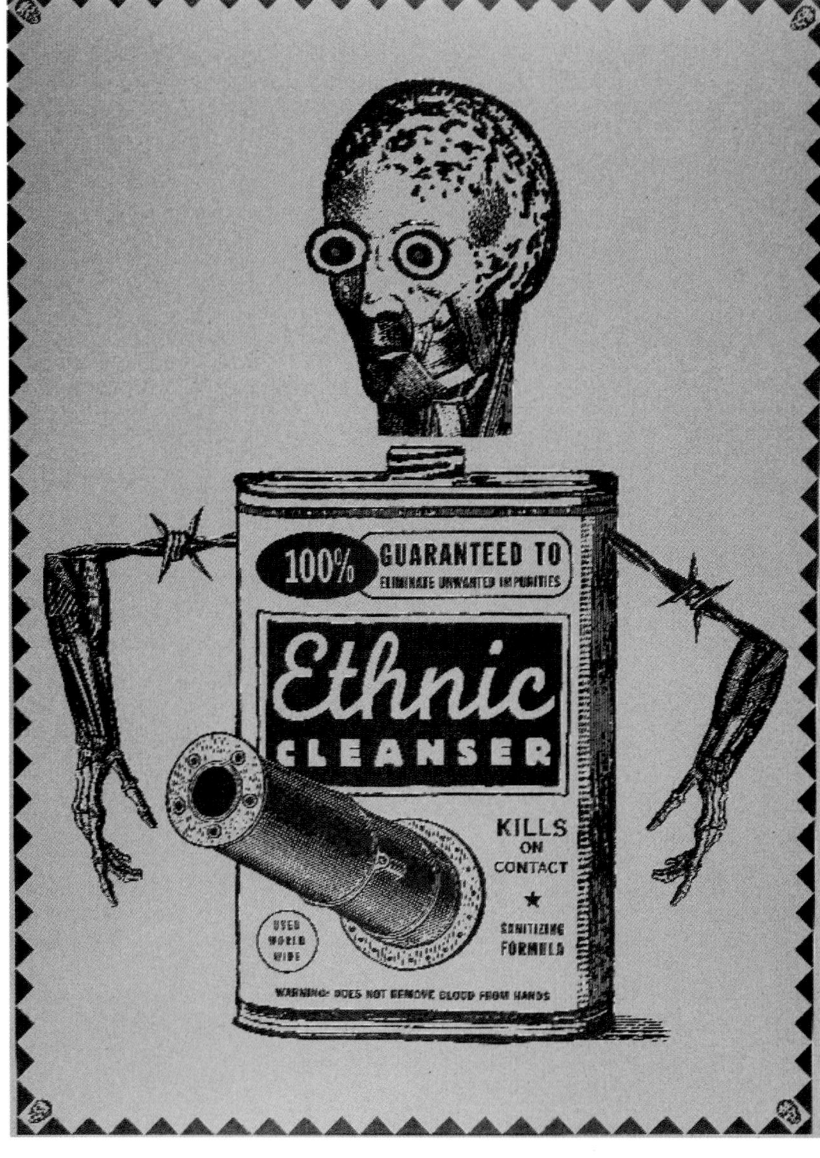

Poster

Design_Jason Schulte
Minneapolis, Minnesota
Art Direction_Charles S. Anderson
Copywriter_Lisa Pemrick

Design Office_Charles S. Anderson Design
Client_French Paper Company

Principal Type_Alpin Gothic and ITC Franklin Gothic

Dimensions_35 x 48 in. (88.9 x 121.9 cm)

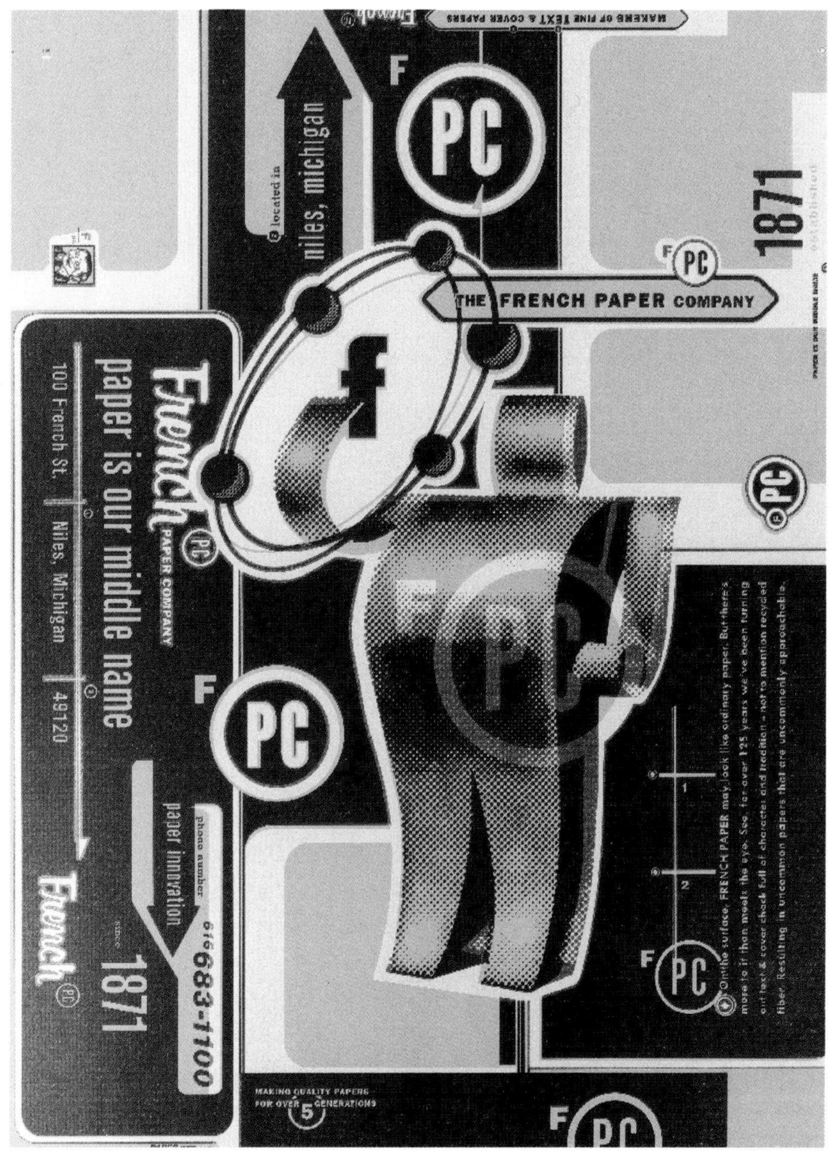

"DeMartino often combines traditional typography, rules,
as well as photography in her work,
and arranges them in ways that evoke a sense of elegance and order" Communication Arts Magazine
STUDIO d DESIGN
a b c d e
STUDIO d DESIGN. 30 N
First Street, Floor 3, Mpls
Minnesota, Zip Code 55401
612|332 3987 FAX 332 0330
DOG
DOTS
56789
TULSA ART DIRECTORS CLUB PRESENTATION:
LAURIE DEMARTINO, STUDIO d DESIGN
THURSDAY NOVEMBER 19, NINETEEN 98, 7:30PM
THE PHILBROOK MUSEUM OF ART
2727 SOUTH ROCKFORD ROAD

Design_Uwe Melichar and
Katrin Schmidt
Hamburg, Germany
Art Direction_Uwe Melichar
Creative Direction_Uwe Melichar

Design Office_Factor Design
Client_HKF Film–und
Fernsehproduktion

Principal Type_Bank Gothic,
Alternate Gothic, and Ariston BQ

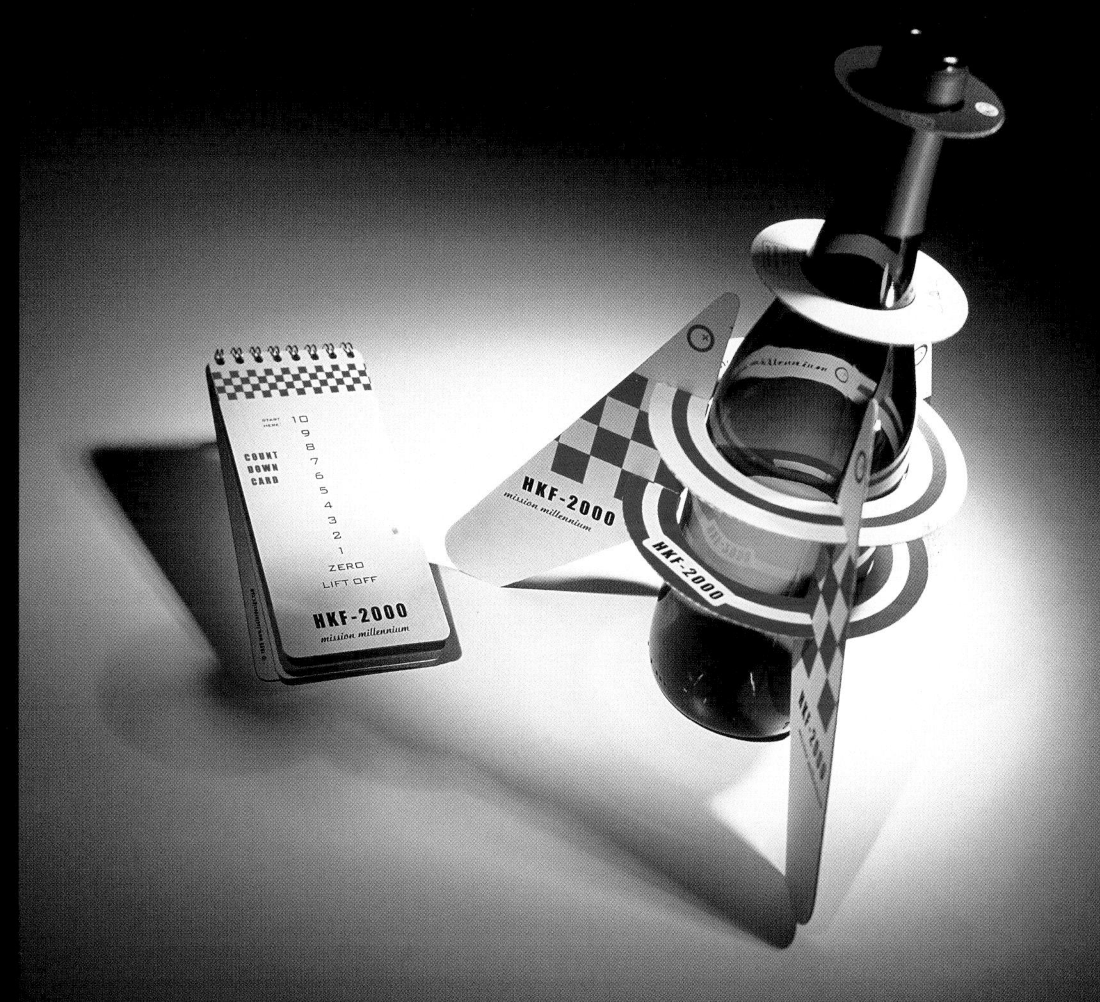

Poster

Design_Takafumi Kusagaya
and Miki Sekigushi
Tokyo, Japan
Art Direction_Takafumi Kusagaya

Design Office_Kusagaya Design, Inc.
Client_Takeo, Inc.

Principal Type_Original type
Takafumi Miyajima

Dimensions_28 11/16 x 40 9/16 in.
(72.8 x 103 cm)

I Like You — I Like You — I Like You — I Like You — I Like You
I Like You — I Like You — I Like You — I Like You — I Like You
I Like You — I Like You — I Love You — I Like You — I Like You
I Like You — I Like You — I Like You — I Like You — I Like You
I Like You — I Like You — I Like You — I Like You — I Like You

Poster

Design_Paul Bichler
Chicago, Illinois
Art Direction_Paul Bichler
Creative Direction_Chris Froeter

Design Office_Froeter Design Co., Inc.
Client_The David and Alfred Smart Museum of Art

Principal Type_OCR-B and DIN Mittelschrift

Dimensions_24 x 18 in. (61 x 45.7 cm)

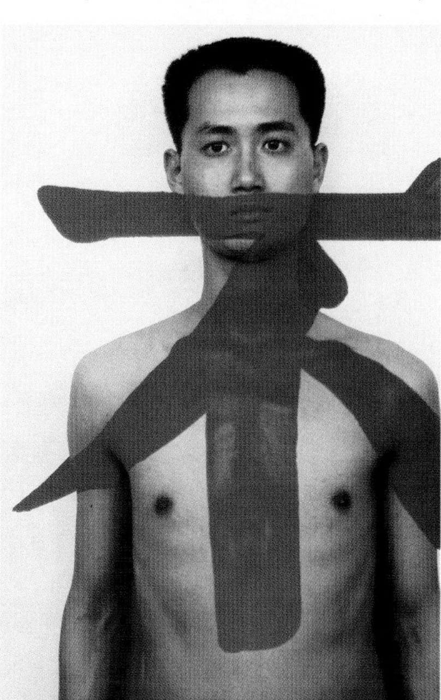

Design_Fons M. Hickmann
Berlin, Germany
Lettering_Tom Croll's Mother
Art Direction_Fons M. Hickmann

Creative Direction_Fons M. Hickmann
Studio_Fons M. Hickmann
Client_Theaterhau

Principal Type_Tom Croll's Mother's Typewriter

Dimensions_39 3/8 x 27 9/16 in. (100 x 70 cm)

Invitation

Design_David Salanitro and Ted Bluey, San Francisco, California
Art Direction_David Salanitro
Creative Direction_David Salanitro
Illustration_Heather Layne

Design Office_Oh Boy, A Design Company
Client_Tracy Chaney

Principal Type_Century Schoolbook and Twentieth Century

Dimensions_4 7/8 x 6 7/8 in. (12.4 x 17.4 cm)

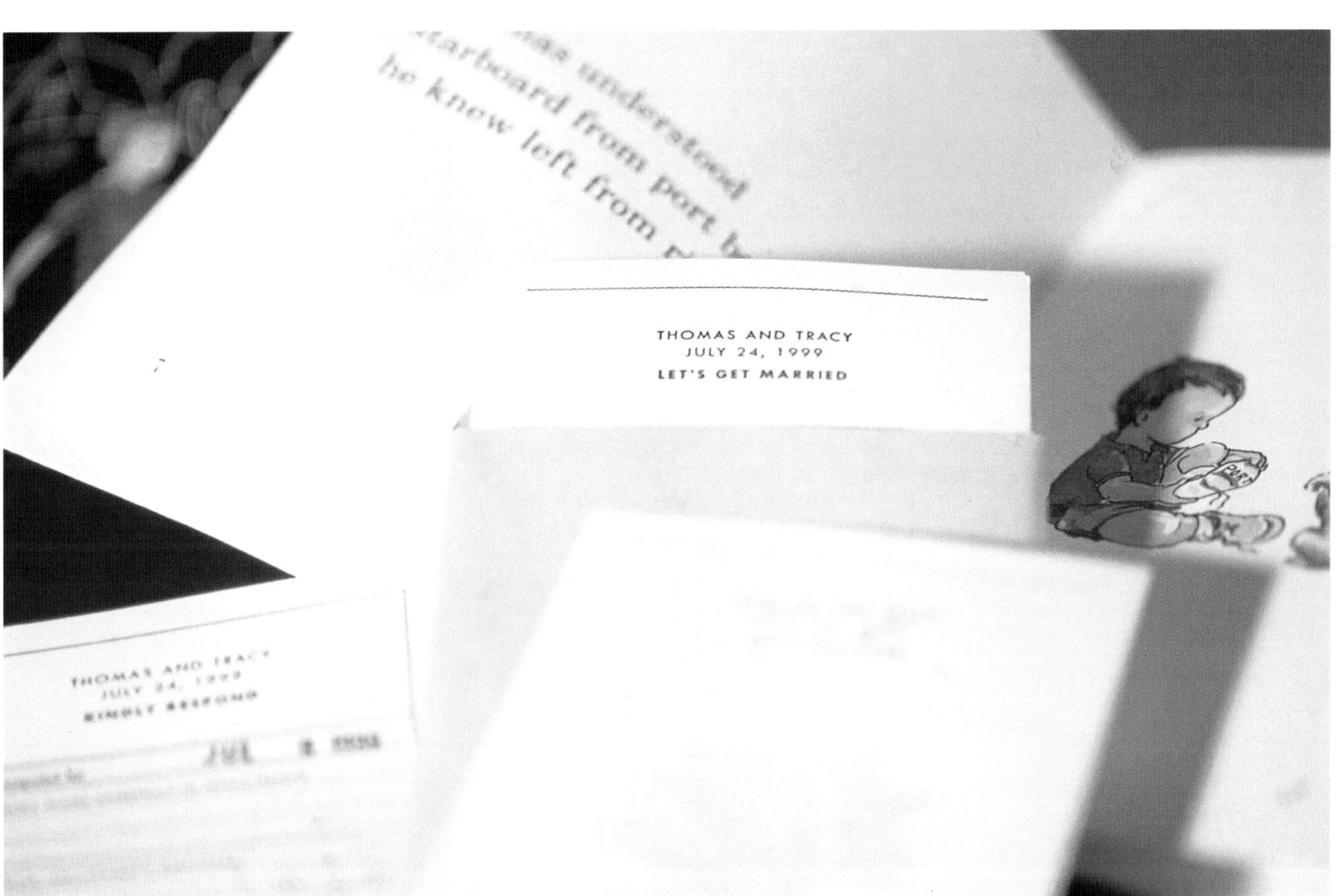

Design_Laurie DeMartino
Minneapolis, Minnesota
Art Direction_Laurie DeMartino
Photography_Aaron Dimmel
Seed Art Illustration_David Steinlicht
Printer_Holm Graphic Service

Studio_Studio d Design
Client_Art Directors Association of Iowa

Principal Type_Handlettering with seeds

Dimensions_17 x 24 in. (43.2 x 61 cm)

Poster

Design_Akihiko Tsukamoto
Tokyo, Japan
Art Direction_Akihiko Tsukamoto
Printer_Twin-Eight Co., Ltd.

Studio_Zuan Club
Client_Amaguri-Taro, Inc.

Principal Type_ITC Snap Italic, ITC Kokoa, and Hiragino Gyosho Extra Bold

Dimensions_40 9/16 x 28 11/16 in. (103 x 72.8 cm)

Wenedikt Jerofejew

Die Reise nach Petuschki

Ein Poem / Ein Theaterstück

Eine Produktion des
fringe ensemble Frank Heuel
in Coproduktion mit dem
Forum Freies Theater, Düsseldorf

THEATER IM BALLSAAL

1999
DESIGN SHOW OF EXCELLENCE

WHAT TO ENTER

WHO MAY ENTER

CATEGORIES

ANNUAL REPORTS 01
BOOKS 02
BROCHURES/CATALOGS 03
DIRECT MAIL 04
ENVIRONMENTAL DESIGN 05
INVITATIONS/ANNOUNCEMENTS 06
LOGOS/MARKS 07
MISCELLANEOUS 08
MULTIMEDIA: WEBSITES, CD ROMS, ETC. 09
NEWSLETTERS/PUBLICATIONS 10
PACKAGING 11
POSTERS 12
SELF-PROMOTION 13
STATIONERY SYSTEMS 14
STUDENT WORK 15
CAMPAIGNS/SERIES 16

ENTRY RULES

11.03

deadlines

preparation of print entries

preparation of interactive multimedia entries

preparation of packages

FEES AND PAYMENTS

entry fees

exhibit fees

Design_Catherine Knaeble
Minneapolis, Minnesota
Lettering_Elvis Swift
Art Direction_Catherine Knaeble
Creative Direction_Connie Soteropolis

Design Office_Dayton's/Hudson's/Marshall Field's

Principal Type_Bembo, Harting, and handlettering

Dimensions_Various

Poster and Brochure

Design_Veress Tamás
Budapest, Hungary
Lettering_Veress Tamás
Art Direction_Veress Tamás
Creative Direction_Simon Attila
Illustration_Veress Tamás

Studio_Art Force Studio

Principal Type_Gill Sans
and handlettering

Dimensions_16 9/16 x 23 1/4 in.
(42 x 59 cm)

HI FIVE! JUNE 5TH IS THE DSVC END-OF-THE-YEAR PARTY AND CRAWFISH BOIL. BRING 5 FRIENDS, 5 FAMILY MEMBERS OR JUST BRING YOURSELF, BUT ABOVE ALL BRING A BIG APPETITE.

JUNE

DIG YOUR FINGERS INTO A MESS OF CRAWFISH AND GET YOURSELF A GEN-U-INE CAJUN MANICURE.

FIVE GREAT REASONS TO COME: CRAWFISH, CAJUN MUSIC, BEER, FUN AND GAMES FOR KIDS.

FIVE DELICIOUS INGREDIENTS: SUCCULENT CRAWFISH, POTATOES, CORN, GARLIC AND FINGER LICKIN' SEASONING

Design_Matteo Federico Bologna
New York, New York
Art Direction_Matteo Federico Bologna
Illustration_Robert Padilla

Studio_Mucca Design Corporation
Client_Pastis Restaurant

Principal Type_Pastis Nobel, Pastis Rockwell, and Pastis Geometric Slab Condensed
Tamaye Parry

Dimensions_Various

CAFÉ, LIQUEURS & BIÈRES DE MARQUE

PASTIS

CUISINE TRADITIONNELLE RECOMMANDÉE

CAFE – COMPTOIR – RESTAURANT

PLAT DU JOUR
CHAMPVALLON
MARDI

COCKTAILS AU PASTIS
– 8.00 –

LE CASSE-TÊTE
Anejo Rum, Cognac, Calvados, Pernod

LE CHRYSANTHÈME
Benedictine, Dry Vermouth, Suze

LE FEU ROUGE
Stoli Pepper Vodka, Ricard, Fresh Lemon Juice

LE SAZERAC
Bourbon, Fresh Lemon Juice, Casanis

LE PERROQUET
Pernod and Mint Syrup

L'AMANDE PASTIS
Ricard, Almond Syrup and Soda Water

Coffee 2.00
Espresso 2.50
Cappuccino 3.00
Café au Lait 3.00

HORS D'OEUVRES

Onion Soup Gratinée 6.00
Leeks Vinaigrette 7.00
Beet, Endive, Roquefort and Walnut Salad 8.00
Rillettes Fermière 8.00
Mixed Green Salad .... 7.00 w/Goat Cheese . 8.00
Grilled Sardines 8.00
Pissaladière - Caramelized Onion Tart 6.00
Frisée Lardons and a Poached Egg 8.00
Gratin of Mussels and Spinach 7.00
Grilled Octopus and White Bean Salad 9.00
Oysters on the Half Shell .... P/A
Fritto Misto 11.00

ENTREES

Skate au Beurre Noir 15.00
Grilled Salmon, Sauce Verte 16.00
Trout Amandine 16.00
Shellfish Stew w/Chorizo 15.00
Grilled Whole Fish of the Day .... P/A
Half Roast Lobster w/Garlic Butter and Fries .... P/A
Full Roast Lobster w/Garlic Butter and Fries .... P/A
Poussin Rôti with Garlic Confit 16.00
Glazed Pork w/Lentils 17.00
Roast Leg of Lamb w/Flageolets 16.00
Steak Frites w/Béarnaise 17.00
Butcher's Tender w/Marrow and Shallots 18.00
Blanquette de Veau 16.00
Tripes Gratinées 14.00
Braised Beef w/Glazed Carrots 17.00

PATES

Penne Puttanesca 13.00
Spaghetti Carbonara 12.00
Mushroom Ravioli w/Sage and Butter 12.00
Rabbit Pappardelle 14.00
Penne Primavera 13.00

GARNITURES

Légumes Verts 4.50
Ratatouille 5.00
Carottes Vichy 4.50
French Fries 5.00
Gratin Dauphinois 5.50

– CARAFE MAISON –

BLANC

CÔTES DE GASCOGNE
verre 6.00 / demi 10.00 / carafe 13.00

BORDEAUX BLANC
verre 7.00 / demi 11.00 / carafe 15.00

ROUGE

VINS DE PAYS D'OC '94
verre 6.00 / demi 10.00 / carafe 14.00

MARCILLAC '97
verre 7.00 / demi 11.00 / carafe 15.00

BREAKFAST	TOUTE LA SEMAINE	9.00 AM - 12.00 PM
LUNCH	MONDAY FRIDAY	12.00 PM - 5.00 PM
DINNER	TOUTE LA SEMAINE	6.00 PM - 12.00 AM
SUPPER	SUNDAY THURSDAY	12.00 AM - 2.00 AM
	FRIDAY SATURDAY	12.00 AM - 3.00 AM
BRUNCH	SATURDAY SUNDAY	12.00 PM - 4.00 PM

20% gratuities added to parties of 8 or more

CHEFS DE CUISINE
Riad Nasr & Lee Hanson

DINNER

TARIF DES CONSOMMATIONS

HORS D'OEUVRES	TAXES AND SERVICE NOT INCLUDED	PATES	TAXES AND SERVICE NOT INCLUDED
Onion Soup Gratinée	6.00	Penne Puttanesca	13.00
Leeks Vinaigrette	7.00	Spaghetti Carbonara	12.00
Beet, Endive and Walnut Salad	8.00	Mushroom Ravioli with Sage and Butter	12.00
Rillettes Fermière	8.00	Rabbit Pappardelle	14.00
Mixed Green Salad	6.00	Penne Primavera	13.00
Mixed Green Salad with Goat Cheese	7.00		
Grilled Sardines	8.00	ENTREES	
Pissaladière - Caramelized Onion Tart	6.00	Skate au Beurre Noir	
Frisée Lardons with a Poached Egg	8.00	Grilled Salmon, Sauce Verte	
Gratin of Mussels and Spinach	7.00	Trout Amandine	
Grilled Octopus and White Bean Salad	9.00	Shellfish Stew with Chorizo	
Oysters on the Half Shell	P/A	Grilled Whole Fish of the Day	
Fritto Misto	11.00	Half or Full Roast Lobster with French Fries	
		Poussin Rôti with Garlic Confit	
SALADES		Glazed Pork with Lentils	
Grilled Chicken Paillard	14.00	Roast Leg of Lamb with Flageolets	
Salade Niçoise	14.00	Steak Frites with Béarnaise	
Grilled Vegetable Salad	12.00	Butcher's Tender with Marrow and Shallots	
		Blanquette de Veau	
SANDWICHS		Tripes Gratinées	
Pressed Mozzarella, Basil and Peperonata	9.00	Braised Beef with Glazed Carrots	
Confit of Pork and Chutney	10.00		
Hamburger	9.00	GARNITURES	
Cheeseburger	8.00	Légumes Verts	
Hamburger à Cheval	10.00	Ratatouille	
		Carottes Vichy	
Omelette aux Fines Herbes w/French Fries	10.00	French Fries	
		Gratin Dauphinois	

20% gratuities added to parties of 10 or more

CHEFS DE CUISINE Riad Nasr & Lee Hanson

BUVEZ UN PASTIS APÉRITIF ANISÉ

PASTIS

DESSERTS $6

Apple Tart
Crêpes Suzette
Ile Flottante
Riz au Lait (Rice Pudding)
Gratin de Fruits
Tarte Tropézienne
Mousse au Chocolat
Poire Belle-Hélène,
(Poached Pear with Vanilla Ice Cream & Chocolate Sauce)
Tarte au Citron
Pastis Chocolate Layer Cake

Ice Cream/Sorbet $5

DESSERT WINES

Muscat de Rivesaltes Gautier '97
Glass 6.00
Half Bottle 16.00

Beaumes de Venise Beaumalric '96
Glass 8.00
Half Bottle 18.00

CAFE - COMPTOIR - RESTAURANT

9 Ninth Avenue – New York – NY 10014
Phone (212) 929.4844 – Fax (212) 929.5676
E-mail: frontdesk@pastisny.com

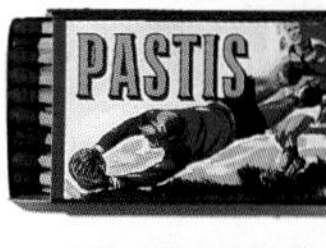

BISTROT FRANÇAIS
Little West 12th Street
(corner of ninth avenue)
☎ (212) 929 4844
CUISINE TRADITIONNELLE

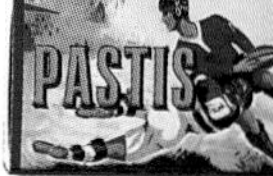

LEUCHTENDE GRÜSSE PARTYLIGHT TISCHKARTE SCHATTENWERFER LEUCHTENDE GRÜSSE

05

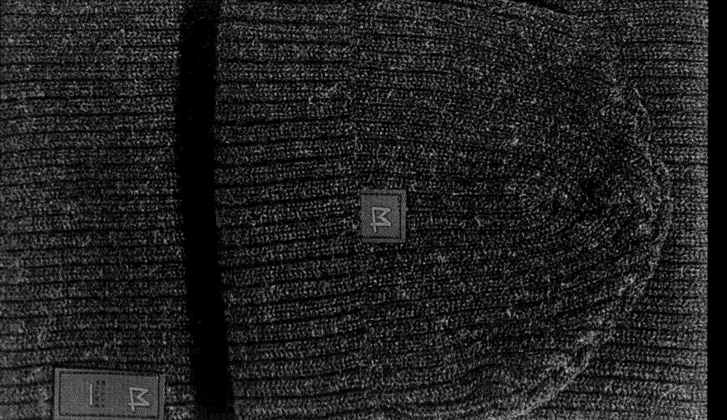

Design_Jennifer Sterling
San Francisco, California
Art Direction_Jennifer Sterling
Creative Direction_Jennifer Sterling

Design Office_Jennifer Sterling Design
Client_Spike Networks

Principal Type_Garamond No. 3, Orator, and Cottonwood

Dimensions_Various

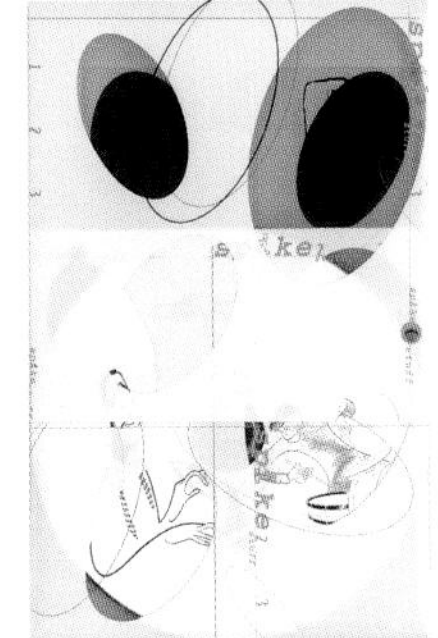

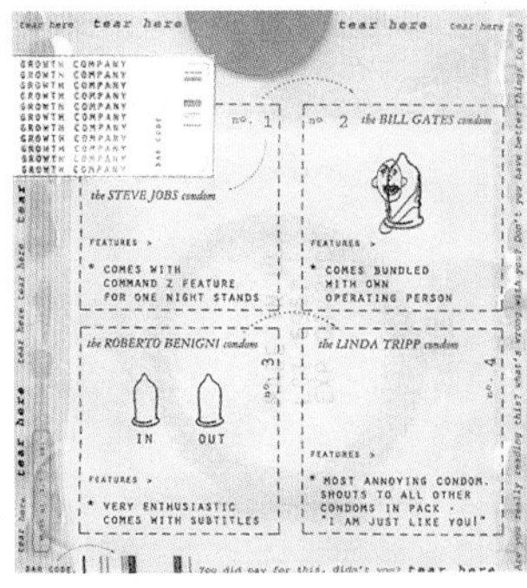

Advertisement

Design_David Covell and Joe Peila
Burlington, Vermont
Art Direction_David Covell
Creative Direction_Michael Jager

Studio_Jager Di Paola Kemp Design
Client_Champion International

Principal Type_Nobel, Trade Gothic, and Russell Square

Dimensions_37 ¼ x 22 ½ in. (94.6 x 57.2 cm)

Design_Anuthin Wongsunkakon
Bangkok, Thailand
Art Direction_Anuthin Wongsunkakon

Studio_Graphic Behaviour
Client_Type Behaviour and Kitsch Publishing

Principal Type_Son Gothic, Key Stone State, Aspirin, and Metamorphosis

Dimensions_4 x 6 in. (10.2 x 15.2 cm) and 4 x 8 in. (10.2 x 20. 3 cm)

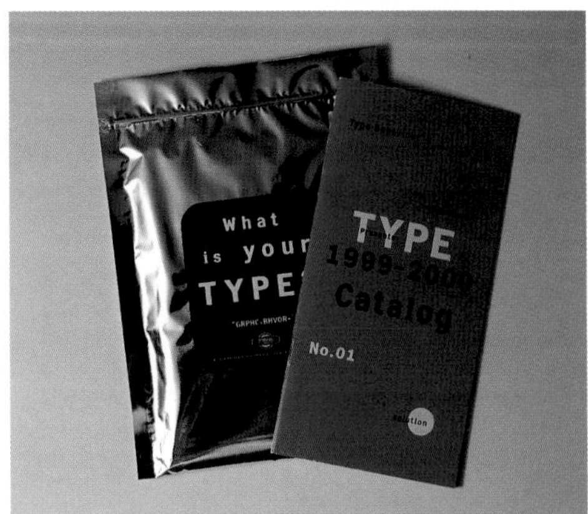

Design_Michael Petersen
Chicago, Illinois
Lettering_Mchael Petersen
Art Direction_Ken Fox and
Michael Petersen

Agency_VSA Partners
Client_Harley-Davidson
Motor Company

Principal Type_Akzidenz Grotesk,
Bulmer, Trade Gothic, and
handlettering

Dimensions_24 x 36 in.
(61 x 91.4 cm)

Design_Teeranop Wangsillapakun
Chicago, Illinois
Art Direction_Carlos Segura
Creative Direction_Carlos Segura

Studio_Segura Inc.
Client_yosho.com

Principal Type_Helvetica

Dimensions_24 x 36 in.
(61 x 91.4 cm)

Poster

Design_Malcolm Buick
Burlington, Vermont
Art Direction_Malcolm Buick
and Michael Jager
Creative Direction_Michael Jager

Studio_Jager Di Paola Kemp Design

Principal Type_Malcy.1

Dimensions_24 x 24 in.
(61 x 61 cm)

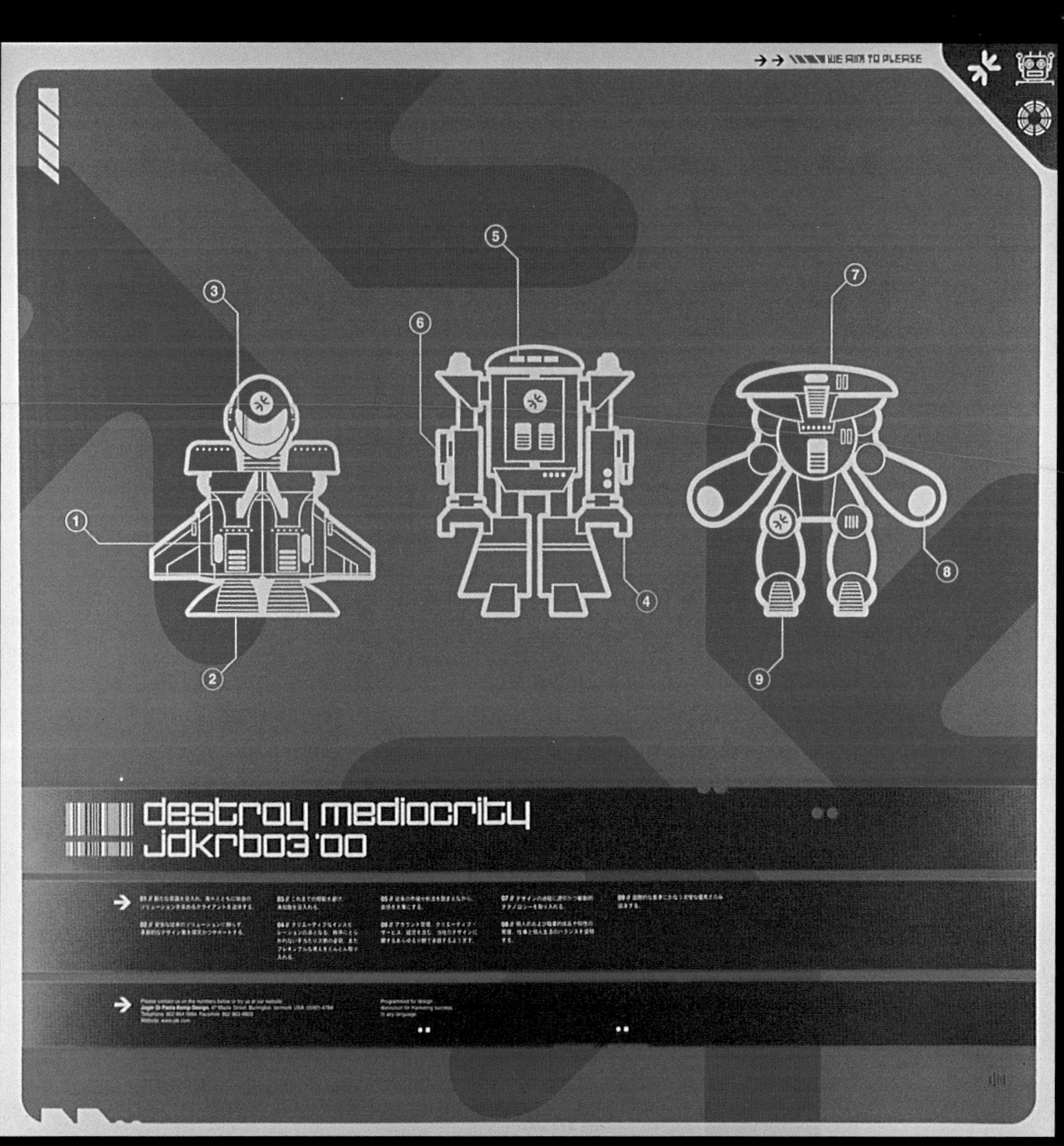

Design_Leslie Chan Wing Kei
Taipei, Taiwan
Lettering_Leslie Chan Wing Kei
Art Direction_Leslie Chan Wing Kei
Creative Direction_Leslie Chan Wing Kei
Photography_Justin Chin and Larcher Chao

Design Office_Leslie Chan Design Co., Ltd.
Client_Macau Designers Association

Principal Type_Chapbook

Dimensions_39 3/8 x 27 9/16 in.
(100 x 70 cm)

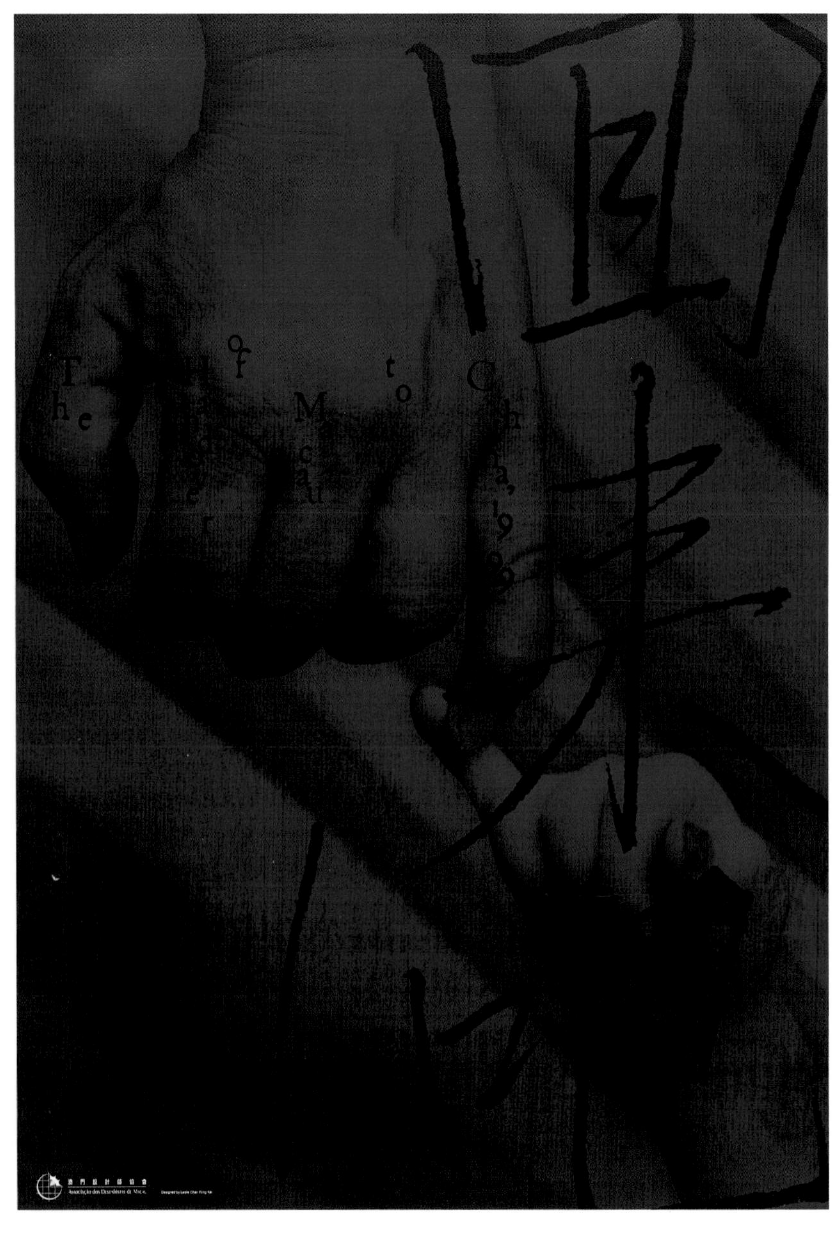

Campaign

Design_Lance Rusoff and Jeremy Dean
Philadelphia, Pennsylvania
Art Direction_Lance Rusoff and Jeremy Dean
Creative Direction_Sue Otto

Studio_Urban Outfitters

Principal Type_Helvetica

Dimensions_18 x 36 in. (45.7 x 91.4 cm)

Design_Todd Piper-Hauswirth, Charles S. Anderson, Jason Schulte, Kyle Hames, and P.J. Chmiel
Minneapolis, Minnesota
Art Direction_Charles S. Anderson
Illustration_Charles S. Anderson and Kyle Hames
Copywriter_Lisa Pemrick

Design Office_Charles S. Anderson Design
Client French Paper Company

Principal Type_Trade Gothic and Univers

Dimensions_Various

Brochure

Design_Tom Brown
Coquitlam, British Columbia, Canada
Art Direction_Tom Brown

Studio_TBA+D
Client_Fredrik Broden

Principal Type_Akzidenz Grotesk

Dimensions_3 5/8 x 5 in.
(9.2 x 12.7 cm)

Design_Michael Bierut and Jacqueline Thaw New York, New York
Art Direction_Michael Bierut
Photography_Melissa Hayden, Neal Slavin, Maria Robledo, Emily Mott, Byron Lee, and Shepard Fairey
Illustration_Andy Cruz, Rich Roat, and Christoph Niemann

Editors_Michael Bierut and Jacqueline Thaw
Writers_Michael Bierut, Andrea Moed, Lorraine Wild, Peter Hall, Andrew Tilin, Steven Heller, and Stuart Henley
Design Office_Pentagram
Client_Mohawk Paper Mills

Principal Type_Vendetta, Cooper Black, and Alternate Gothic

Dimensions_7 x 4 ¼ in. (17.8 x 10.8 cm)

Poster

Design_Shuichi Nogami
Osaka, Japan
Art Direction_Shuichi Nogami

Design Office_Nogami Design Office

Principal Type_Tear Drop

Dimensions_40 9/16 x 28 11/16 in.
(103 x 72.8 cm)

Design_Jennifer Sterling
San Francisco, California
Lettering_Jennifer Sterling
Creative Direction_Jennifer Sterling
Art Direction_Jennifer Sterling
Creative Direction_Jennifer Sterling

Design Office_Jennifer Sterling
Design

Principal Type_Garamond No. 3,
FF Meta, and handlettering

Dimensions_6 x 9 in.
(15.2 x 22.9 cm)

Poster

Design_Paula Scher
and Keith Daigle
New York, New York
Art Direction_Paula Scher

Design Office_Pentagram
Client_Metropolis

Principal Type_Helvetica

Dimensions_24 x 18 in.
(61 x 45.7 cm)

Design_Slavimir Stojanovic
Ljubljana, Slovenia
Art Direction_Slavimir Stojanovic
Creative Direction_Slavimir Stojanovic

Design Studio_Kompas Design
Client_JDP

Principal Type_Helvetica Black

Dimensions_26 x 18 ⅛ in.
(66 x 46 cm)

Brochure

Design_Scott Lambert
Los Angeles, California
Art Direction_Scott Lambert
Creative Direction_Douglas Joseph
Photography_Eric Tucker
Writer_Scott Lambert

Design Office_Douglas Joseph Partners
Client_Spicers Paper Inc.

Principal Type_Perpetua, Bell Gothic, Variex, and Univers

Dimensions_7 x 8 ½ in. (17.8 x 21.6 cm)

encoreteknologies

Our Mega tek Team *(left to right)*: Glenn Freaksley PhD., Senior Researcher. Glenn heads the laser proton voice activated system division. Alfred Boringski, Product Engineer. Alfred has guided the *Inyerface* cranial cover development team since 1999. Wil DeNerd, Senior Vice President of Product Development. Wil joined the *Inyerface* team in late 1998 and has worked extensively on the communications device system which drives the laser network.

The Rapid Communication Matrix (RCM) market is rapidly growing and the Etek R&D group is moving to capitalize from sales of the Inyerface product. To meet the market demands, Eteknologies is developing new light-speed laser algorithms, engineering new light weight helmet materials and creating focused solutions that will enable our customers to embrace the latest teknology.

Eteknologies R&D investment, which remained strong at 32% of revenues in fiscal 2005, will continue to be a key component of our company strategy.

9

Design_Lisa Schulze Oechtering and Marcus Kraus
Frankfurt, Germany
Art Direction_Marcus Kraus
Creative Direction_Lisa Schulze Oechtering

Agency_Feine Werbung
Client_Jung Dentaltechnik

Principal Type_Univers and Bembo

Dimensions_8 ¼ x 8 ¼ in. (21 x 21 cm)

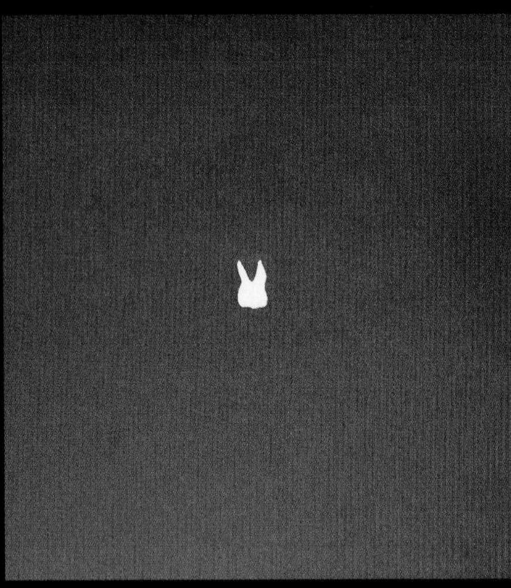

1 | 1 · EINS

BESONDERE Präzision erfordert die sogenannte Kombinationstechnik, bei der fester und herausnehmbarer Zahnersatz über spezielle Verankerungselemente verbunden sind. Hierzu dienen zum Beispiel Geschiebe, Druckknopfverankerungen, Stege oder Doppelkronen.

ZAHNERSATZ dieser Art ist im Behandlungsablauf und in der zahntechnischen Herstellung sehr aufwendig. Er ist hinsichtlich Ästhetik und

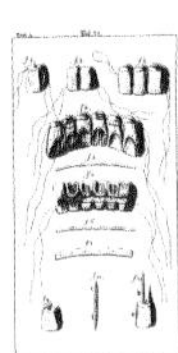

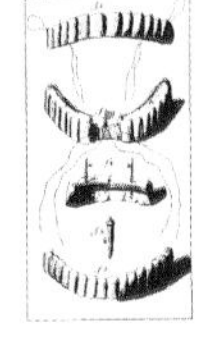

Abb. 13)

Claude Mouton (gest. 1786) erfand eine Prothesenbasis mit kleinen, den Zahnfächern ähnelnden Löchern, in denen nach oben Stifte herausragten, auf die echte menschliche Zähne aufgesetzt wurden, die knapp unterhalb des Zahnhalses abgeschnitten worden waren.

Sicherheit vielfach den klammerverankerten Prothesen überlegen.

DIESE VORTEILE kommen jedoch nur zum Tragen, wenn die einzelnen Elemente mit äußerster Genauigkeit aufeinander abgestimmt sind und sich zu einem funktionstüchtigen und harmonischen Ganzen verbinden. In Zusammenarbeit mit den Zahnärzten kreative Lösungen zu entwickeln und minutiös zu realisieren gehört zu den Ansprüchen, die wir an uns selbst stellen.

Abb. 13) Der Franzose Pierre Fauchard (1678 bis 1761) faßte das zahnmedizinische Wissen der westlichen Welt zu seiner Zeit zusammen und systematisierte es. In seinem Werk »Le chirurgien dentiste« (1728) gibt er einen Überblick über die damalige Brücken- und Prothesentechnik.

12 13

back karen mok
back karen mok

Design_Susanne Fritsch, Andreas Uebele, and Jutta Boxheimer
Stuttgart, Germany
Lettering_Jutta Boxheimer
Art Direction_Andreas Uebele and Susanne Fritsch

Agency_Büro Uebele, Visuelle Kommunikation
Client_Lothar Bertrams

Principal Type_Akzidenz Grotesk

Dimensions_8 ¾ x 11 ⅞ in. (22.3 x 30.2 cm)

Brochure

Design_Mark Geer
Houston, Texas
Creative Direction_Mark Geer

Studio_Geer Design Inc.
Client_Domtar Paper

Principal Type_Caslon Oldstyle No.337, Rosewood Fill, Linotext, and Texas Hero

Dimensions_8 ⅜ x 11 ¾ in. (21.3 x 29.9 cm)

Every educated man during the Middle Ages and Renaissance knew his sign and planet. The Church sponsored several schools of astronomy which incorporated astrology. Astromica, the study of astronomy, supplied the base knowledge; while astrologia, the study of astrology, was its applied science

Design_Michael Daiminger
Munich, Germany
Creative Direction_Michael Daiminger and Claus Lehmann
Photography_Infrarot GmbH

Design Office_Infrarot GmbH
Client_Fastfood Theater

Principal Type_Berthold Akzidenz Grotesk Condensed

Dimensions_23 ⅝ x 33 ⅛ in. (53.4 x 84.1 cm)

It's new typeface originally designed by N.D.O.

Brochure

Design_Jon Olsen
Portland, Oregon
Art Direction_Jon Olsen

Creative Direction_Steve Sandstrom
Illustration_Jeff Foster
and John Hersey
Copywriter_Matt Elhardt

Principal Type_Century Schoolbook

Dimensions_8 ½ x 11 in.
(21.6 x 27.9 cm)

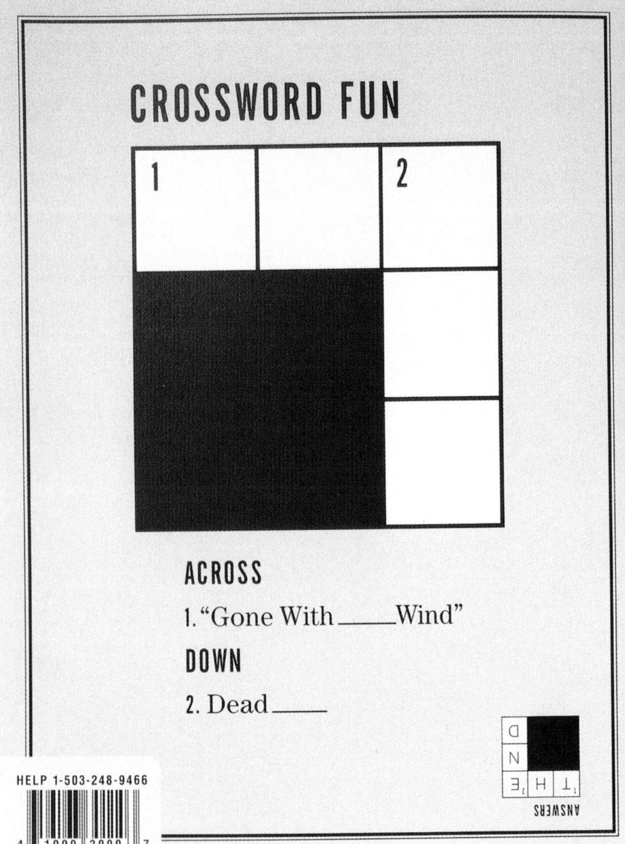

Brochure

Design_Venus D'Amore and Erik Olsen
San Francisco, California
Art Direction_Erik Olsen

Design Office_Erik Olsen Graphic Design
Client_Spinal Diagnostics and Treatment Center

Principal Type_Avenir

Dimensions_5 x 8 in. (12.7 x 20.3 cm)

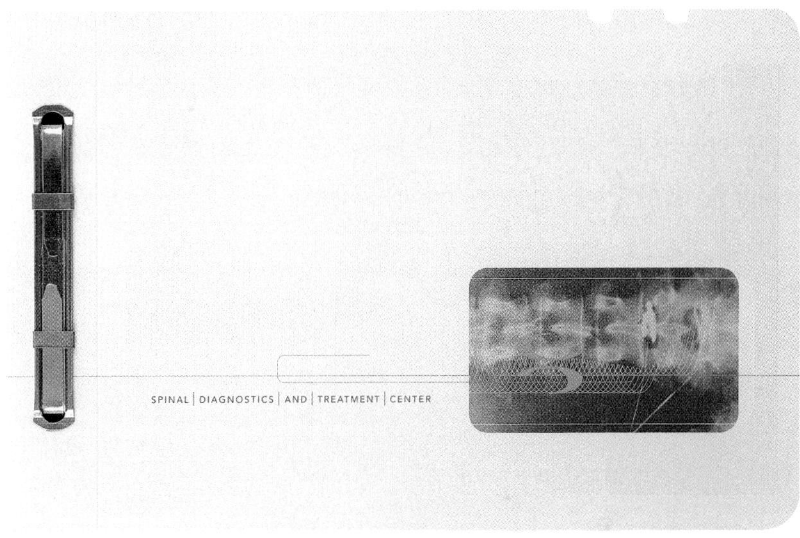

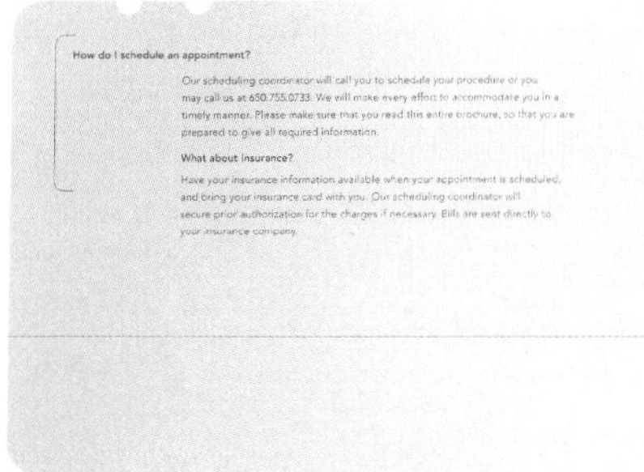

Design_David Handschuh
Urbana, Illinois
School_University of Illinois
Urbana-Champaign

Client_Montage

Principal Type_Typewriter, Times New Roman, and handlettering

Dimensions_6 ¼ x 7 ⅛ in.
(15.9 x 18.1 cm)

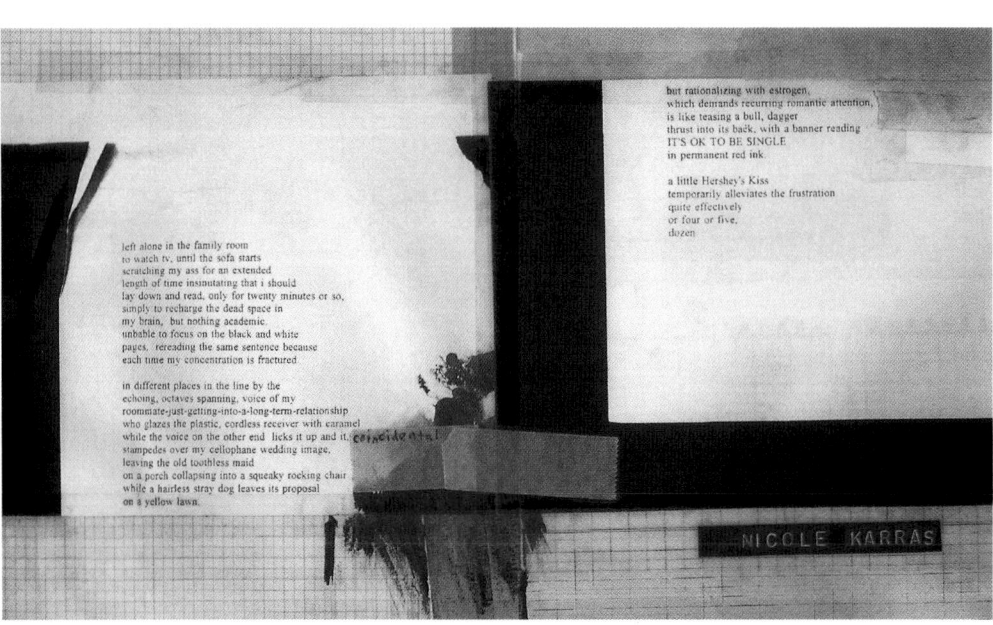

Brochure

Design_Giorgio Pesce
Lausanne, Switzerland
Art Direction_Giorgio Pesce
Creative Direction_Giorgio Pesce

Agency_Atelier Poisson
Client_Théâtre Arsenic

Principal Type_Triumvirate and Trade Gothic

Dimensions_Envelope:
7 11/16 x 3 3/8 in. (19.5 x 8 cm)
Program: 21 5/16 x 15/16 in.
(54.2 x 2.1 cm)

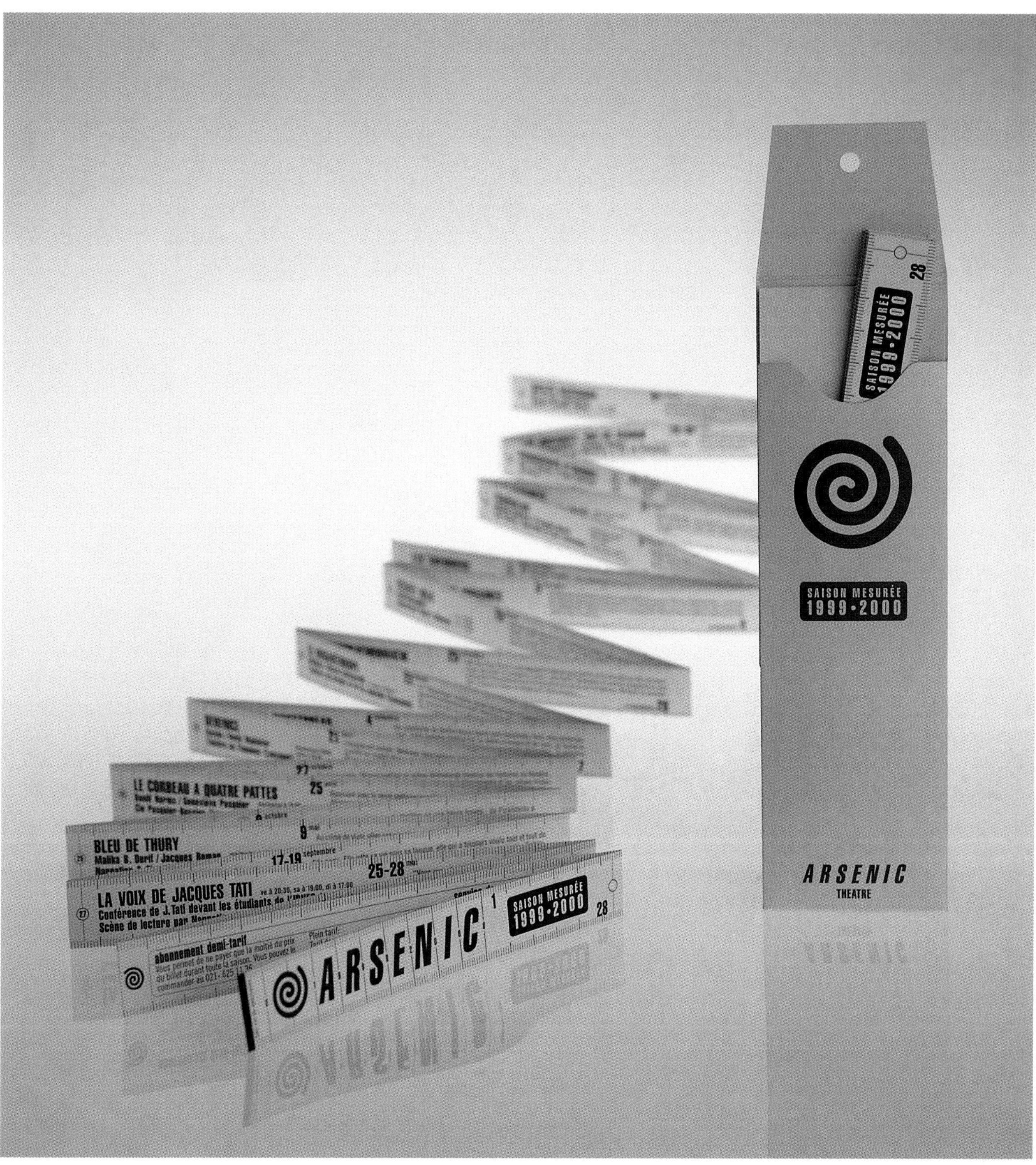

Design_Aaron Dietz
Farmington, Connnecticut
Art Direction_Aaron Dietz
Creative Direction_Mike Scricco
Illustration_James Yang,
Laura Ljungkvist, and Jack Unruh

Agency_Keiler & Company
Client_Crane's

Principal Type_Jigsaw,
Subluxation, and Mrs. Eaves

Dimensions_6 x 9 in.
(15.2 x 22.5 cm)

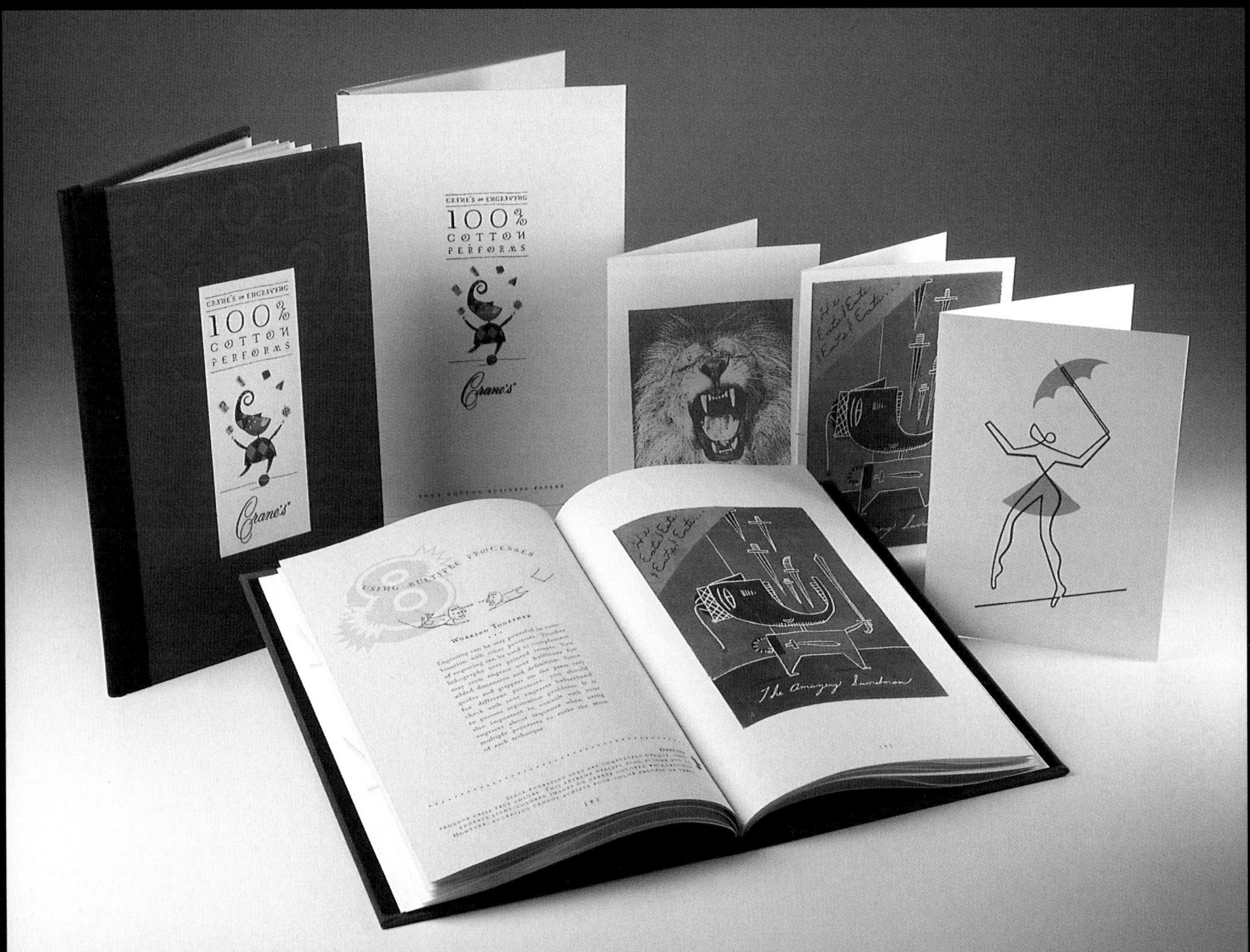

Design_Liz Dzilenski
Farmington, Connnecticut
Lettering_Carolyn Fisher
Art Direction_Liz Dzilenski
Creative Direction_Mike Scricco
Illustration_Ed Fotheringham, Nishan Akgulian, Eric Panke, Raymond Verdaguet, and Carolyn Fisher

Agency_Keiler & Company
Client_Crane's

Principal Type_Mrs. Eaves, Isonorm, and handlettering

Dimensions_6 x 9 in. (15.2 x 22.5 cm)

Design_Frank Baseman
Jenkintown, Pennsylvania
Art Direction_Frank Baseman
Creative Direction_Frank Baseman
Photography_Frank Baseman

Studio_Frank Baseman Design
Client_Philadelphia College of Textiles & Science

Principal Type_Bulmer, Egiziano, Kuenstler Script, and ITC Franklin Gothic Extra Condensed

Dimensions_19 ½ x 26 in. (49.5 x 66 cm)

SCHOOL OF architecture AND design

PHILADELPHIA COLLEGE OF TEXTILES & SCIENCE

Architecture Graphic Design Industrial Design Interior Design

Spring

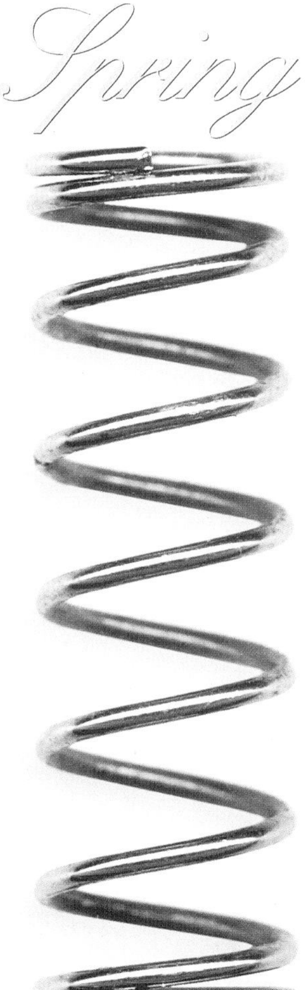

fig. [a] spring

JANUARY 8, 6:00pm
IAN LIDDELL
Structural Engineer
Buro, Happold Engineers
London, England
"The Millennium Dome Project"
Media Room, Gutman Library
Sponsored by Fabric Architecture Magazine

MARCH 16, 6:00pm
URSULA DAYENIAN
Interior Designer
Legat Architects, Chicago
"Creative and Strategic Thinking in Interior Design"
Media Room, Gutman Library

MARCH 24, 6:00pm
CHIP KIDD
Graphic Designer/Art Director/Writer
Alfred A. Knopf Publishing Co., New York
Downs Hall
Sponsored by The American Institute of Graphic Arts, Philadelphia chapter and Potlatch Corporation

APRIL 8, 6:00pm
ROBERT BLAICH
Industrial Designer, Design Management and Strategic Planning Consultant
Aspen, Colorado
"Design Leadership"
Downs Hall
Sponsored by the Industrial Design Society of America, Philadelphia chapter

APRIL 15, 6:00pm
DANIEL LIBESKIND
Architect
Daniel Libeskind and Nina Libeskind
Berlin, Germany
Downs Hall
Sponsored by Francis Cauffman Foley Hoffmann Architects, Philadelphia

APRIL 21, 6:00pm
DAVID PISCUSKAS
Architect
1100 Architect, New York
David Piscuskas and Juergen Riehm, partners
Downs Hall
Sponsored by Vitetta Group

Sponsored by Asten, Inc. as part of the Dietrich Asten Global Awareness Project

For more information contact the School of Architecture and Design (215)951-2896 or www.philacol.edu

1.9.9.9

spring lecture SERIES

Brochure

Design_Clive Piercy
Santa Monica, California
Art Direction_Clive Piercy
and Michael Hodgson

Design Office_Ph.D
Client_Friend + Johnson

Principal Type_Trade Gothic,
Perpetua, and Interstate

Dimensions_7 x 11 in.
(17.8 x 27.9 cm)

Design_Vanessa Eckstein and Frances Chen
Toronto, Canada
Art Direction_Vanessa Eckstein

Design Studio_Blok Design
Client_The Partners Film Company

Principal Type_Trade Gothic

Dimensions_8 ½ x 11 in. (21.6 X 27.9 cm)

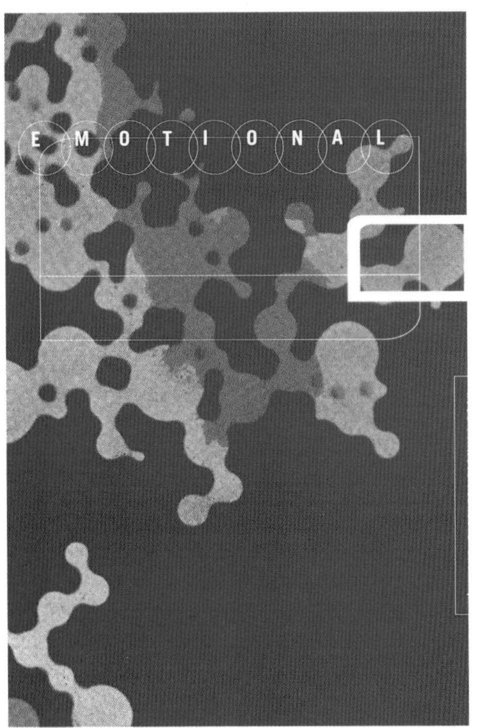

Poster

Design_Lanny Sommese
State College, Pennsylvania
Art Direction_Lanny Sommese
Creative Direction_Lanny Sommese

Studio_Sommese Design
Client_Penn State School of Visual Arts

Principal Type_Gill Sans and Helvetica

Dimensions_26 x 40 in. (66 x 101.6 cm)

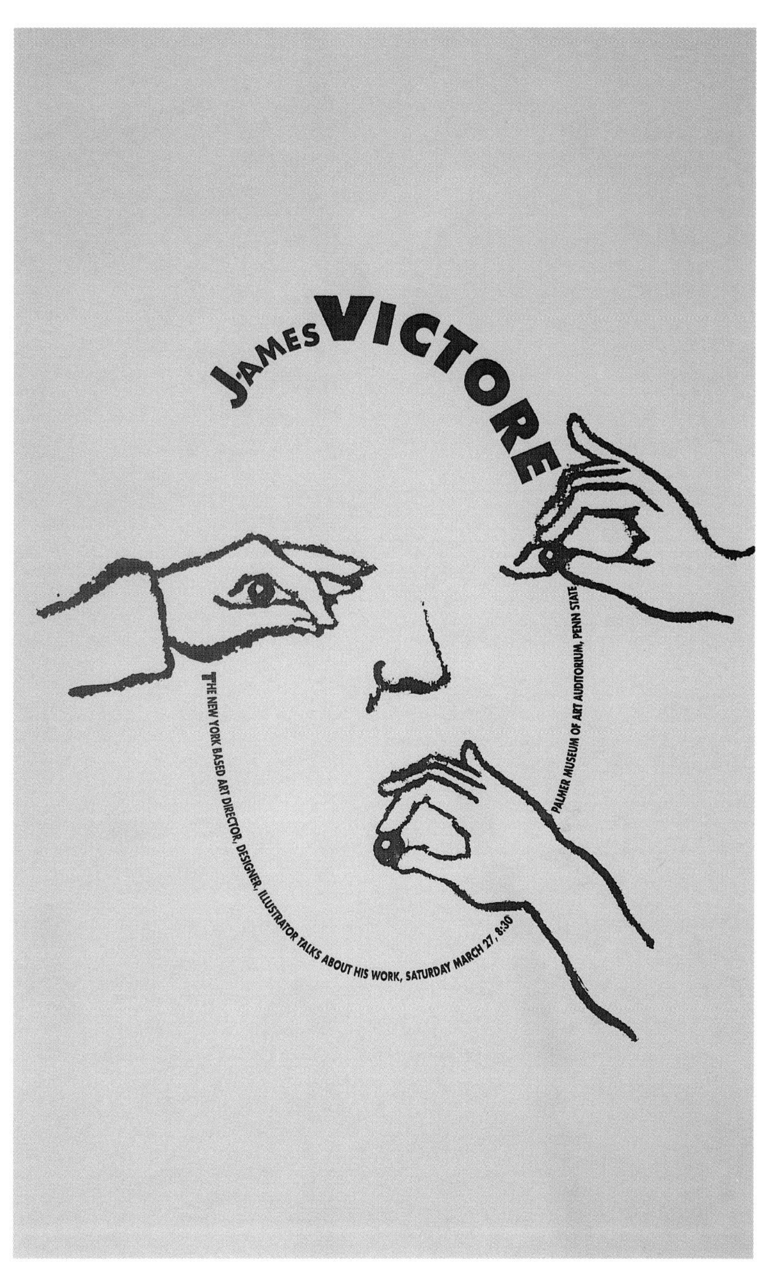

Design_Catherine Knaeble and Karl Wolf
Minneapolis, Minnesota
Lettering_Elvis Swift
Art Direction_Catherine Knaeble
Creative Direction_Connie Soteropolis

Design Office_Dayton's/Hudson's/Marshall Field's

Principal Type_Bembo, Harting, and handlettering

Dimensions_22 x 28 in. (55.9 x 71.1 cm) and 14 x 22 in. (35.6 x 55.9 cm)

Design_Steve Sandstrom
Portland, Oregon
Art Direction_Steve Sandstrom
Creative Direction_Steve Sandstrom

Principal Type_Aviator

Dimensions_10 ½ x 5 x 3 in.
(26.7 x 12.7 x 7.6 cm)

Design_Shinnoske Sugisaki
Osaka, Japan
Art Direction_Shinnoske Sugisaki
Creative Direction_Nob Fukuda
Copywriter_Osamu Nakasuji

Studio_Shinnoske Inc.
Client_Tojuso Center

Principal Type_Morisawa MB31 and Morisawa MB101

Dimensions_21¼ x 15¾ in. (54 x 40 cm)

Poster

Design_Pedro Falcão
Lisbon, Portugal
Art Direction_Pedro Falcão
Photography_Mariana Viegas

Studio_Secretonix
Client_André Guedes

Principal Type_ITC Charter

Dimensions_16 ⅝ x 23 ¹³⁄₁₆ in.
(42 x 60.5 cm)

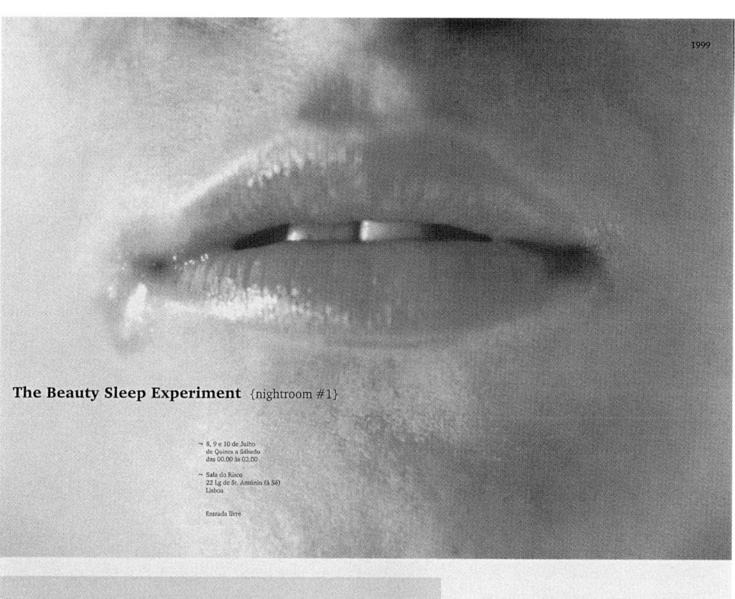

Acordar — ao deitar

Sem mentira — nem verdade
Pulsação branca — de cores
Saltar — a realidade
Embebida — no transparente
Vertida — assim

Vestido — um silêncio
Despe-se de mim — para mim
Dispersa-se
O tempo — deixou de se fazer em saudade

Contidos — os pés submersos
Deixaram — de pisar ovos
Próximos — distantes
São outros — estão novos

Esvaziei — o lugar
Um mergulho — no denso
intenso
Preenchi — outro estar
Deitei-o — e deixei-o acordar

Design_Lisa Hoffman
San Diego, California
Art Direction_Lisa Hoffman
Editors_Amanda Burt
and Summer Oram

Studio_Lisa Hoffman Design
Client_English Department,
California Polytechnic State
University, San Luis Obispo

Principal Type_Rosewood, Caslon Book BE, Caslon Regular BE, Minaret, and Byzantine

Dimensions_6 ½ x 8 ½ in.
(16.5 x 21.6 cm)

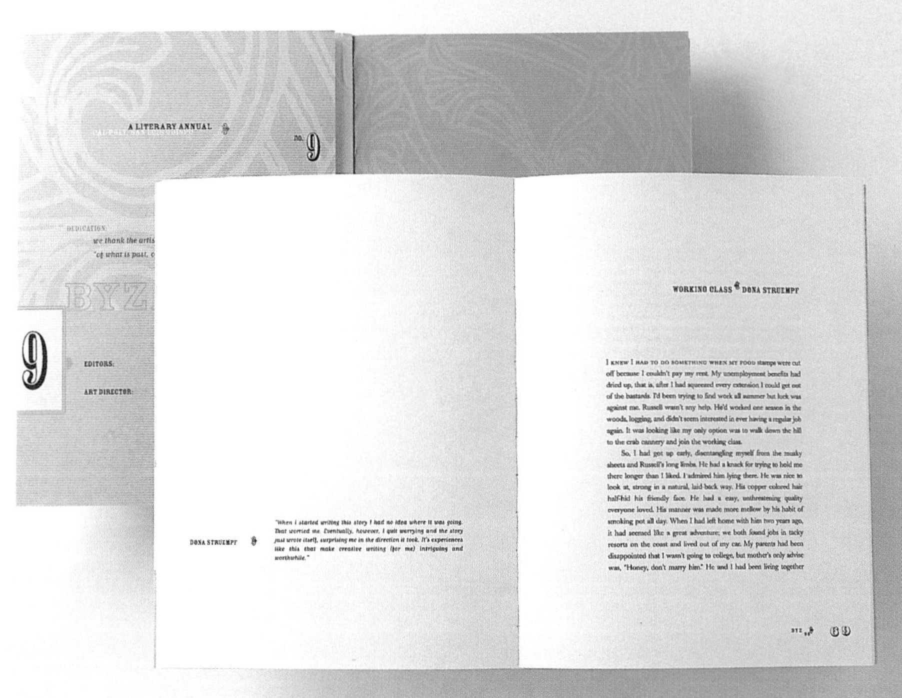

Brochure

Design_Tim Hagedorn
Bremen, Germany
Art Direction_Karsten Unterberger
Creative Direction_Almut Roeper
Project Manager_Sven Ruschek

Agency_in(corporate communciation + design GmbH
Client_Lang + Schwarz Wertpapierhandel AG

Principal Type_ITC Weidemann and News Gothic

Dimensions_7 11/16 x 7 11/16 in. (19.5 x 19.5 cm)

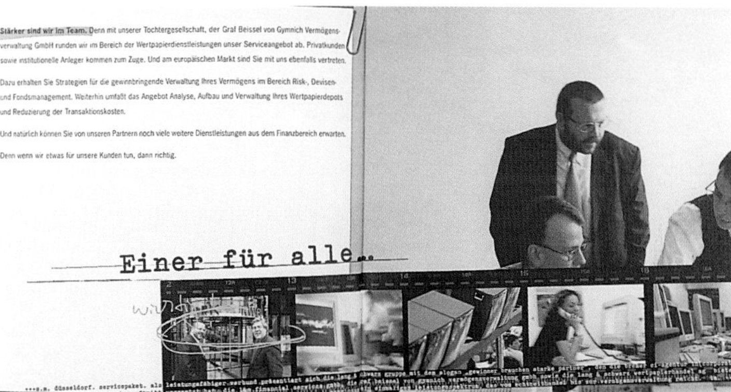

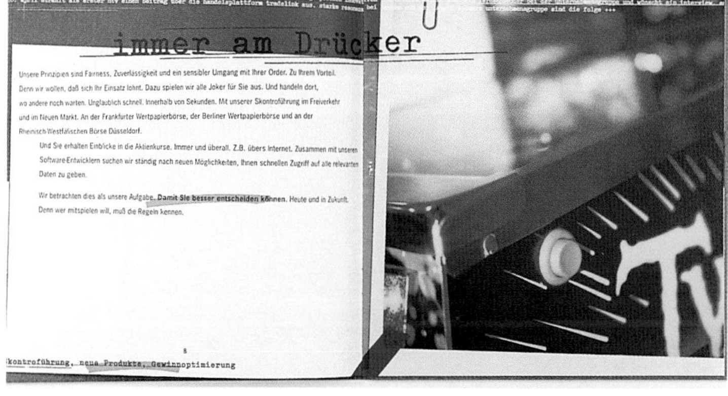

Design_Joerg Bauer
Stuttgart, Germany
Art Direction_Joerg Bauer
Creative Direction_Reiner Hebe and Joerg Bauer

Agency_HEBE Werbung + Design
Studio_Joerg Bauer Design
Client_HEBE Werbung + Design

Principal Type_Adobe Clarendon, Trade Gothic, Leucadia, FB Magneto Bold, FB Magneto Bold Extended, and FB Magneto Super Bold

Dimensions_9 ⅝ x 11 ⅝ in. (24.5 x 29.5 cm)

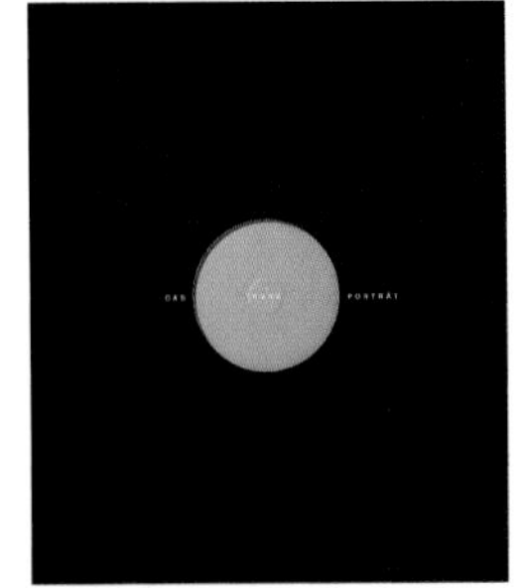

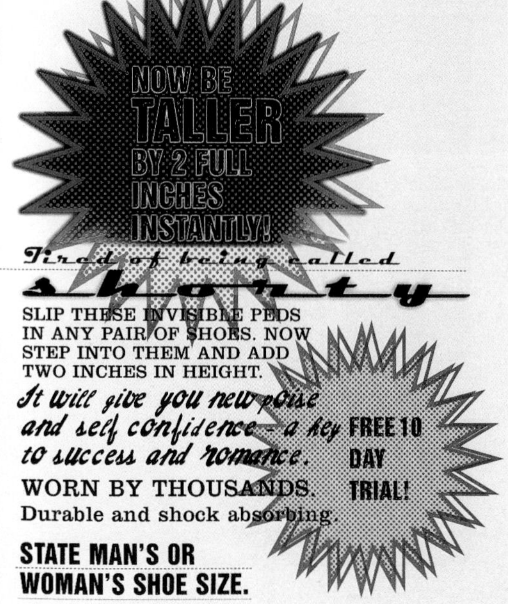

Poster

Design_Wang Xu
Guangzhou, China
Art Direction_Wang Xu
Creative Direction_Wang Xu

Studio_Wang Xu & Associates Ltd.
Client_Shanghai Graphic Designers Association

Principal Type_Bauer Bodoni

Dimensions_23 3/8 x 33 1/16 in. (59.4 x 84 cm)

when the well is dry we know the worth of water

当井水枯干时
我们才知道水
是多么的珍贵

Design_David Beck Dallas, Texas
Lettering_Duane Michals
Art Direction_David Beck
Creative Direction_David Beck

Design Office_Sibley Peteet Design
Client_Dallas Society of Visual Communications

Principal Type_Univers

Dimensions_22 x 30 in. (55.9 x 76.2 cm)

Design_Bob Johnson
Sonoma, California
Lettering_Blair O'Neil
Art Direction_Bob Johnson
Creative Direction_Bob Broman
Printer_Dan Reimer Aurora Press

Agency_JohnsonLynch Advertising
Client_Bob Broman Winery

Principal Type_Goudy Handtooled (modified)

Dimensions_1 ⅞ x 2 ¾ in. (4.8 x 7 cm)

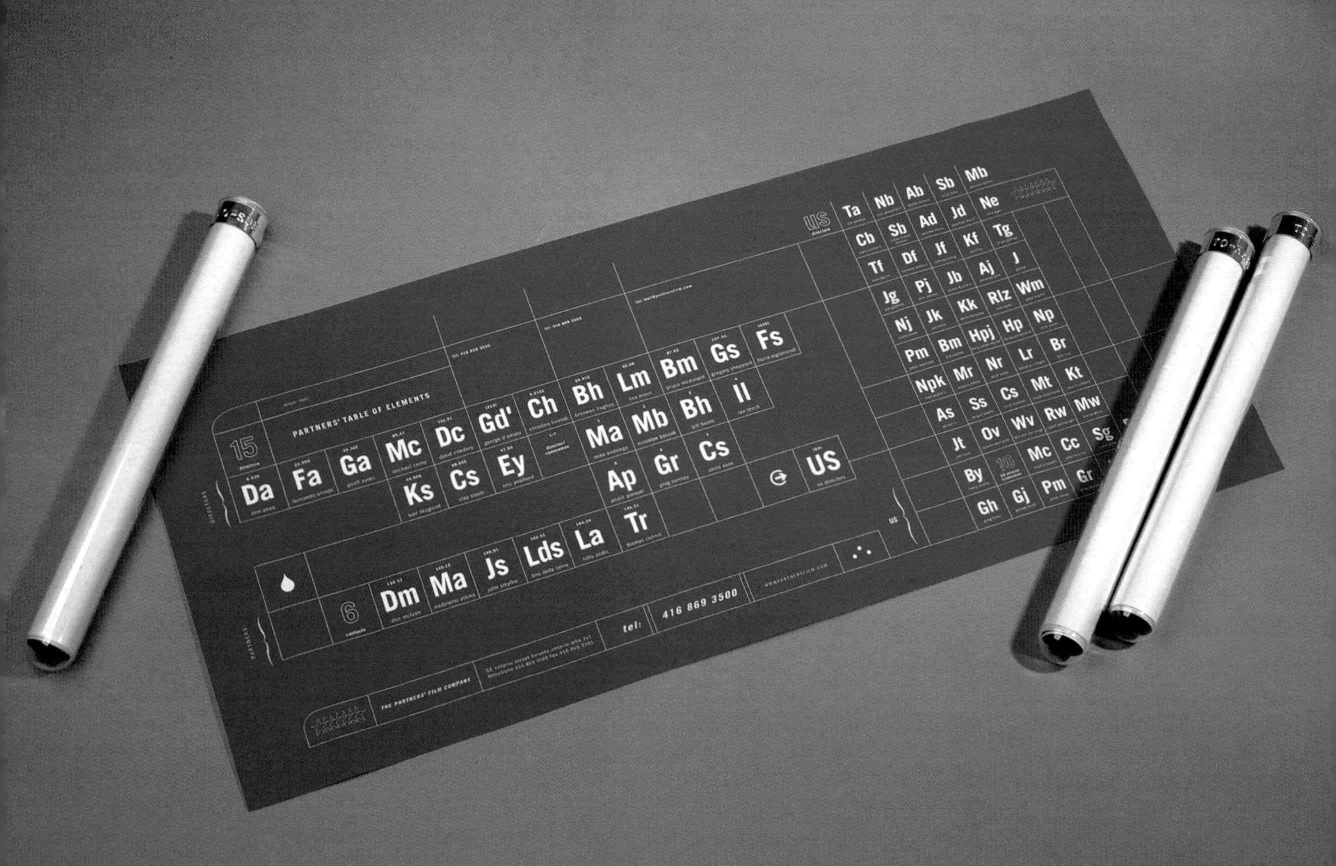

PARTNERS' TABLE OF ELEMENTS
15
directors
Da
Fa
Ga
Mc
Dc
Gd'
Ch
Bh
Lm
Bm
Gs
Fs
Ks
Cs
Ey
Ma
Mb
Bh
Il
Ap
Gr
Cs
US
Tr
La
Lds
Js
Ma
Dm
6
contacts
tel:
416 869 3500
THE PARTNERS' FILM COMPANY
US
Ta
Nb
Ab
Sb
Mb
Cb
Sb
Ad
Jd
Ne
Tf
Df
Jf
Kf
Tg
Jg
Pj
Jb
Aj
J
Nj
Jk
Kk
Rlz
Wm
Pm
Bm
Hpj
Hp
Np
Npk
Mr
Nr
Lr
Br
As
Ss
Cs
Mt
Kt
Jt
Ov
Wv
Rw
Mw
By
10
Mc
Cc
Sg
Gh
Gj
Pm
Gr

Design_Greg Lindy
Los Angeles, California
Art Direction_Greg Lindy
Creative Direction_Greg Lindy

Design Office_Intersection Studio
Client_School of Thought Records

Principal Type_Interstate and Section

Dimensions_5 ¾ x 4 ¾ in. (14.6 x 12.1 cm)

Poster

Design_Michael Bierut
and Nicole Trice
New York, New York
Art Direction_Michael Bierut

Design Office_Pentagram
Client_The Architectural League
of New York

Principal Type_Interstate Bold

Dimensions_23 ½ x 38 ½ in.
(59.7 x 97.8 cm)

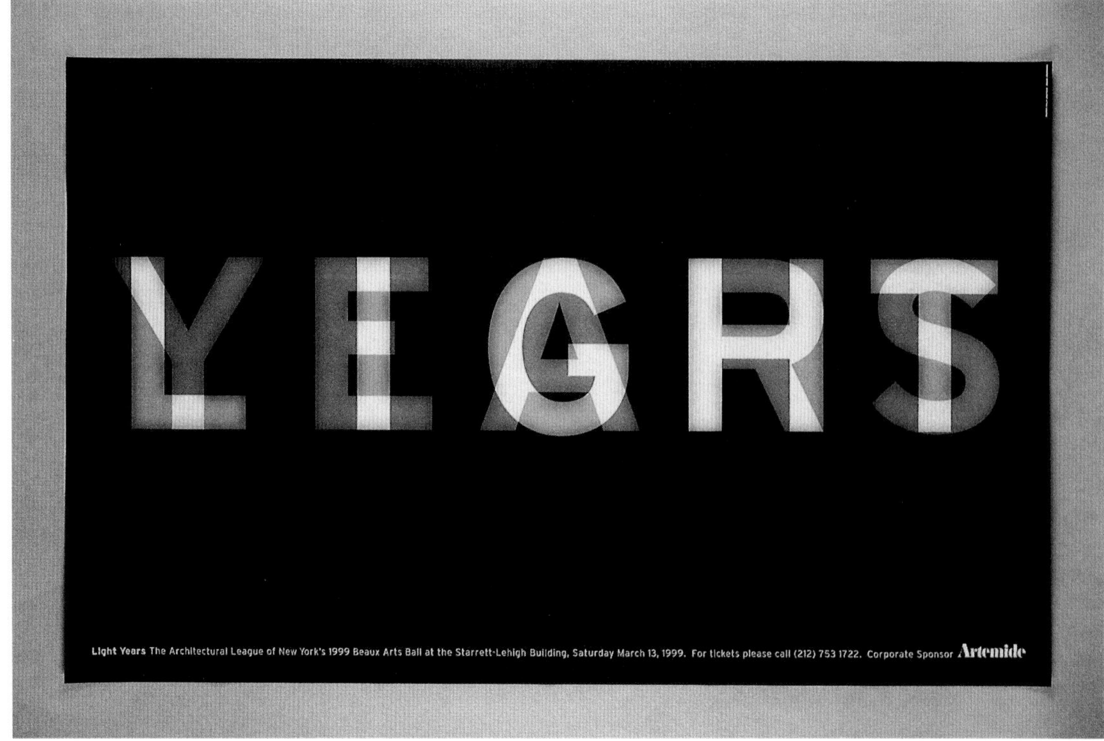

Poster

Design_Norio Kudo Tokyo, Japan
Art Direction_Norio Kudo
Photography_Takahito Sato
Copywriter_Juri Sakuma

Design Office_Strike Co., Ltd.
Client_Japan Graphic Designers Association, Inc.

Principal Type_Helvetica Bold

Dimensions_40 9/16 x 28 5/8 in. (103 x 72.8 cm)

Design_Joerg Bauer and Jan Maier
Stuttgart, Germany
Art Direction_Joerg Bauer, Jan Maier, and Nils Schubert
Photography_Nils Schubert and Joerg Bauer

Design Office_Joerg Bauer Design
Client_Undercover

Principal Type_Cholla Unicase Ligatures, Citizen, Dot Matrix, Digital, Helvetica, and Helvetica Neue Black

Dimensions_18 ⅛ x 24 in. (46 x 61 cm)

Design_Mario L'Écuyer
Ottawa, Canada
Art Direction_Mario L'Écuyer
Creative Direction_Jean-Luc Denat and Mario L'Écuyer
Photography_Headlight Innovative Imagery
Copywriter_Bianca Bohanan

Agency_Iridium marketing + design (formerly Aartvark Communications)
Client_Rolland Inc.

Principal Type_Arbitrary Sans, Calvino Hand, and Keedy Sans

Dimensions_10 x 14 in. (25.4 x 35.6 cm)

La première qualité
Le verre est-il à moitié vide ou à moitié plein?
Number Two tries harder
Ouvert 24 hres — 7 jrs
MEDIOCRITY is simply a conceptual point of reference.
MÉDIOCRITÉ
“The future bel
« L'avenir
to cr wds”
— DON DeLILLO

Design_Paula Scher
and Keith Daigle
New York, New York
Art Direction_Paula Scher

Design Office_Pentagram
Client_Metropolis

Principal Type_Trade Gothic

Dimensions_44½ x 31½ in.
(113 x 80 cm)

Student Work

Design_Sibylle Reichelt and Maike Truschkowski Kassel, Germany
Photography_Werner Maschmann, Constantin Meyer, Sibylle Reichelt, and Maike Truschkowski

School_Kunsthochschule Kassel
Instructors_Christof Gassner and Jörg Stürzebecher

Principal Type_Univers Bold Condensed

Dimensions_15 ¾ x 11 ¹¹⁄₁₆ in. (40 x 29.7 cm)

03

Brochure

Design_John Fairley
London, England
Art Direction_John Fairley
Creative Direction_John Fairley

Design Office_MCS Design
Client_BDO Stoy Hayward/Kite (UK) Limited

Principal Type_Perpetua and Mason

Dimensions_11 ⁹⁄₁₆ x 10 ¹⁵⁄₁₆ in. (29.3 x 27.5 cm)

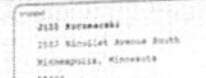

K

Jill Kuczmarski | (Kōs'mär skē) 3507 Nicollet Avenue South Minneapolis, MN 55404

Date/Month/Year

Mr. or Ms. Addressee
Company Name
Street Address
City, State Zip Code

Dear Name of Addressee,

I was born in Rhinelander, Wisconsin. The world I grew up in was small but the energy was high. We lived on a farm, and aside from all the broken bones and emergency room visits, life was pretty quiet. Naturally, this has had an effect. In my case it has made me a risk taker, and has given me an understanding of how the beautiful can be useful, and vice versa.

The first time I remember noticing graphic design was helping my dad shop for tractor parts at Mill's Fleet Farm. I love all the images and objects at Fleet Farm, with its simple signage, packaging and layout. It really fertilizes the imagination (no pun intended). However, I actually made the decision to go into design as a career when I realized that design is one of the only professions where being strange is acceptable and I could talk about the aesthetic value of a beat-up Buick without the threat of being locked up in a padded room. Right now, my style tends toward the (underline one): conservative/exotic/classical/funky/irreverent/other: delinquent Catholic schoolgirl.

This stationery system represents layers. On one hand it shows my passion for literature and old printed matter; on the other it represents my love for the eclectic. The only thing that was a given in this project was using French Paper. I chose Dur-O-Tone Newsprint Extra White because it is reminiscent of the vintage encyclopedias I used to ravish as a kid. Everything else was fill in the blank.

Since I am a little hard to follow at times, I would like to bring a certain clarity to my designs. I want to make people experience design, not just look at it. As for the future, I never want to grow up and I hope I can still be awed by at least two things a day until I die.

Sincerely,

Jill Kuczmarski
Design Student

Phone

Design_Masahiko Kimura
Tokyo, Japan
Art Direction_Masahiko Kimura

Client_Libreria Giannino Stoppani

Principal Type_Dante and HonMincho

Dimensions_11 11/16 x 8 3/8 in. (29.7 x 21.2 cm)

Design_Vittorio Costarella
Seattle, Washington
Lettering_Vittorio Costarella
Art Direction_Vittorio Costarella
Creative Direction_Mitch Nash

Studio_Modern Dog Design Co.
Client_Blue Q

Principal Type_Handlettering

Dimensions_2 ½ x 4 x 1¾ in.
(6.4 x 10.2 x 4.5 cm)

Design_Douglas Dearden
Salt Lake City, Utah
Lettering_J. Otto Seibold
Art Direction_Douglas Dearden
Illustration_J. Otto Seibold

Design Office_AND
Client_Bink

Principal Type_Seibold and Courier

Dimensions_6 x 9 in.
(15.2 x 22.9 cm)

1

Birth Annoucement

Design_David Plunkert
Baltimore, Maryland
Art Direction_David Plunkert

Design Office_SPUR Design LLC

Principal Type_Akzidenz Grotesk and Shelley

Dimensions_4⅛ x 5¼ in. (10.5 x 13.3 cm)

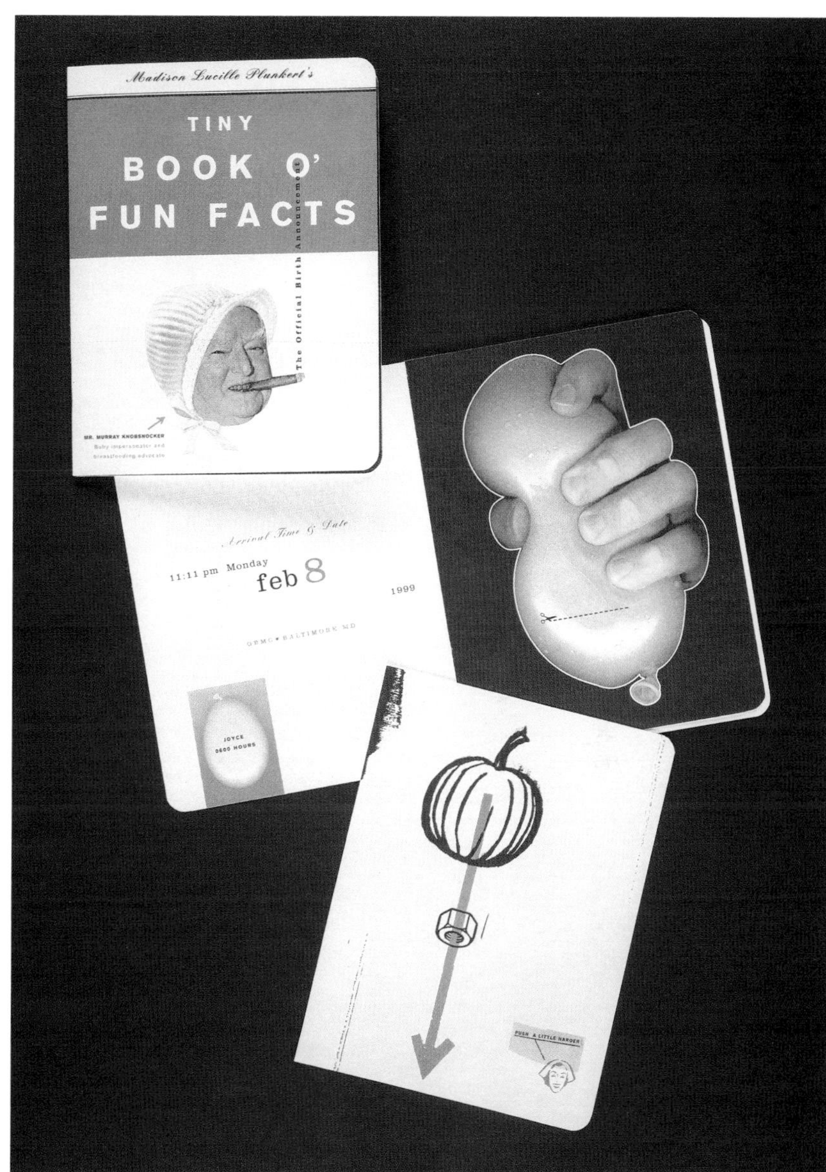

Design_Samantha Davenport
Atlanta, Georgia
Art Direction_David Cannon

Design Office_EAI
Client_Georgia Pacific Papers

Principal Type_ITC Franklin Gothic

Dimensions_6 x 8 in.
(15.2 x 20.3 cm)

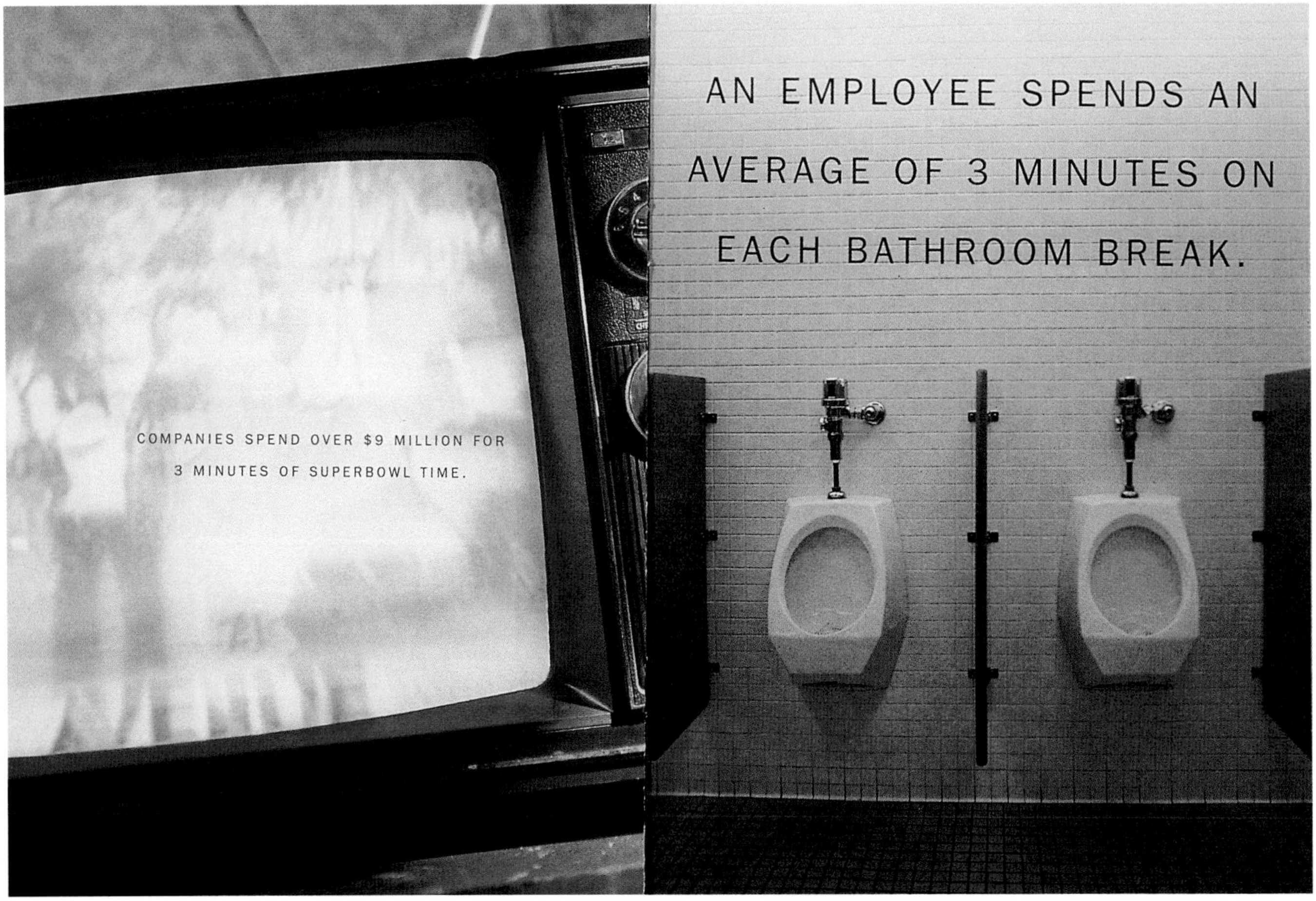

COMPANIES SPEND OVER $9 MILLION FOR
3 MINUTES OF SUPERBOWL TIME.

AN EMPLOYEE SPENDS AN
AVERAGE OF 3 MINUTES ON
EACH BATHROOM BREAK.

1

Student Work

Design_Justyna Zareba
Passaic, New Jersey

School_School of Visual Arts
Instructor_James Victore

Principal Type_Zurich

Dimensions_6 x 9 in.
(15.2 x 22.9 cm)

All life is an experiment. The more experiments you make the better. What if they are a little coarse, and you might get your coat soiled or torn? What if you do fil, and get fairly rolled in the dirt once or twice? Up again, you shall never be so afraid of a tumble.

Knowledge, love, power-
there is the complete life

Design_Christian Toensmann
Hamburg, Germany

School_University for Applied Science, Bielefeld
Instructor_Professor Gerd Fleischmann

First Place

Principal Type_Trade Gothic Regular and Monotype Baskerville Italic

Dimensions_8 11/16 x 10 5/8 in. (22 x 27 cm)

Poster

Design_Mirko Ilić
New York, New York
Art Direction_Mirko Ilić

Studio_Mirko Ilić Corp.
Client_International Design Center

Principal Type_Based on Helvetica

Dimensions_27⅝ x 39⅜ in.
(70 x 100 cm)

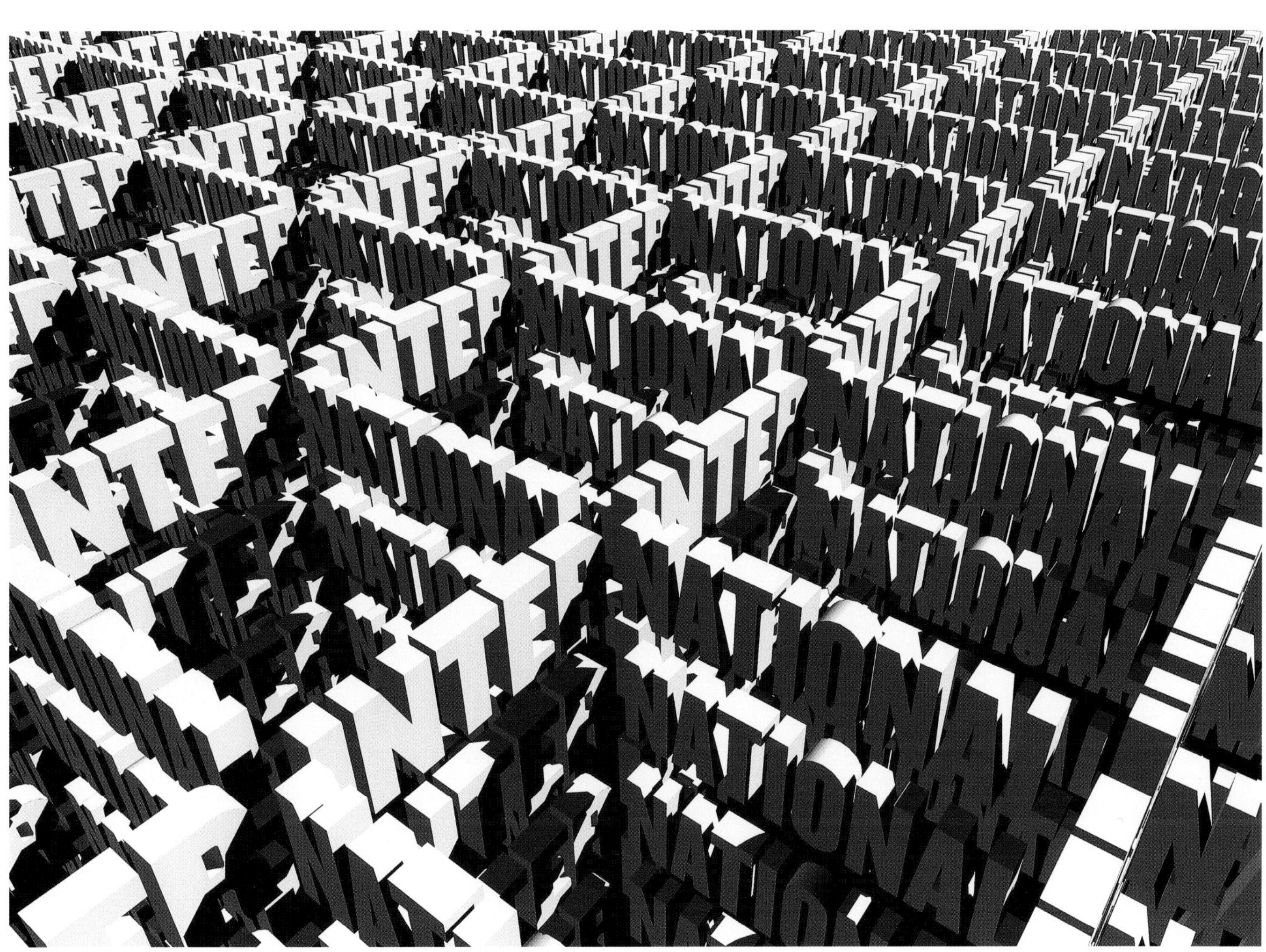

Student Work

Design_Elizabeth Ackerman
New York, New York
Instructor_Carin Goldberg

School_School of Visual Arts

Principal Type_Trade Gothic

Dimensions_13 x 8 in.
(33 x 20.3 cm)

Student Work

Design_Yoshiko Kusada
New York, New York
Instructor_L. Richard Poulin

School_School of Visual Arts

Third Place

Principal Type_Centaur

Dimensions_8 x 4 ¾ in. (20.3 x 12.1 cm)

Facedown in ignorance Your mouths spilling words

You, created only a little lower than
The angels, have crouched too long in
The bruising darkness
Have lain too long

Armed for slaughter.

The Rock cries out to us today,

Here, on the pulse of this fine day
You may have the courage to look up and out and upon me,
The Rock, the River, the Tree, your country.
No less to Midas than the mendicant.
No less to you now than the mastodon then.

Here on the pulse of this new day
You may have the grace to look up and out
And into your sister's eyes,
And into your brother's face,

Your country,

and say simply very simply ———— with hope

so say

the Asian
the Jew
the Native American
The Catholic
the French
The Irish
the Priest
The Gay
the Preacher
the homeless

the Hispanic
The African
the Sioux
the Muslim
the Greek
the Rabbi
the Sheik
the Straight
The privileged
the Teacher

The Creator gave to me when I and the Tree and the Rock were one.

Before cynicism was a bloody sear across your brow
And when you yet knew you still knew nothing.
The River sang and sings on.

There is a true yearning to respond to the singing River and the wise Rock.

They hear. They all hear the speaking of the Tree.

MIXER

MÜNCHEN>13.10.99_WERKBAR ZÜRICH>14.10.99_ROHSTOFFLAGER FRANKFURT>19.10.99_KING KAMEHAMEHA
DÜSSELDORF>20.10.99_THE ROOM HAMBURG>27.10.99_MODERN EROTIC ART MUSEUM
BERLIN>28.10.99_WMF___START JEWEILS 21 UHR.

CLUBABEND MIT LIVE-MIXES AUS STILLS [TONY STONE], FILM FOOTAGE [ENERGY FILM LIBRARY] UND MUSIK. MIT VIDEO-ARTIST ULLEVÅN UND DJ DIXON SOWIE LOKALEM DJ. ANMELDUNG ERFORDERLICH. DETAILS: HTTP://WWW.TONYSTONE.DE / E-MAIL: MIXER@TONYSTONE.COM

TONY STONE BILDERWELTEN

ENERGY FILM-LIBRARY

Design_Katsunori Nishi
Tokyo, Japan
Art Direction_Katsunori Nishi

Design Office_Brahman Company Limited
Client_Tower Records Inc.

Principal Type_Puzzle

Dimensions_40 ⁹⁄₁₆ x 28 ⁵⁄₈ in. (103 x 72.8 cm)

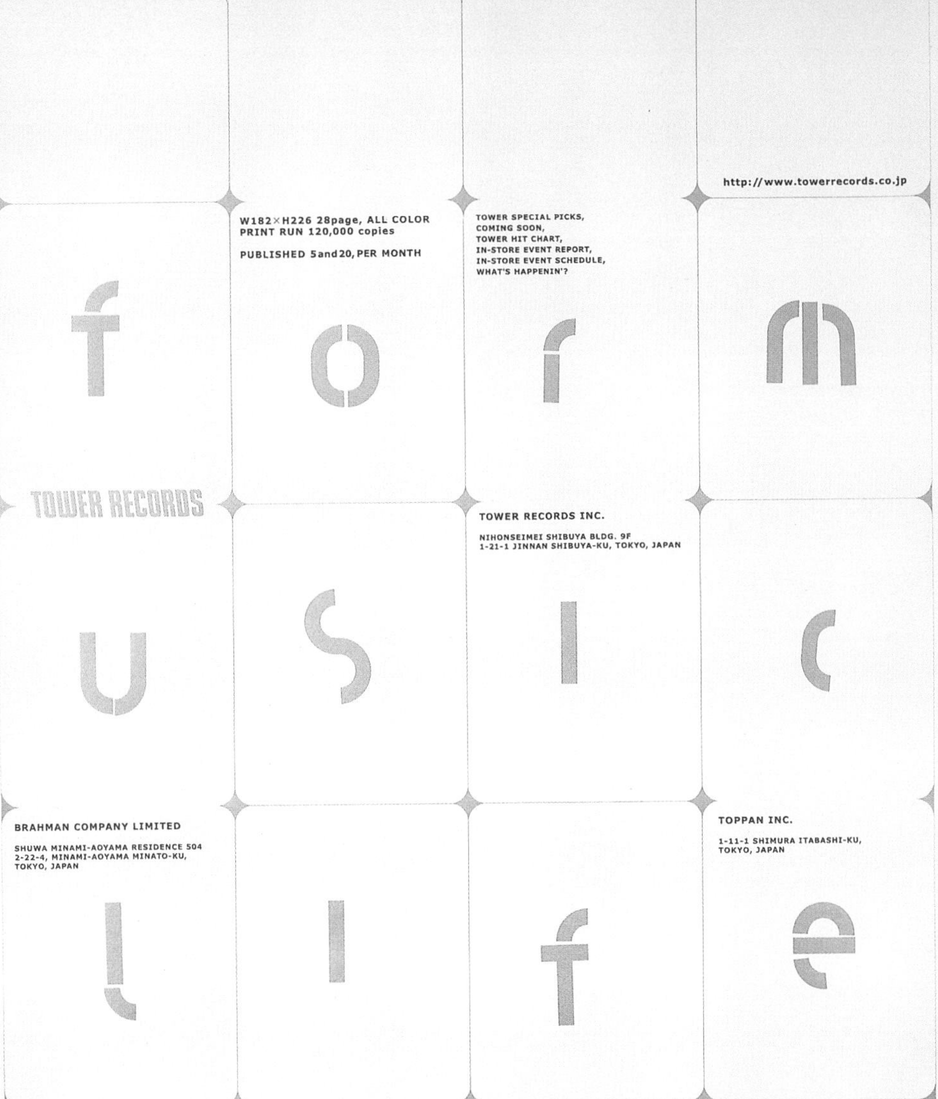

Design_Abigail Arafeli
New York, New York
Instructor_Kingsley Parker

School_Fashion Institute of Technology

Principal Type_Lunatix and Helvetica

Dimensions_60 x 35 in. (23.6 x 88.9 cm)

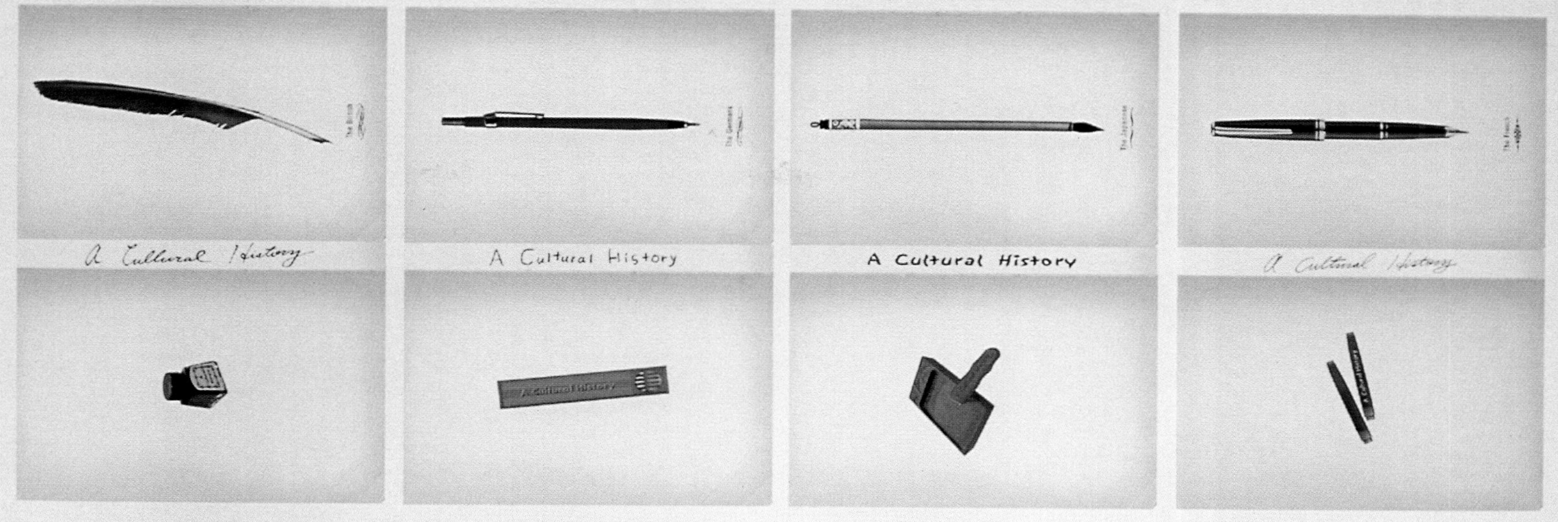
The British
A Cultural History
The Germans
A Cultural History
A Cultural History
The Japanese
A Cultural History
The French
A Cultural History
A Cultural History

Student Work

Design_Simone Mutert
Düsseldorf, Germany
Instructor_Prof. Helfried Hagenberg

School_Fachhochschule Düsseldorf

Second Place

Principal Type_Univers and Joanna

Dimensions_Various

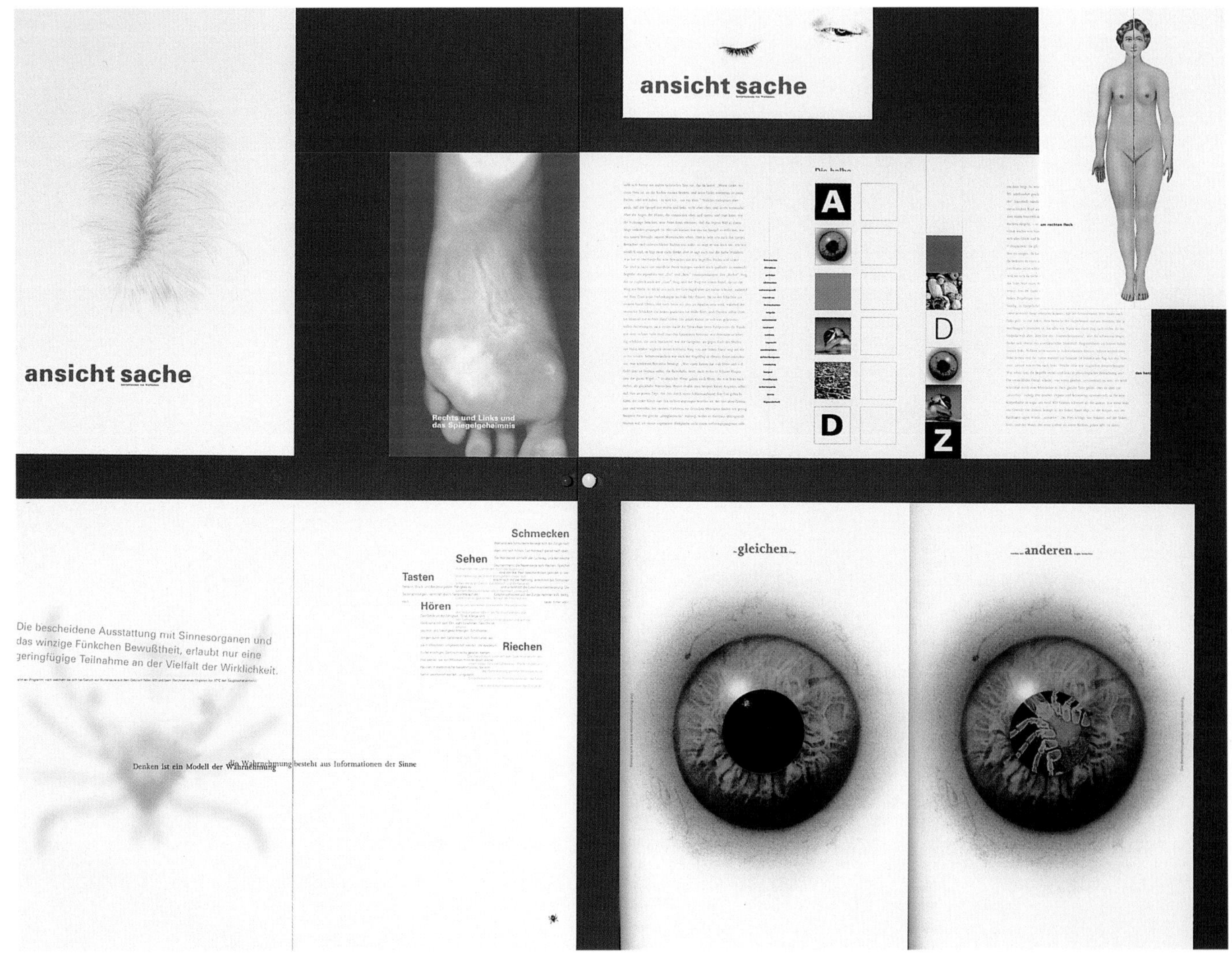

Brochure

Design_Régine Thienhaus
Hamburg, Germany
Art Direction_Régine Thienhaus
Creative Direction_Prof.
Peter Wippermann
Photography_Nathanel Goldberg
and Claudia Kempf

Agency_Büro Hamburg JK.PW.
Client_Trendbüro B.K.W.

Principal Type_OCR Buero
and ITC Officina

Dimensions_8 ¼ x 11 11/16 in.
(21 x 29.7 cm)

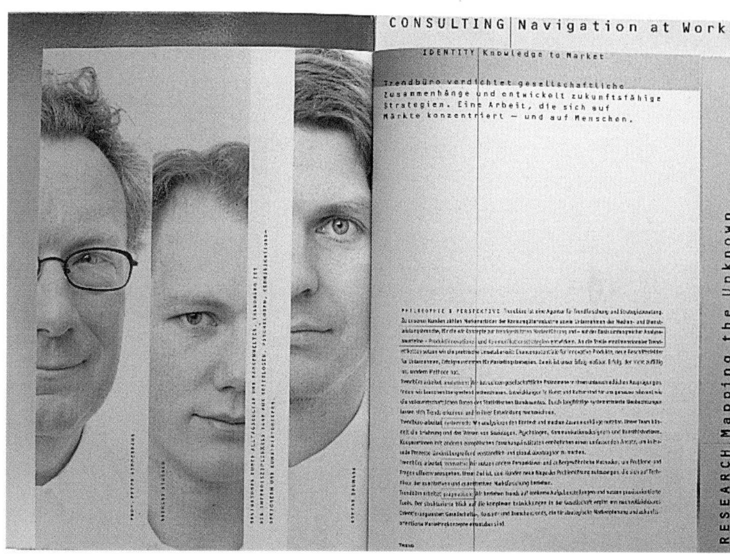

1

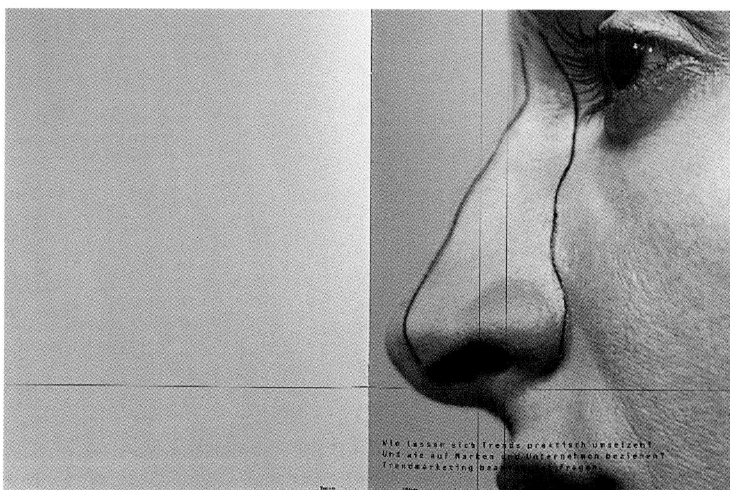

Design_Harry Pearce
Twickenham, England
Art Direction_Harry Pearce
and Domenic Lippa
Creative Direction_Harry Pearce
and Domenic Lippa

Studio_Lippa Pearce Design

Principal Type_AG Old Face,
HTF Champion Gothic, Didot,
and Bitstream Clarendon

Dimensions_8 11/16 x 7 in.
(22 x 18 cm)

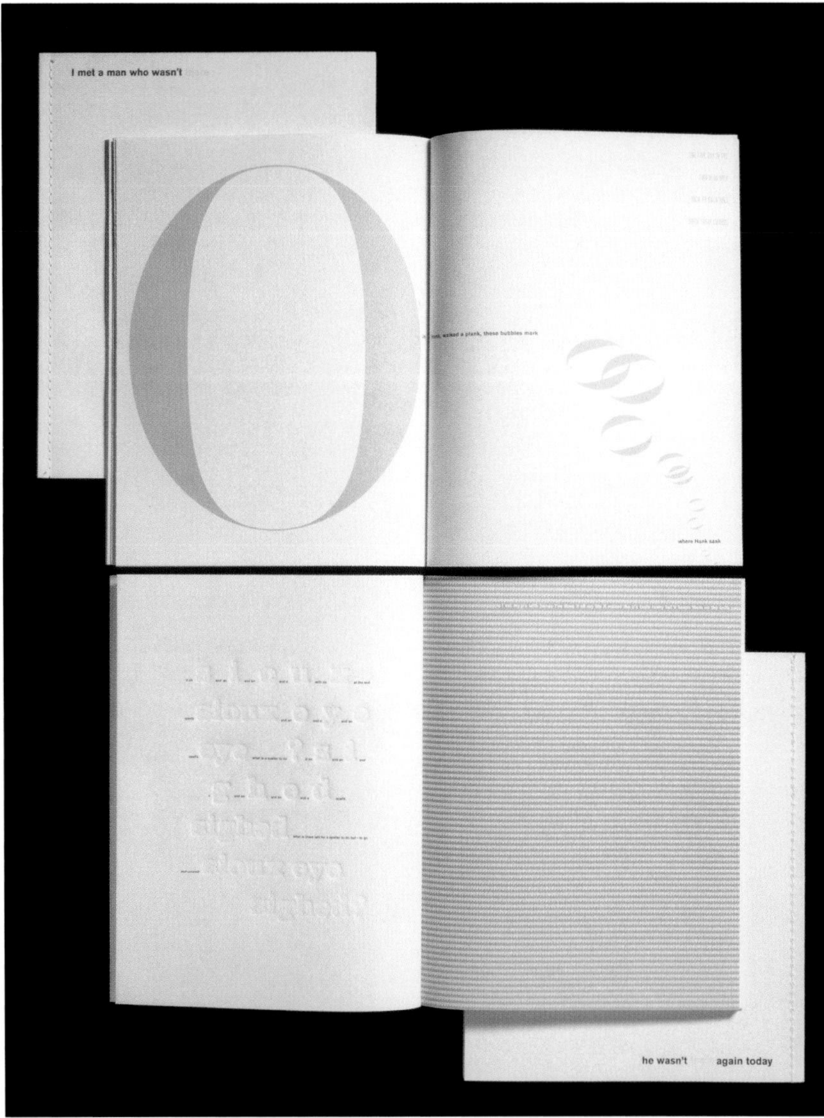

Poster

Design_Minao Tsukada
Tokyo, Japan
Art Direction_Minao Tsukada
Photography_Takahito Sato
Copywriter_Azusa Kajita

Studio_Strike Co., Ltd.

Principal Type_Morisawa MB 101

Dimensions_40 9/16 x 28 5/8 in.
(103 x 72.8 cm)

3

KIM

what needed to be done and how they needed to record their data. I told him I was ready to do it. Receiving the therapy was simple, not complicated at all. It wasn't uncomfortable or painful and best of all, I didn't have the depression, loss of appetite and hair loss that I had with chemotherapy.

They monitored me closely, collecting data every step of the way. Waiting in the hospital for results was the hardest part -- even though I actually felt shrinkage almost immediately. Because my tumors were on my ovaries, I actually felt the tumors shrinking inside me. I was told that other patients had similar kinds of experiences. With my first CT scan after I left the hospital, the doctor said it looked excellent and that they couldn't see tumors. There was scarring left over from the shrinkage of tumors, but the tumors were gone. I stayed in remission for five years.

In 1998, I had a feeling something was wrong because I could feel tightness in my throat. The doctor found a mass on the outside of my esophagus -- the cancer was back. Luckily, the tumors on my ovaries were still gone, but the cancer had found a new place in my body. I got the news of relapse, but my doctor said he'd treat me again. In June, I received another Bexxar treatment. So much progress had been made on the therapy since my first treatment five years ago. It was like going to the doctor for a little procedure. First, they did blood work and all the preliminary pre-therapy steps, and then I had the treatment the same day. I was sent home without staying in the hospital overnight. Because of the radiation from the therapy, I shouldn't be around anyone for long periods of time for the first week. That was painless. I had scans to determine what the treatment had done. There was no tumor. Again, my lymphoma is gone. Now, I need to see my doctor every three months. When I'm in remission for a year, I'll only see him every six months. I feel fine.

I'm very thankful for this new drug which certainly helped me -- but my attitude helped me, too. I don't see things quite the same way. I try not to look in a negative way at things. We're all human and I'm no saint. But I realize I'll only be alive for a certain length of time and I really need to make the best of it while I'm here. Non-Hodgkin's lymphoma has made me realize that family and friends are most important in my life. I've been with my partner now for 10 years. He's been a real rock to lean on during this whole thing. When I talk to other non-Hodgkin's lymphoma patients, I tell them about this drug. I also tell them to keep a very positive attitude. Depend on the people that you love. No one can go through this alone. You need support.

ALIVE & WELL

GREAT JAZZ MUSIC IN THE SCULPTURE GARDEN AT THE SHELDON MEMORIAL ART GALLERY
ADMISSION IS FREE
MUSIC BEGINS AT 7PM
JAZZ IN JUNE IS SPONSORED BY THE NEBRASKA ART ASSOCIATION
CORPORATE FUNDING FROM NORWEST BANKS
JAZZ in June
Live Performance
Instrumental and Vocal
HOT SUMMERTIME GROOVE
(Every Tuesday Evening in June)
IRIE/The Gulizia Bros., June 02–Kevin Mahogany, June 09
Musa Nova, June 16–Bruce Katz, June 23
Ivan Paduart, June 30
57-60005
Made in U.S.A.
NOT LICENSED FOR RADIO BROADCAST
DEDICATED TO THE MEMORY OF KATHERINE FARREL
MEDIA SPONSOR IS KFOR
SPECIAL THANKS TO BAILEY LAUERMAN & ASSOC., NEBRASKA BUSINESS PRINTING, QUALI.GRAPHS, AND THE UNIVERSITY PROGRAM COUNCIL/UNL

Art Direction_Darren Namaye
Creative Direction_Wendy Blattner

Principal Type_MT News Gothic, ITC New Baskerville, Rosewood, and Eurostile

Dimensions_8 ¼ x 10 ¼ in. (21 x 26 cm)

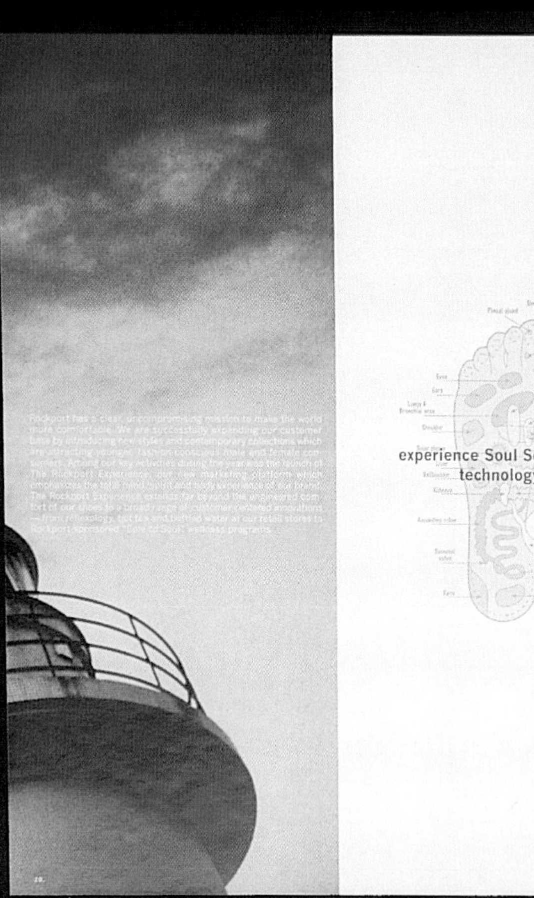

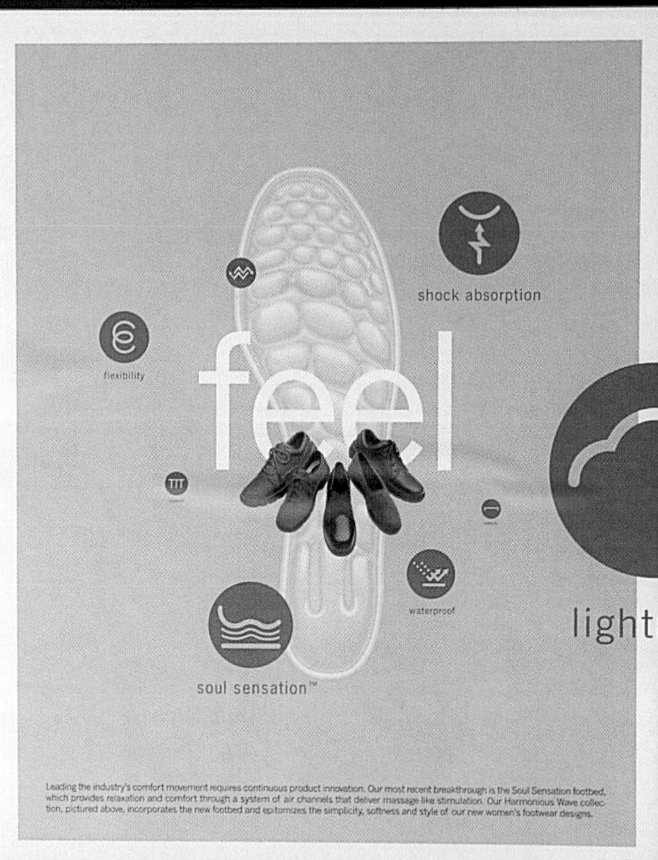

Design_Darren Namaye
New York, New York
Art Direction_Darren Namaye
Creative Direction_Wendy Blattner

Design Office_Nuforia, Inc.
Client_Reebok International, Ltd.

Principal Type_MT News Gothic, ITC New Baskerville, Rosewood, and Eurostile

Dimensions_8 ¼ x 10 ¼ in. (21 x 26 cm)

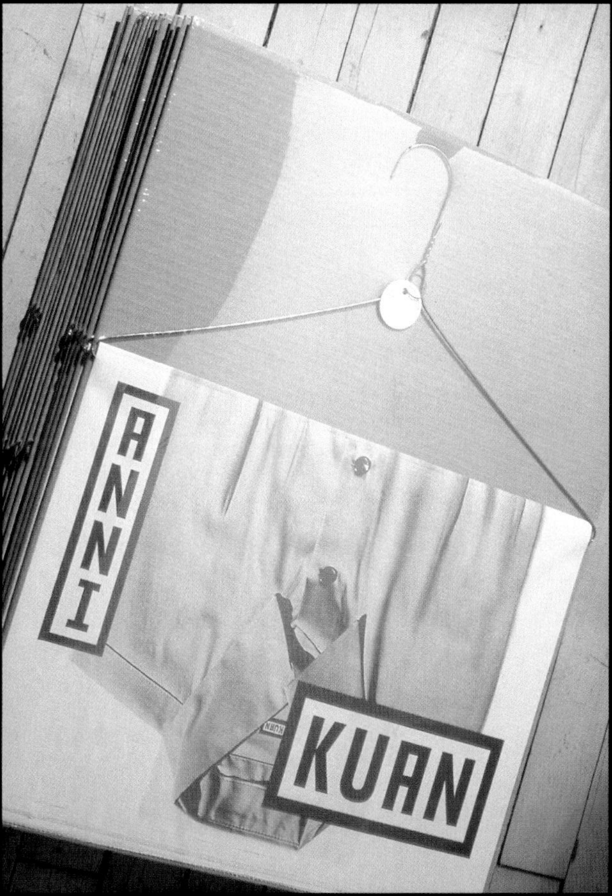

Design_Ken Fox and Fletcher Martin
Chicago, Illinois
Creative Direction_Curtis Schreiber

Agency_VSA Partners
Client_Harley-Davidson Motor Company

Principal Type_Bulmer, Adobe Cheltenham, Adobe Century, and BT Futura

Dimensions_20 x 35 in. (50.8 x 88.9 cm)

Poster

Design_Giorgio Pesce
Lausanne, Switzerland
Art Direction_Giorgio Pesce
Creative Direction_Giorgio Pesce

Agency_Atelier Poisson
Client_Théâtre Arsenic

Principal Type_Triumvirate
and Trade Gothic

Dimensions_50 ⅜ x 35 7/16 in.
(128 x 90 cm)

Design_Todd Simmons
San Francisco, California
Art Direction_Bill Cahan
Creative Direction_Bill Cahan
Photography_Robert Schlatter
Illustration_Bill Barminski
Copywriter_Karen Langdon

Design Office_Cahan & Associates
Client_The Doctor's Company

Principal Type_Futura Heavy Oblique and HTF Champion Gothic

Dimensions_6 ¼ x 9 in. (15.9 x 2.9 cm)

Poster

Design_Katsuyuki Tanaka
Osaka, Japan
Art Direction_Katsuyuki Tanaka
Creative Direction_Katsuyuki Tanaka

Design Office_KPlant Co., Ltd.
Client_"S" Wonderland Co., Ltd.

Principal Type_Art Factory

Dimensions_40 9/16 x 28 11/16 in.
(103 x 72.8 cm)

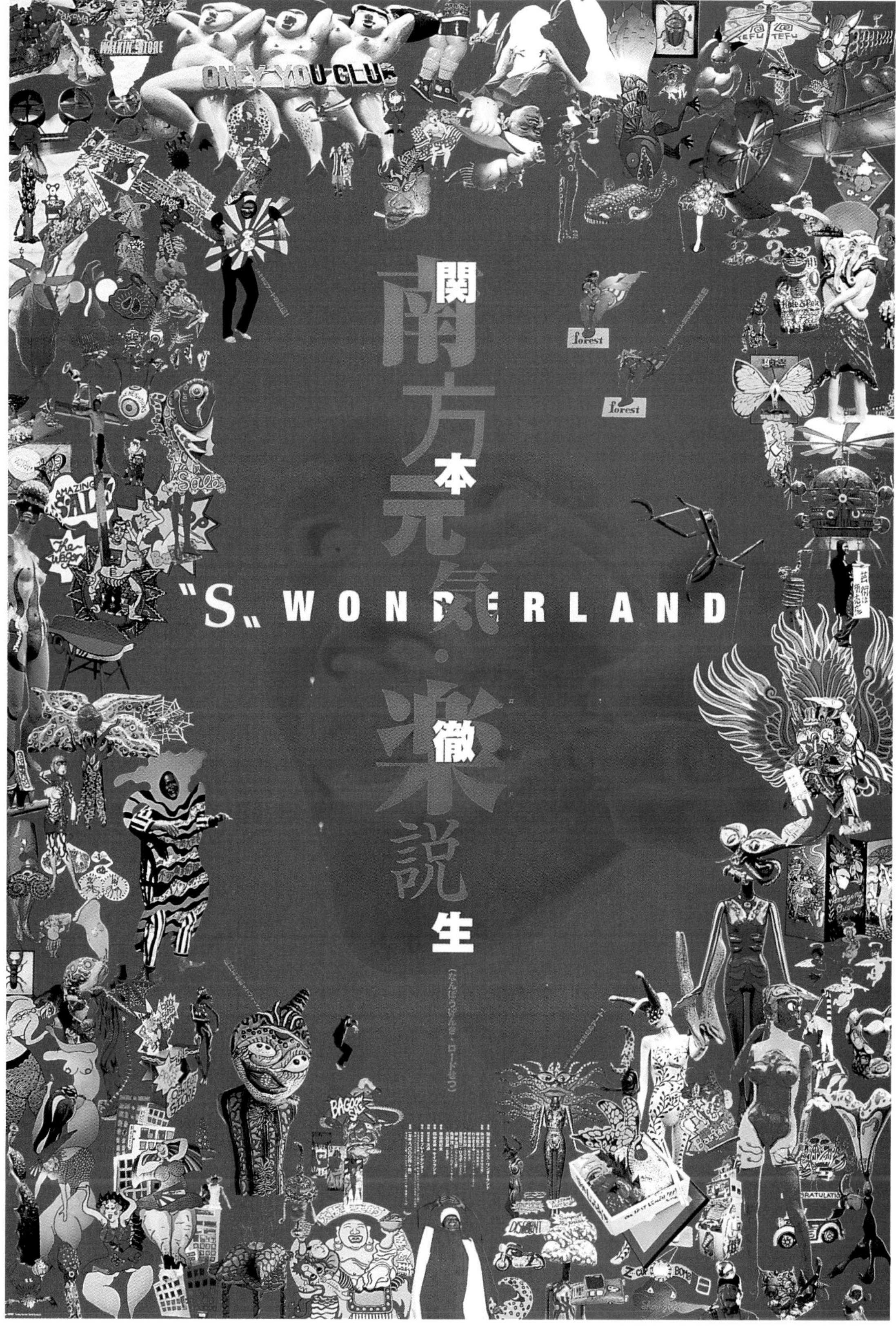

Design_Chris Froeter
Chicago, Illinois
Art Direction_Chris Froeter
Creative Direction_Chris Froeter

Design Office_Froeter Design Co., Inc.
Client_American Institute
of Graphic Arts/Chicago

Principal Type_Charcoal
and Bodoni

Dimensions_Various

Catalog

Design_Matt Eller and Topher Sinkinson
Portland, Oregon
Creative Department_Alicia Johnson, Matt Eller, Amie Champagne, Kimberly Harrington, and Topher Sinkinson
Creative Direction_Alicia Johnson and Matt Eller

Production Team_Deborah Hyde and Alan Foster
Design Firm_Johnson & Wolverton
Client_Photonica USA

Principal Type_Univers

Dimensions_9 x 11¾ in. (22.9 x 30 cm)

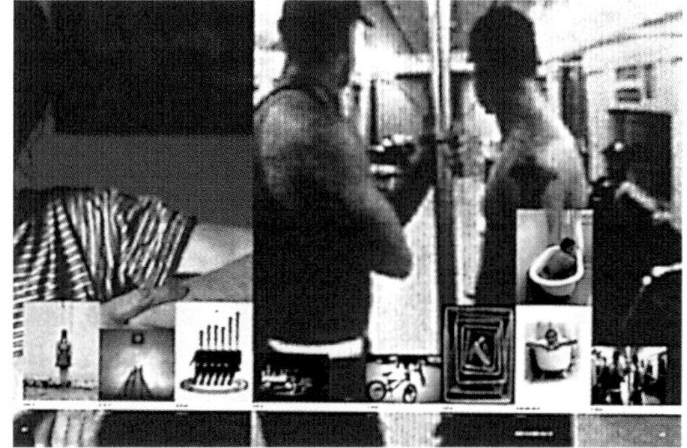

Design_Takafumi Kusagaya
Tokyo, Japan
Art Direction_Takafumi Kusagaya

Design Office_Kusagaya Design, Inc.
Client_TGV Inc.

Principal Type_Custom

Dimensions_28 1/16 x 40 9/16 in.
(72.8 x 103 cm)

Brochure

Design_Sharon Werner and Sarah Nelson
Minneapolis, Minnesota
Lettering_Todd ap Jones
Art Direction_Sharon Werner
Illustration_Allen Brewer, Tom Garrett, Eric Hanson, Dan Picasso, Elvis Swift, Jack Molloy, and Joe Sorren

Design Studio_Werner Design Werks, Inc.
Client_Joanie Bernstein, Art Rep

Principal Type_Adobe Clarendon, Univers Extended, News Gothic, and handlettering

Dimensions_10 x 12 in. (25.4 x 30.5 cm)

Design_David Covell and Joe Peila
Burlington, Vermont
Art Direction_David Covell
Creative Direction_Michael Jager

Studio_Jager Di Paola Kemp Design
Client_Champion International

Principal Type_Clicker, Nobel, Emperor Eight, Carplate, and Orator

Dimensions_7 x 5¾ in. (17.8 x 14.6 cm)

Annual Report

Design_Kevin Roberson
San Francisco, California
Art Direction_Bill Cahan
Creative Direction_Bill Cahan
Photography_Robert Schlatter, Ken Probst, Bill Phelps, and Christine Alicino

Design Office_Cahan & Associates
Client_Collateral Therapeutics

Principal Type_OCR B and Adobe Caslon

Dimensions_6 7/8 x 8 3/4 in. (17.5 x 22.2 cm)

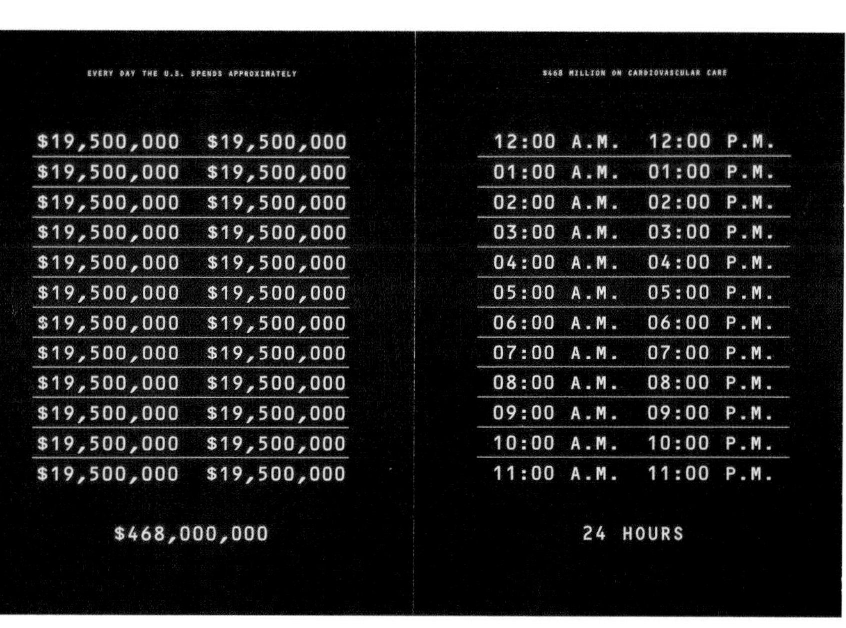

Design_Patrick Bittner and Isabel Bach Saarbruecken, Germany
Art Direction_Patrick Bittner
Creative Direction_Ivica Maksimovic
Photography_Patrick Bittner and Isabel Bach

Agency_Maksimovic & Partners
Client_Versorgungs – und Verkehrsgesellschaft Saarbruecken

Principal Type_DIN Mittelschrift and Engschrift

Inhalt → Seite ↓

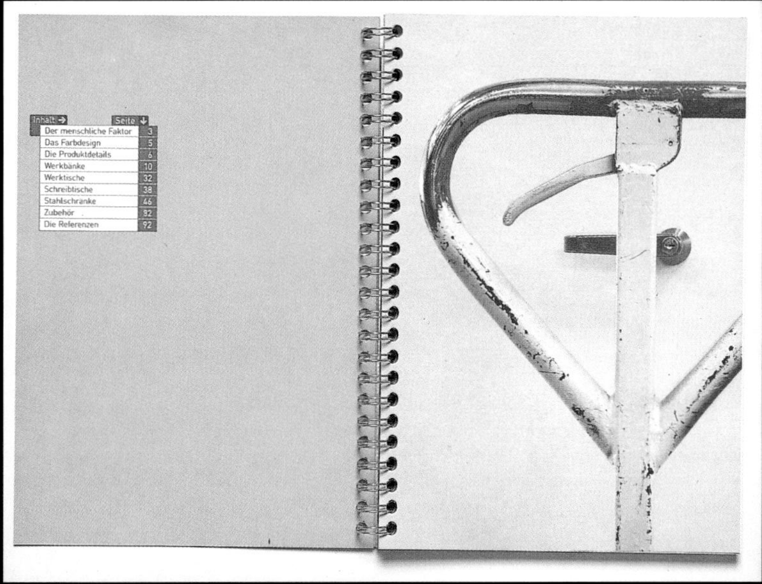

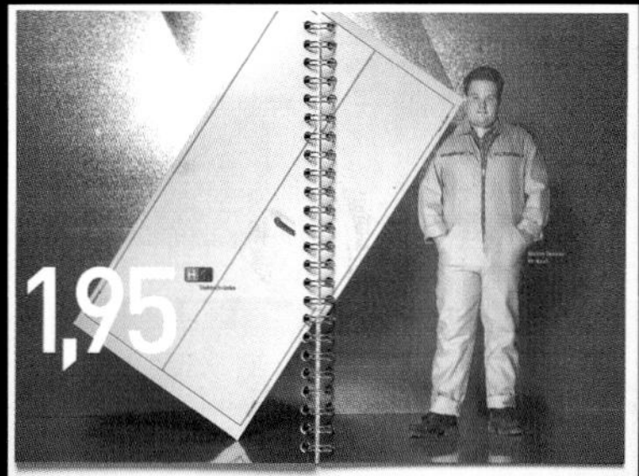

Poster

Design_Paul Sahre
New York, New York

Client_Rob Weisbach Books

Principal Type_HTF
Champion Gothic

Dimensions_20 x 30 in.
(50.8 X 76.2 cm)

★ THE ★
MUHAMMAD ALI
READER
WITH
NORMAN MAILER
JOYCE CAROL OATES
HUNTER S. THOMPSON
TOM WOLFE
GAY TALESE ★ A.J. LIEBLING
GEORGE PLIMPTON
ROGER KAHN
★ EDITED BY GERALD EARLY
ROB WEISBACH BOOKS
AN IMPRINT OF WILLIAM MORROW & COMPANY

1

Catalog

Design_Peter Bain and Paul Shaw
Brooklyn, New York, and
New York, New York

Design Offices_Peter Bain Design
and Paul Shaw/Letter Design
Client_American Printing
History Association

Principal Type_Zentenar Fraktur,
Stempel Schneidler, and
Monotype Grotesque

Dimensions_7½ x 10½ in.
(19.1 x 26.7 cm)

Design_Allison Williams, Mats Hakansson, Yael Eisele, Abby Clawson, and J.P. Williams
Art Direction_Allison Williams
Photography_Anita Calero

Studio_Design: M/W
Client_Takashimaya New York

Principal Type_Akzidenz Grotesk

Dimensions_7¼ x 9 in. (18.4 x 22.9 cm)

TOP RIGHT: Explore the universe of rice, vast and nutritious. Our collection of stainless steel rice pressers let you sculpt in a new medium, turning a serving of rice into one of three Japanese symbols of good fortune and longevity. Also ideal for shaping cookies, timbales or vegetables. Each piece is boxed, wrapped and tied with raffia. Fan, (5A) $12; Bamboo, (5B) $12; and Plum Flower, (5C) $12. • The perfect accompaniment is Rick Rodgers' book "On Rice" (not shown). It contains more than 60 international recipes for sauces, stews and stir-fries to serve over the many diverse types of this ancient grain. Most of them can be prepared in less than 30 minutes, while your basmati, arborio or black rice cooks. Published by Chronicle Books; 144 pages in paperback, (5D) $16.95.

BOTTOM RIGHT: Beyond bubbles. For more than 200 years, Tokyo artisans have employed a technique known as "glass blowing in the air," creating the distinctively graceful shapes of this glass sake set. Each piece is hand blown and hand finished by a skilled craftsman. The "tokkuri" (decanter) can also hold syrup or cream; the "ochoko" (cup) is ideal for dipping sauces or condiments. 7-oz. bottle and three 1 oz. glasses (one for each of the designers on the project). (5E) $175.

LEFT: Bento boxes give new meaning to our concept of fast food. In Japan's Edo Period (1600-1868), elaborate meals were transported on outings in these tiered lacquer boxes. Similar boxes are now sold to travelers at Japanese railway stations. No need to take this show on the road. The bento box allows individual dishes to retain their separate identities when served together at home. Use it to present several courses simultaneously, as a condiment platter or hors d'oeuvres tray. This wood version, hand crafted in Echizen, Japan, comes with a cover and removable divider. Its subtly-textured Akebono lacquer finish is made using a fine linen fabric. 10.25" x 10.25". (5F) $145. • Our collection of small dishes fits nicely into the bento box or can be used separately. Round red lacquer, 4.5". (5G) $12. Square red lacquer, 4.5" x 4.5". (5H) $12. Square floral handpainted porcelain, 4.25" x 4.25". (5J) $15. Square graphic handpainted porcelain, 4.25" x 4.25". (5K) $15. • Make no bones about it. These stainless steel tweezers, playfully created in the shape of the dish for which they are to be used, allow for easy removal of any small bones remaining in the fish course. 5". (5L) $35. • Cherry blossom, pine, cedar and maple woods each contribute their unique qualities to these hand-carved and lacquered chopsticks. 9". (5M) $40.

Poster

Design_Claudia Schmauder
Zurich, Switzerland
Lettering_Claudia Schmauder
Art Direction_Claudia Schmauder
Creative Direction_Claudia Schmauder

Client_Johann Jacobs Museum

Principal Type_Letters from sales receipts, and screenshots

Dimensions_50⅜ x 35¼ in. (128 x 89.5 cm)

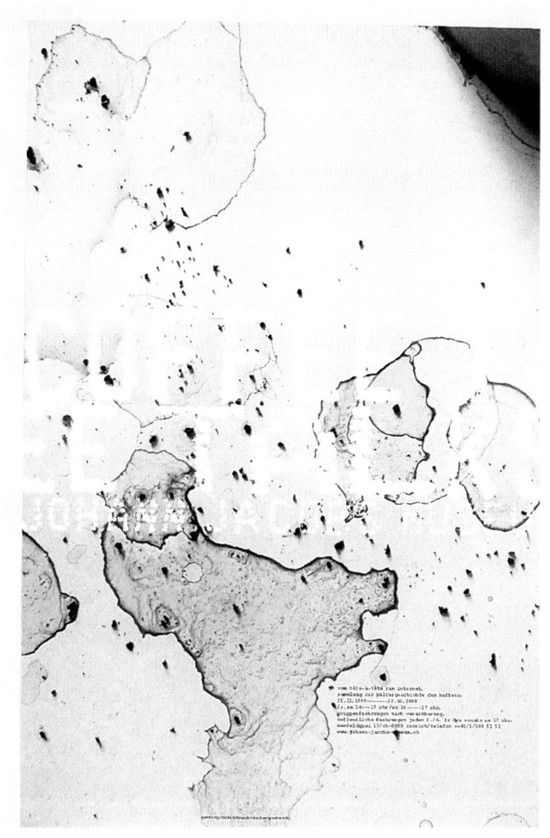

Design_Vince Frost
London, England
Lettering_Vince Frost
and Richard Rolf
Art Direction_Vince Frost
Creative Direction_Vince Frost
Printer_House of Naylor

Studio_Frost Design Ltd.
Client_4th Estate

Principal Type_Wood and
metal type

Dimensions_5½ x 8½ in.
(14 x 21.6 cm)

Brochure

Design_Su Mathews
and JoJo Rhee
New York, New York
Art Direction_Michael Gericke
Photography_Peter Olsen
Copywriter_JoAnn Stone

Design Office_Pentagram
Client_Brooklyn Law School

Principal Type_HTF Hoefler Engraved, Mrs. Eaves, and Trade Gothic

Dimensions_12 x 7 in. (30.5 x 17.8 cm

Design_Monica Peon
and Bob van Dÿk
The Hague, The Netherlands
Lettering_Bob van Dÿk

Agency_Studio Dumbar
Client_Zeebelt Theatre

Principal Type_Handlettering

Dimensions_23 5/8 x 33 1/16 in.
(60 x 80 cm)

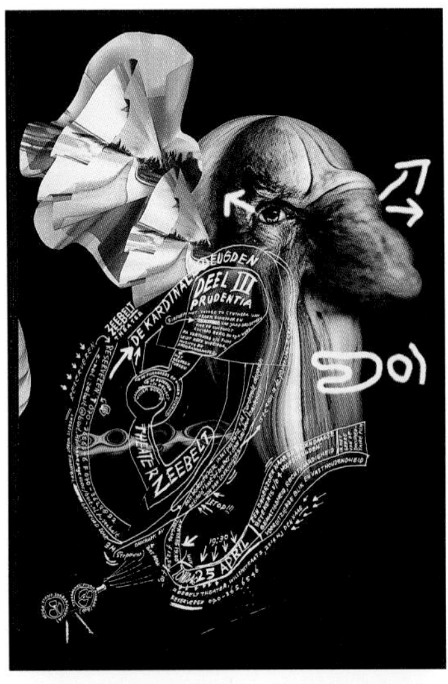

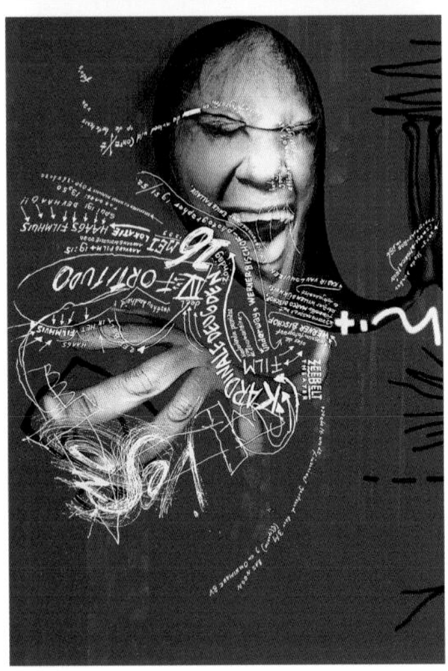

Brochure

Design_Mats Hakansson
New York, New York
Creative Direction_Allison Williams
and J. P. Williams

Studio_Design: M/W
Client_Champion International

Principal Type_Letter Gothic
and FF Scala Sans

Dimensions_5 x 6 ½ in.
(12.7 x 16.5 cm)

Design_Kevin Brainard
New York, New York
Art Direction_Drew Hodges
Creative Direction_Drew Hodges

Agency_Spotco.
Studio_Spot Design

Principal Type_HTF Champion Gothic and Trade Gothic

Dimensions_24 x 24 in. (61 x 61 cm)

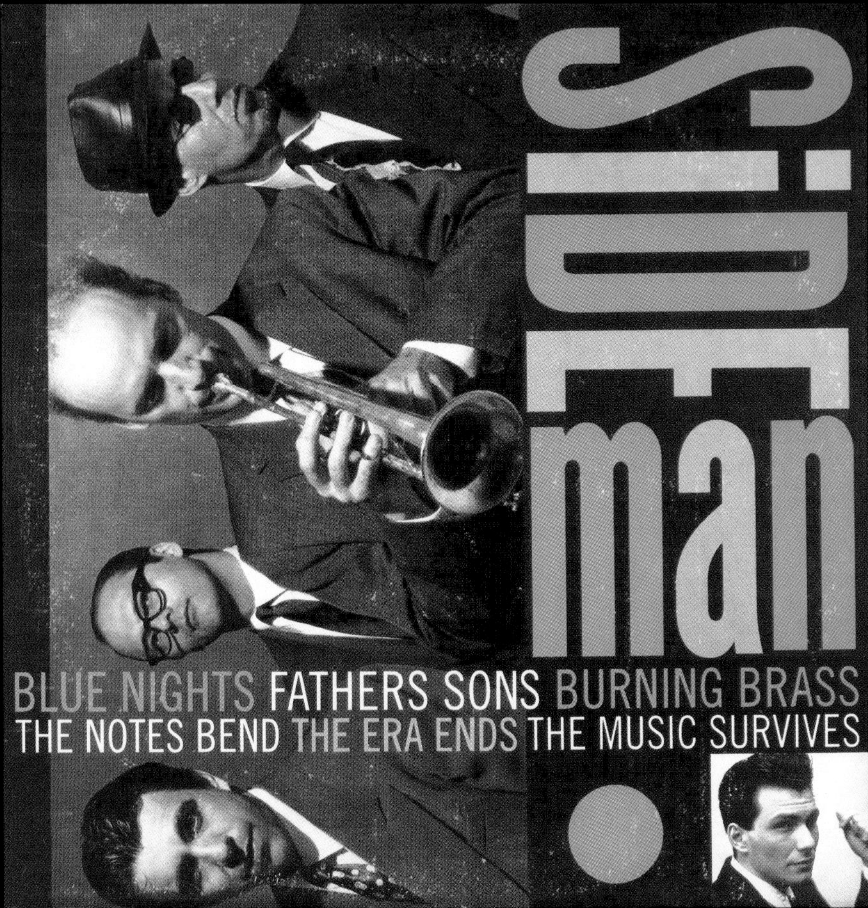

THE MORE
YOU KNOW,
THE LESS
YOU NEED.

Design_Olivier Sténuit, Franck Sarfati, Joël Audenhaege Brussels, Belgium
Art Direction_Olivier Sténuit, Franck Sarfati, Joël Audenhaege
Creative Direction_Olivier Sténuit, Franck Sarfati, Joël Audenhaege

Agency_[sign*]
Client_Encore Bruxelles

Principal Type_Akzidenz Grotesk

Dimensions_27 9/16 x 39 3/8 in. (70 x 100 cm)

1

Poster

Design_Keiko Higashi
Osaka, Japan
Art Direction_Akio Okumura

Studio_Packaging Create Inc.
Client_Inter Medium Institute
Graduate School

Principal Type_Custom
and Univers

Dimensions_$28\frac{11}{16}$ x $40\frac{9}{16}$ in.
(72.8 x 103 cm)

Design_Akio Okumura
Osaka, Japan
Art Direction_Akio Okumura

Studio_Packaging Create Inc.
Client_Musa

Principal Type_Custom

Dimensions_7 3/8 x 6 13/16 x 27 3/8 in.
(18.8 x 17.4 x 69.5 cm)

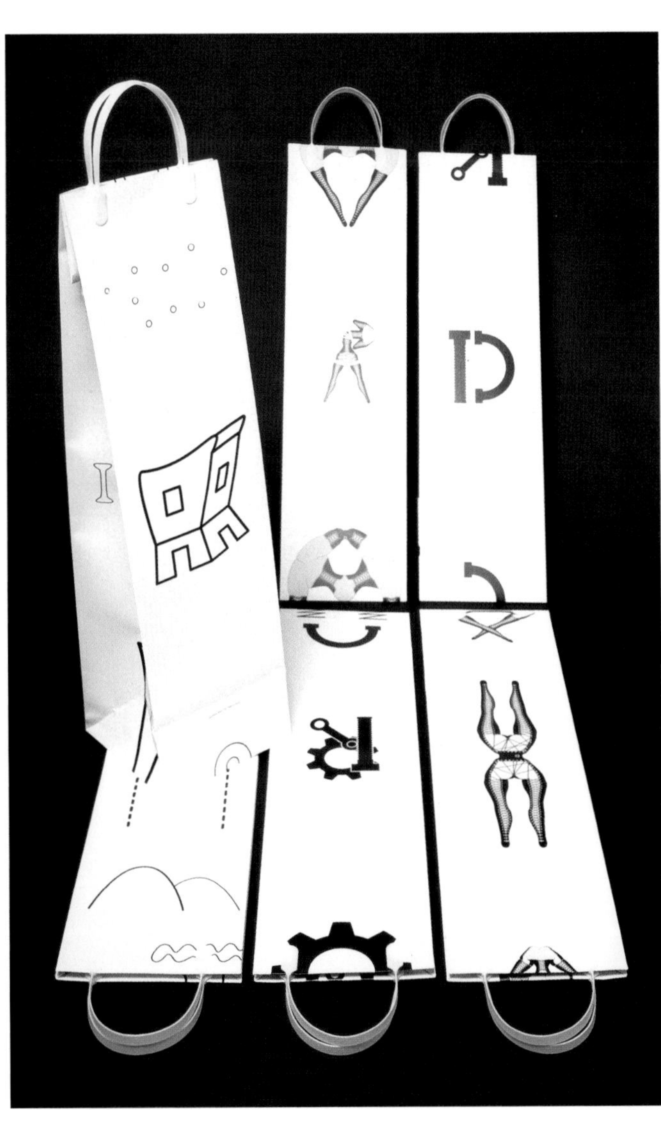

Poster

Design_Joe Scorsone and Alice Drueding
Jenkintown, Pennsylvania
Art Direction_Joe Scorsone and Alice Drueding

Design Office_Scorsone/Drueding

Principal Type_Monoline Script, Schwere, and Franklin Gothic Extra Condensed

Dimensions_30 11/16 x 22 13/16 in. (78 x 58 cm)

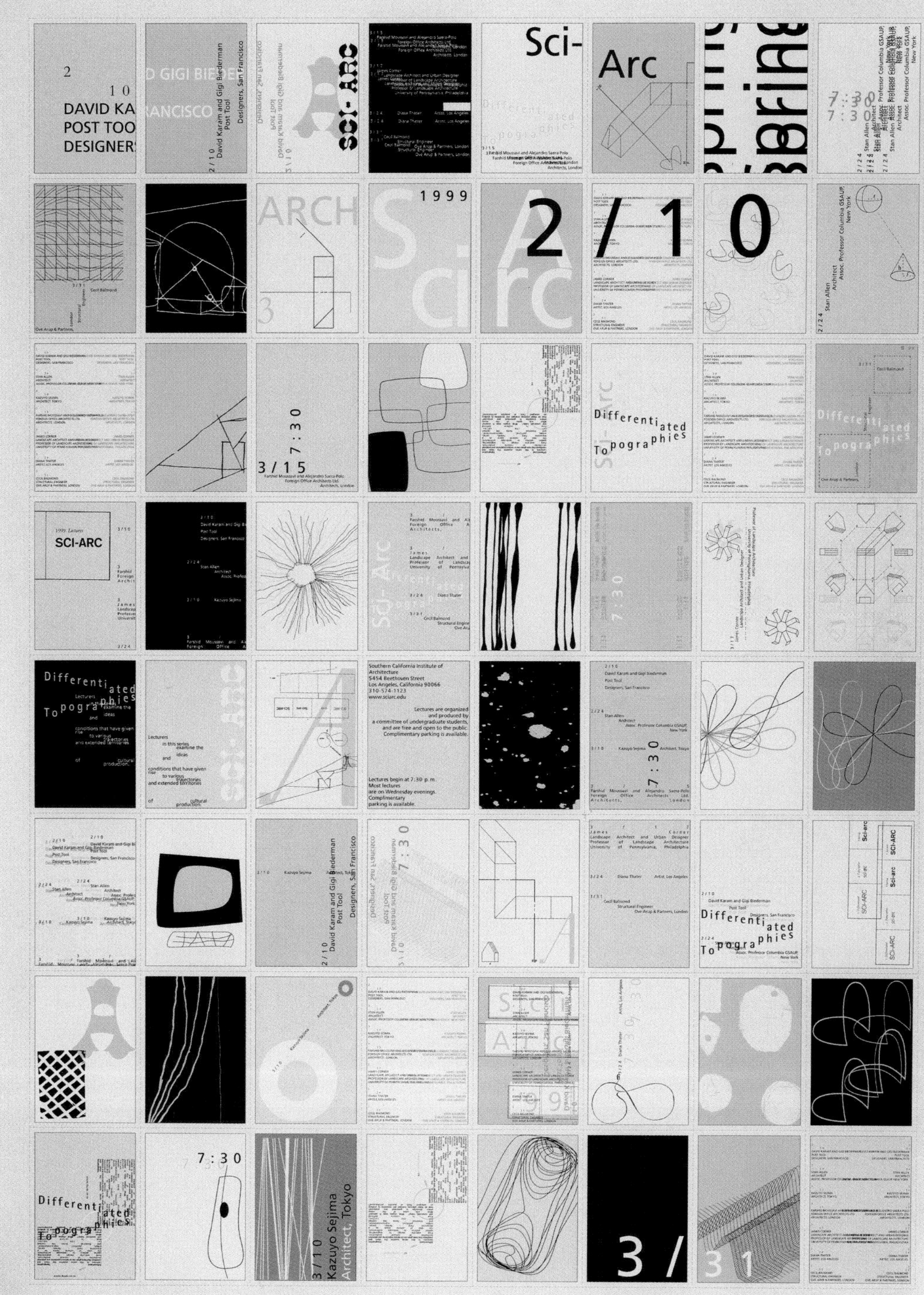

Design_Igors Irbe and Inguna Irbe
Chicago, Illinois
Art Direction_Inguna Irbe
Creative Direction_Igors Irbe
Photography_Maria Astrid Gonzales

Studio_Irbe Design

Principal Type_Orator, Letter Gothic, and FF Bodoni

Dimensions_8 ½ x 11 in. (21.6 x 27.9 cm)

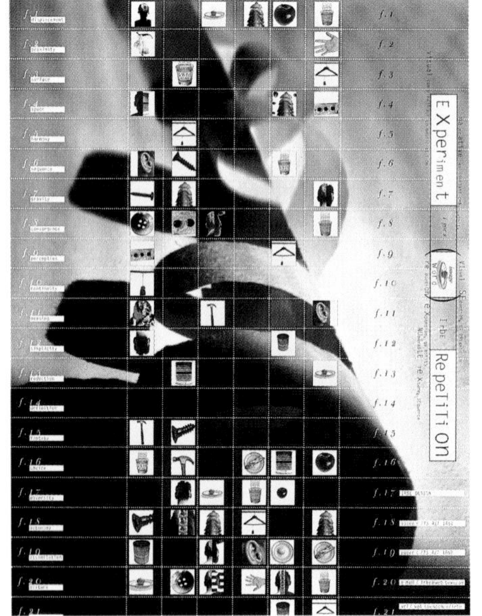

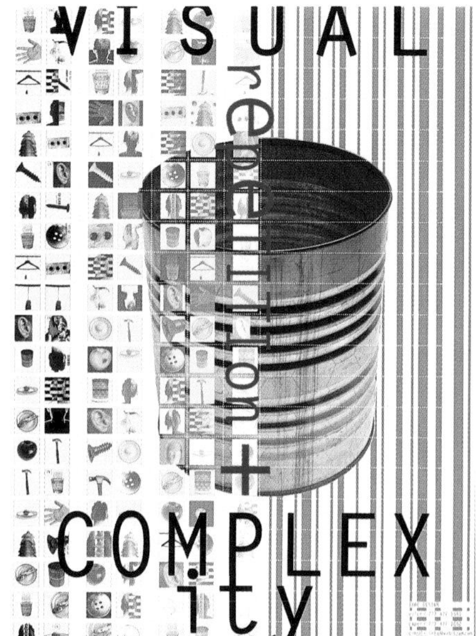

Poster

Design_Charles S. Anderson, Todd Piper-Hauswirth, and Kyle Hames
Art Direction_Charles S. Anderson
Illustration_Charles S. Anderson and Kyle Hames
Copywriter_Lisa Pemrick

Design Office_Charles S. Anderson Design
Client_French Paper Company

Principal Type_Trade Gothic and Univers

Dimensions_18 ½ x 25 in. (47 x 63.5 cm)

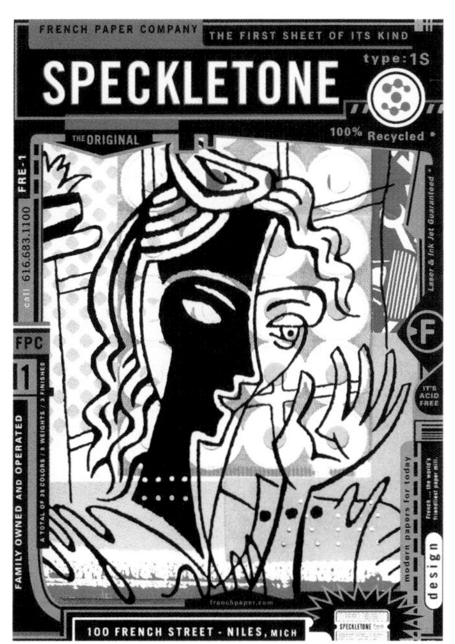

Design_Sandra Planeta
New York, New York
Art Direction_Drew Hodges
Creative Direction_Drew Hodges

Agency_Spotco.
Design Office_Spot Design
Client_Columbia Artists
and Arielle Tepper

Principal Type_Univers
Black Extended

Dimensions_14 x 2 in.
(35.6 x 55.9 cm)

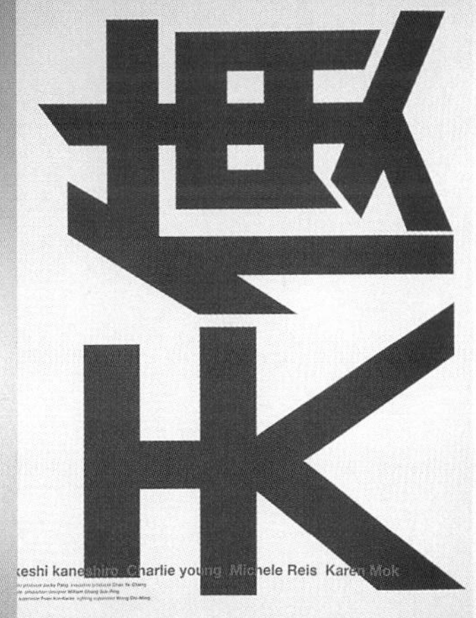

The guideline I gave my designer Wing on the poster of HAPPY TOGETHER was a story about two people. After trying various layouts, from First to Second and Tango to Smoking, I realized the two people were getting closer and closer. Finally, we settled on the most direct image and changed the title to HAPPY TOGETHER.

ATOMIC ENERGY
LAND SPECULATION
FARMERS MINING TOWNS
OPERA HOUSE
ISLAND • ASIAN EXCLUSION ACTS

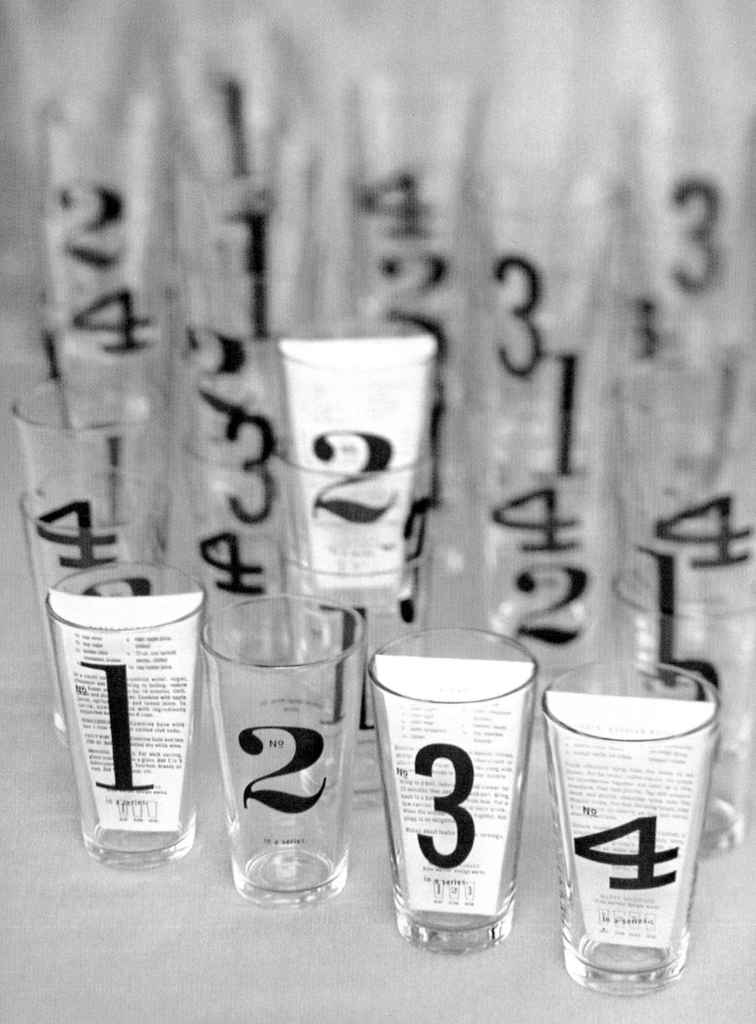

59

Hello, my name is BRAHMAN. I was born in Tokyo in 1997. Remember me, please. Thanks a lot.

BRAHMAN COMPANY LIMITED

SHUWA MINAMI-AOYAMA RESIDENCE 504
2-22-4, MINAMI-AOYAMA MINATO-KU, TOKYO, JAPAN

Design_Giorgio Pesce
Lausanne, Switzerland
Art Direction_Giorgio Pesce

Creative Direction_Giorgio Pesce
Agency_Atelier Poisson
Client_Théâtre Arsenic

Principal Type_Triumvirate and Trade Gothic

Dimensions_50 ⅜ x 35 7/16 i
(128 x 90 cm)

Design_Kevin Krueger
Dundee, Illinois
Art Direction_Kevin Krueger
and Greg Samata
Creative Direction_Kevin Krueger
and Greg Samata

Design Office_SamataMason
Client_Candace Gelman
& Associates

Principal Type_Bembo

Dimensions_6 x 8¼ in.
(15.3 x 21 cm)

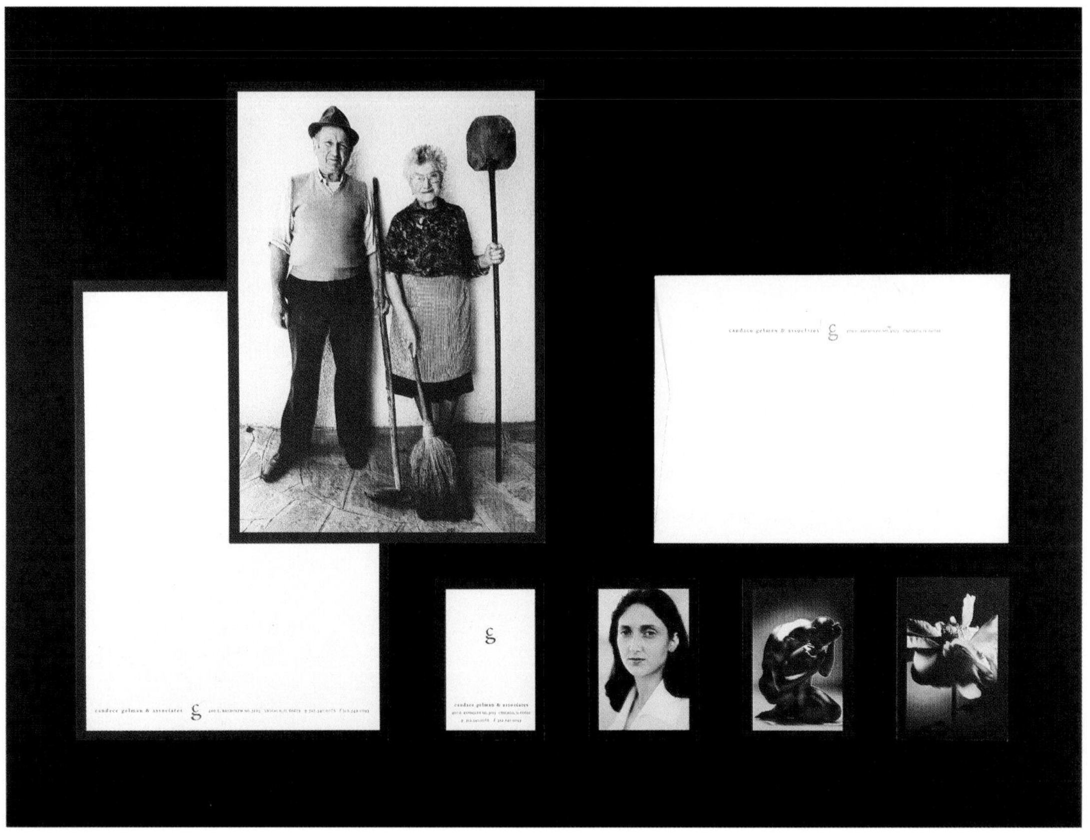

Brochure

Design_Darren Namaye
New York, New York
Art Direction_Darren Namaye
Creative Direction_Darren Namaye, Loid Der, and Brenna Garratt

Design Office_Nuforia, Inc.
Client_Exult

Principal Type_Univers Extended and Univers

Dimensions_13 x 19¾ in. (33 x 50.2 cm)

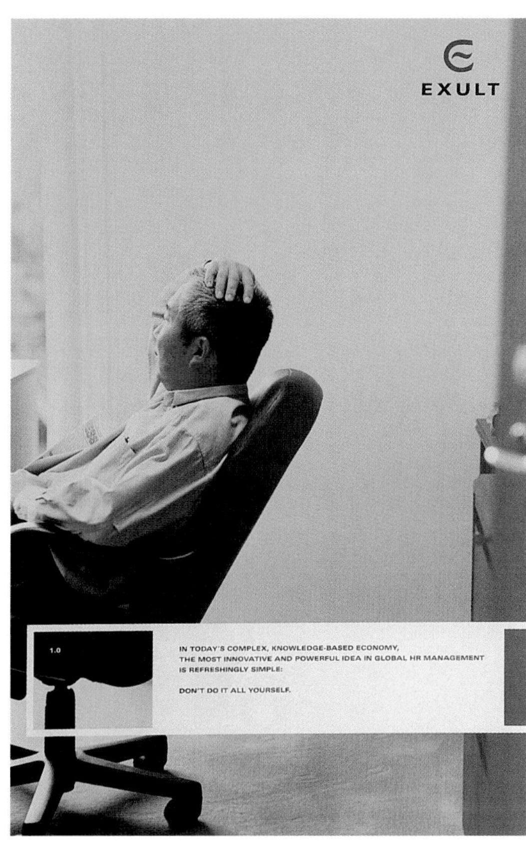

Design_Justin Salvas
Woodstock, Connecticut
Instructor_Valerie Wagner

School_School of Visual Arts

Principal Type_Gothic 13

Dimensions_18 x 24 in.
(45.7 x 61 cm)

THE ART
OF THE
MOTOR
CYCLE

THE ART OF THE MOTORCYCLE
Solomn R. Guggenheim Museum
June 26-September 20, 1998
Education Department, Solomon R. Guggenheim
1071 Fifth Avenue, New York, NY 10128
A Project for the Sacler Center for Arts Education 1998
The Solomon R. Guggenheim Foundation New York
1071 Fifth Avenue, New York, NY 10128
A Project for the Sacler Center for Arts Education 1998
THE ART OF THE MOTORCYCLE
Solomn R. Guggenheim Museum

Student Work

Design_Effendy Wijaya
New York, New York
Instructor_Carin Goldberg

School_School of Visual Arts

Principal Type_Futura Stencil

Dimensions_24 x 32 in.
(61 x 81.3 cm)

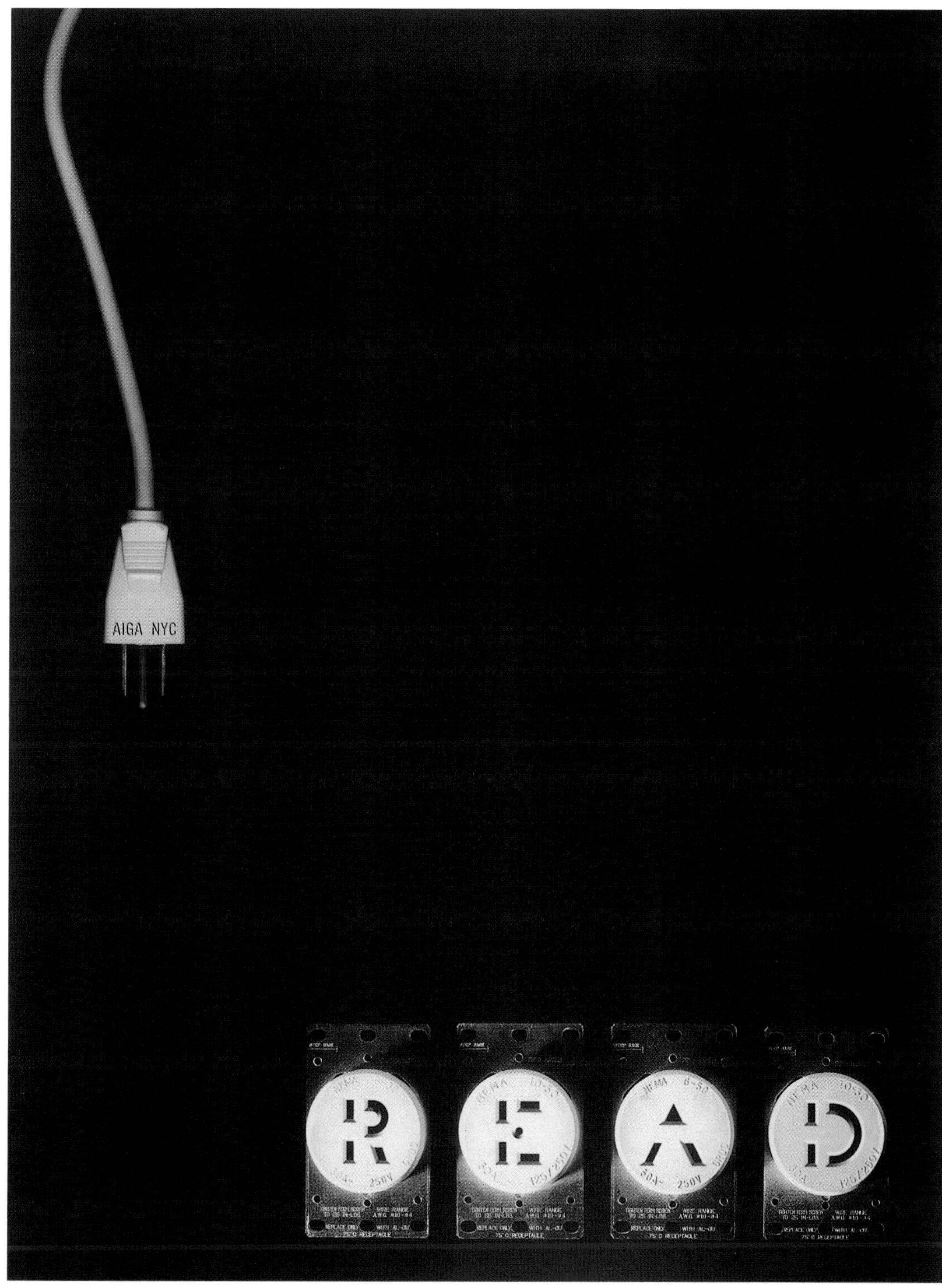

Design_Second-year photography students
Art Direction_Ritva Leinonen and Sakari Nenye

School_Lahti Polytechnic Institute of Design Lahti, Finland

Principal Type_Mrs. Eaves

Dimensions_6 3/8 x 5 9/16 in. (16.2 x 14.2 cm)

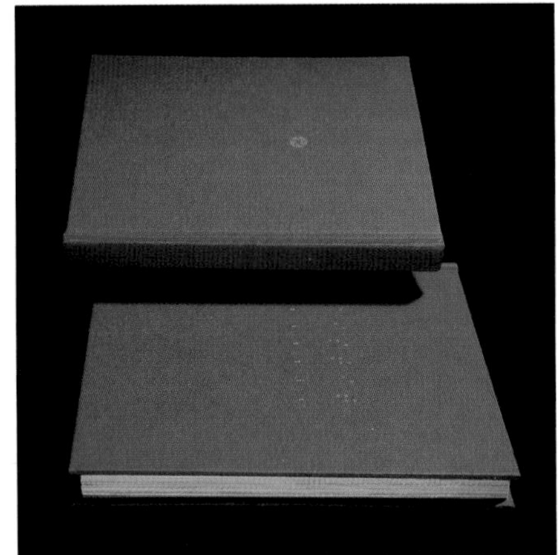

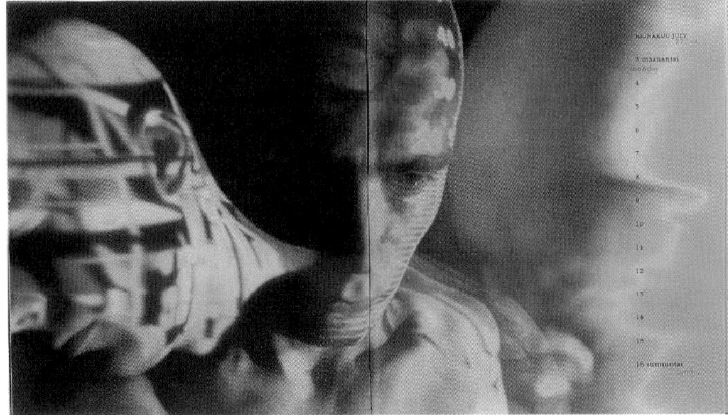

Design_Will de l'Ecluse, Hans Bockting, and David Smith Amsterdam, The Netherlands
Photography_André Thijssen
Typographers_Will de l'Ecluse and David Smith

Design Office_UNA (Amsterdam) designers
Client_Stichting Educatieve Omroep Teleac/NOT

Principal Type_Trinité

Dimensions_9¼ x 12 ⁹⁄₁₆ in. (23.5 x 32 cm)

Design_Susie Stampley
Richardson, Texas
Art Direction_Stephen Zhang
Creative Direction_Tim Hale
and Kosta Kartsotis

Studio_Fossil Design Studio

Principal Type_Interstate
and ITC Officina

Dimensions_5½ x 6½ in.
(14 x 16.5 cm)

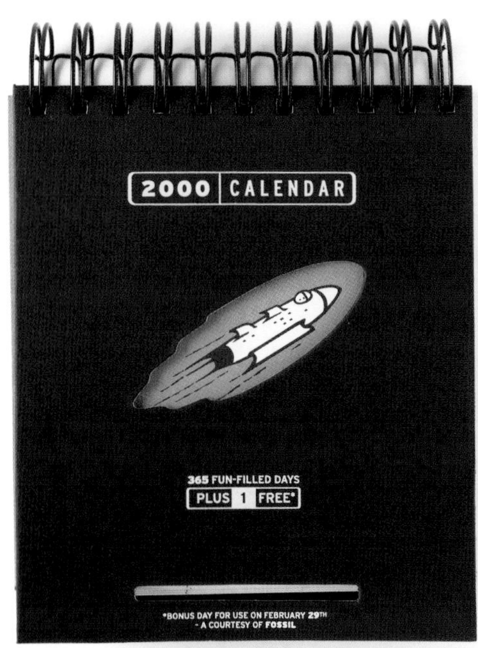

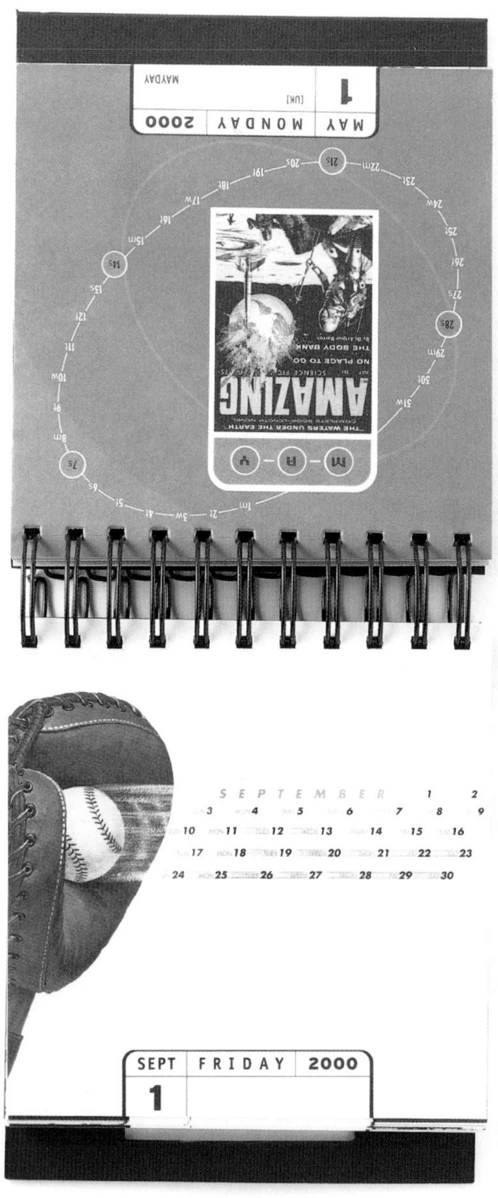

Design_John Pylypczak
Toronto, Canada
Art Direction_Diti Katona and John Pylypczak, Larry Gaudet
Printer_C.J. Graphics Printers & Lithographers

Studio_Concrete Design Communications

Principal Type_New Clarendon

Dimensions_6 ¾ x 7 ¼ in. (17.2 x 18.4 cm)

Design_Richard Bargmann, Assistant Professor Ned Drew, Brenda McManus, Peter Napp, Professor Frank D'Astolfo
Newark, New Jersey

School_The Design Consortium, Rutgers University–Newark

Art Direction_Assistant Professor Ned Drew

Principal Type_Bell Gothic

Dimensions_11 x 15½ in. (27.9 x 39.4 cm)

Poster

Design_Jason Schulte
Minneapolis, Minnesota
Art Direction_Charles S. Anderson
Copywriter_Lisa Pemrick

Design Office_Charles S. Anderson Design
Client_French Paper Company

Principal Type_Custom

Dimensions_19 x 25 in.
(48.3 x 63.5 cm)

Poster

Design_Jun Takechi
Tokyo, Japan
Art Direction_Jun Takechi
Copywriter_Hideyuki Sekikawa

Design Office_Jun Takechi
Client_The Kuricorder Foundation

Principal Type_Custom

Dimensions_40⁹⁄₁₆ x 28¹¹⁄₁₆ in.
(103 x 72.8 cm)

kuricorder quartet
kurihara masaki
kawaguchi yoshiyuki
kondo kenji
sekizima takero

kobo sax quartet
umezu kazutoki
kawaguchi yoshiyuki
nomoto kazuhiro
tada yoko

kuricorder quartet
presents
memorial live showcase for
the postponement of the publication and the morocco tour
kuricorder quartet × kobo sax quartet

'99.9.15 (wed) minamiaoyama mandala
minamiaoyama mandala 03 5474 0411 ¥4,000 (with 1 drink) open-5:30 p.m. start-6:30 p.m.

Poster

Design_Akihiko Tsukamoto
Tokyo, Japan
Art Direction_Akihiko Tsukamoto
Printer_Twin-Eight Co., Ltd.

Studio_Zuan Club
Client_DIG Tokyo Corporation

Principal Type_Kabello Extra Bold and Gill Sans Extra Bold

Dimensions_28 11/16 x 40 9/16 in. (72.8 x 103 cm)

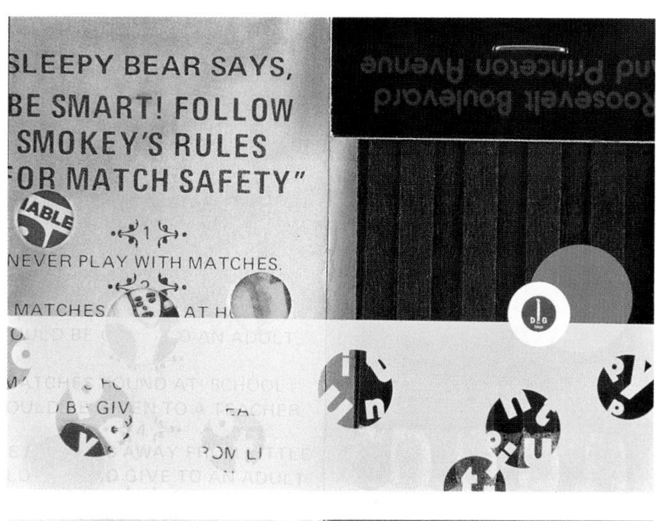

Design_Traci Code
Chicago, Illinois
Art Direction_Robert Petrick
Creative Direction_Robert Petrick
Photography_Jeff Stephens

Design Office_Petrick Design
Client_Ivex Packaging Corporation

Principal Type_ITC Franklin Gothic

Dimensions_8 ¾ x 11 ¾ in.
(22.2 x 29.8 cm)

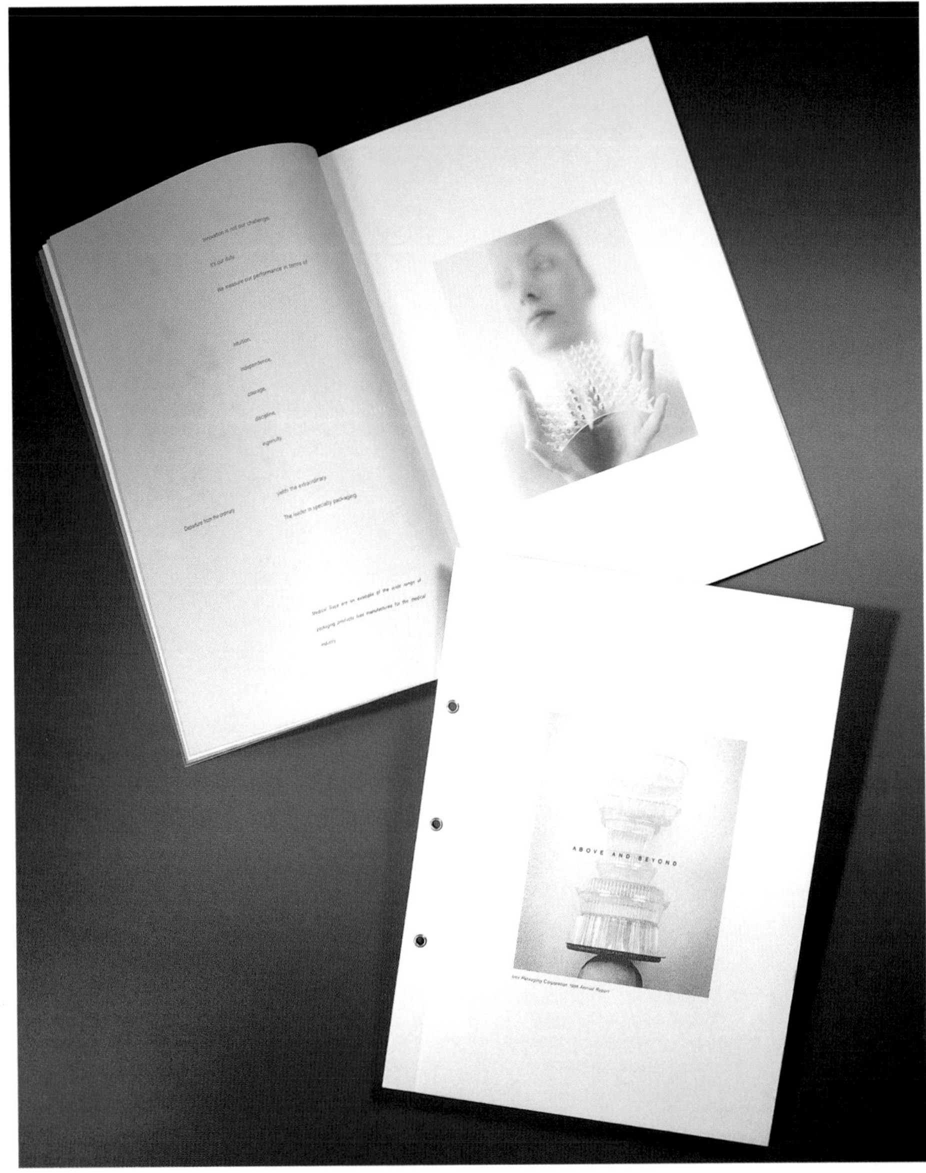

Design_Stephen Zhang
Richardson, Texas
Art Direction_Tim Hale,
Casey McCarr and Stephen Zhang
Creative Direction_Tim Hale
Illustration_Ellen Tanner,
John Vineyard, Susie Stampley,
Paula Wallace, Jennifer Burk,
and Andrea Haynes

Design Studio_Fossil Design Studio

Principal Type_Base
and Mrs. Eaves

Dimensions_7½ x 11 in.
(19 x 27.9 cm)

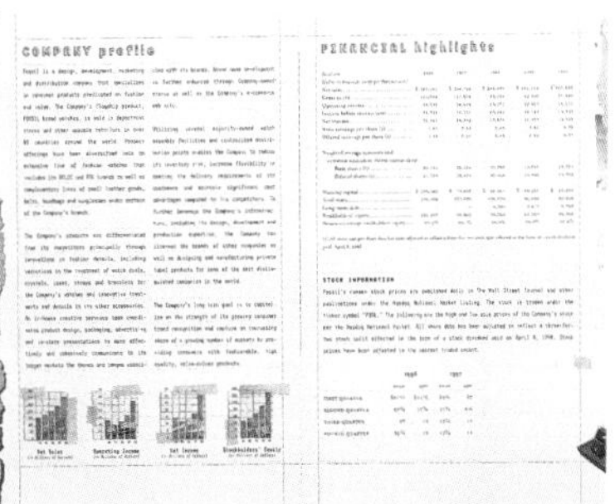

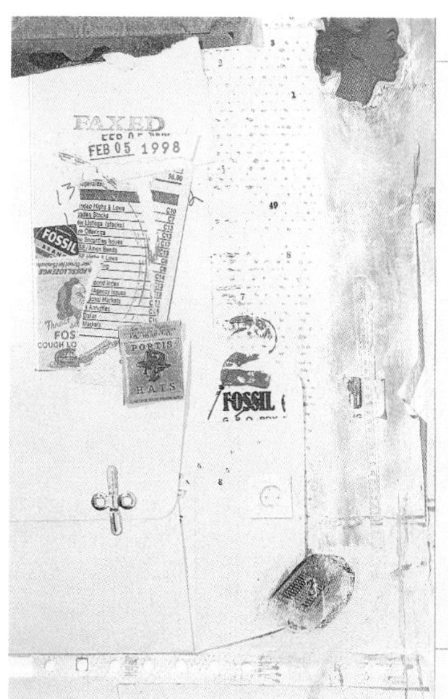

FINANCIAL information

37

INDEPENDENT AUDITORS' REPORT

REPORT OF MANAGEMENT

Design_Vince Frost
London, England
Art Direction_Vince Frost
Creative Direction_Vince Frost
Printer_Artomatic

Studio_Frost Design Ltd.
Client_Chartered Society of Designers

Principal Type_Wood type

Dimensions_28½ x 40 in. (72.4 x 101.6 cm)

Annual Report

Design_Jennifer Sterling
San Francisco, California
Art Direction_Jennifer Sterling
Creative Direction_Jennifer Sterling
Illustration_Jennifer Sterling
and Amy Hayson

Design Office_Jennifer Sterling
Design
Client_DSP

Principal Type_Frutiger,
Garamond No. 3, and handlettering

Dimensions_6¾ x 9¾ in.
(17.2 x 24.8 cm)

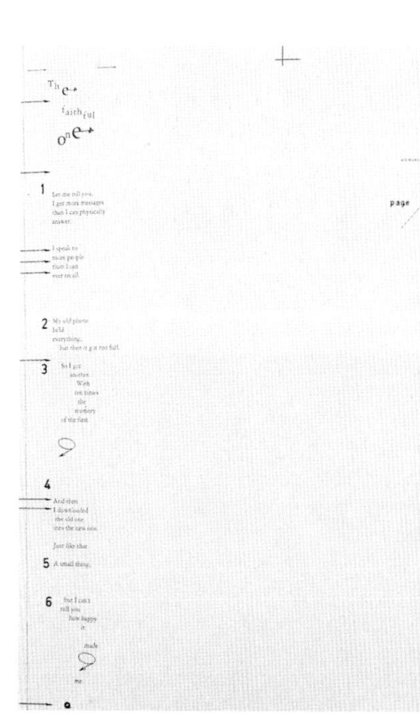

ITALY INSPIRES CANADA

DISEGNO • MACCHINA • MODA
A FESTIVAL OF ITALIAN DESIGN AT THE DESIGN EXCHANGE
OPENING JUNE 29, 1999

DESIGN EXCHANGE

ITALY INSPIRES CANADA

DISEGNO • MACCHINA • MODA
A FESTIVAL OF ITALIAN DESIGN AT THE DESIGN EXCHANGE
OPENING JUNE 29, 1999

DESIGN EXCHANGE

234 Bay St., Toronto, ON tel 416-216-2150 fax 416-368-0684 www.toronto.com/gusto, www.designexchange.org

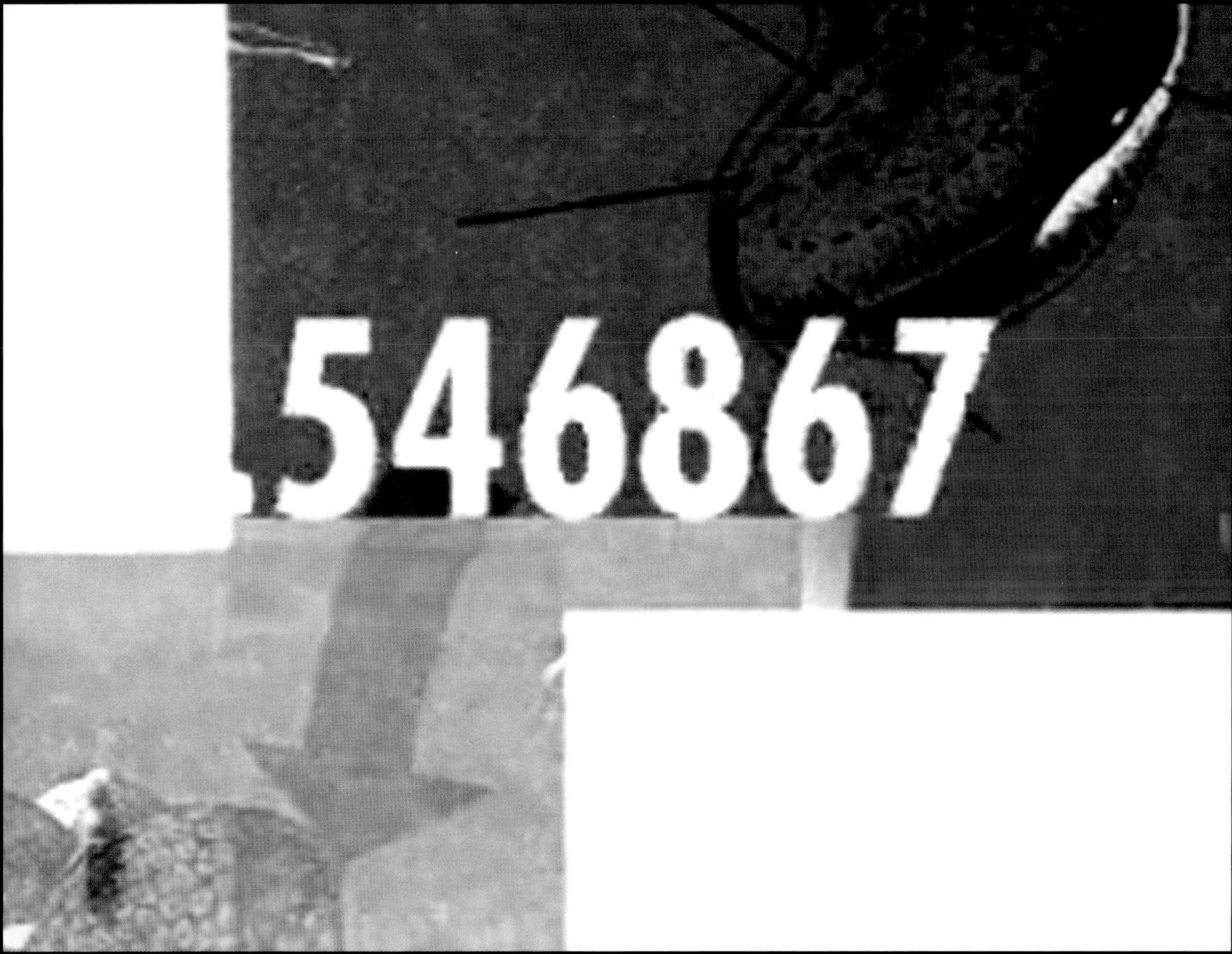

546867

Design_Marion English Powers
Birmingham, Alabama
Art Direction_Marion English Powers
Creative Direction_Terry Slaughter and Marion English Powers

Agency_Slaughter Hanson
Client_Greater Alabama Council

Principal Type_Alternate Gothic, Bell Gothic, and Caslon 540

Dimensions_8¾ x 11½ in. (22.2 x 29.2 cm)

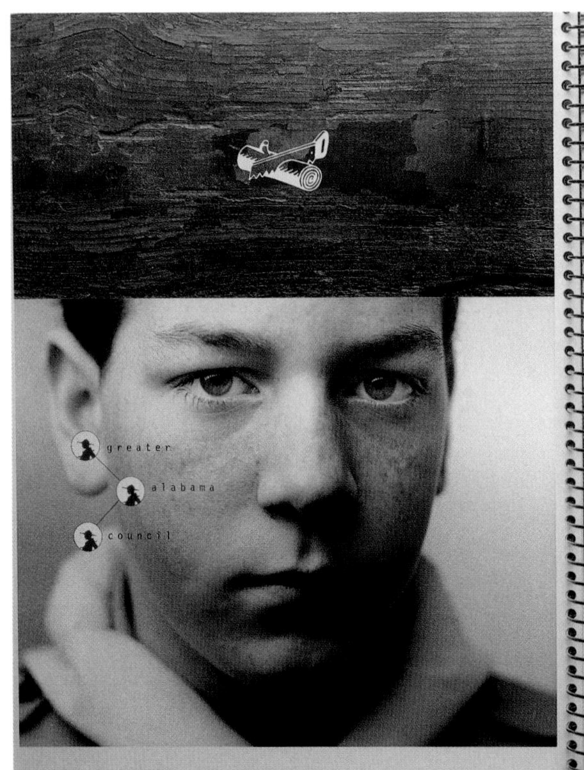

Electronic

Design_Winnie Tan
Singapore
Art Direction_Winnie Tan
Creative Direction_Winnie Tan

Studio_Nimbus Design

Principal Type_Gill Sans
and Bitstream Arrus

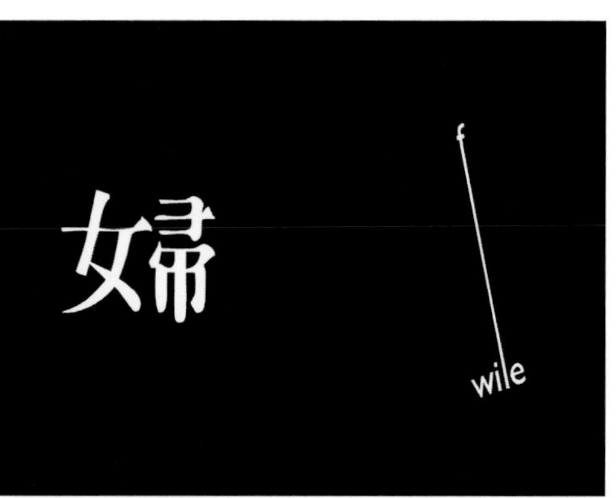

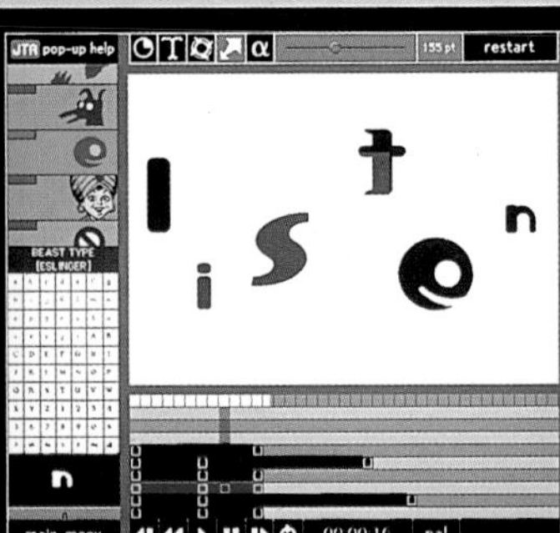

Netscape: just-type-anything.com
Location: http://www.just-type-anything.com/jta.html
What's Related
JTA pop-up help
12 pt
KODAFUJICON
[ESLINGER]
tom e
welcome to www.just-type-anything.com
send
main menu
pal
messaging

spri
ISSEY MIYAKE
LOADING...

Design_Sam Davy, David Eveleigh, and Frances Jackson
London, England
Creative Direction_Tim Fendley
Programmer_David Eveleigh
Technical Director_Andreas Harding

Agency_MetaDesign London
Client_Glasgow 1999: UK City of Architecture and Design

Principal Type_Glasgow 1999

Design_Dominik Mycielski
Köln, Germany

School_Fachhochschule Düsseldorf
Instructors_Professor Phillip Teufel
and Stefan Nowak

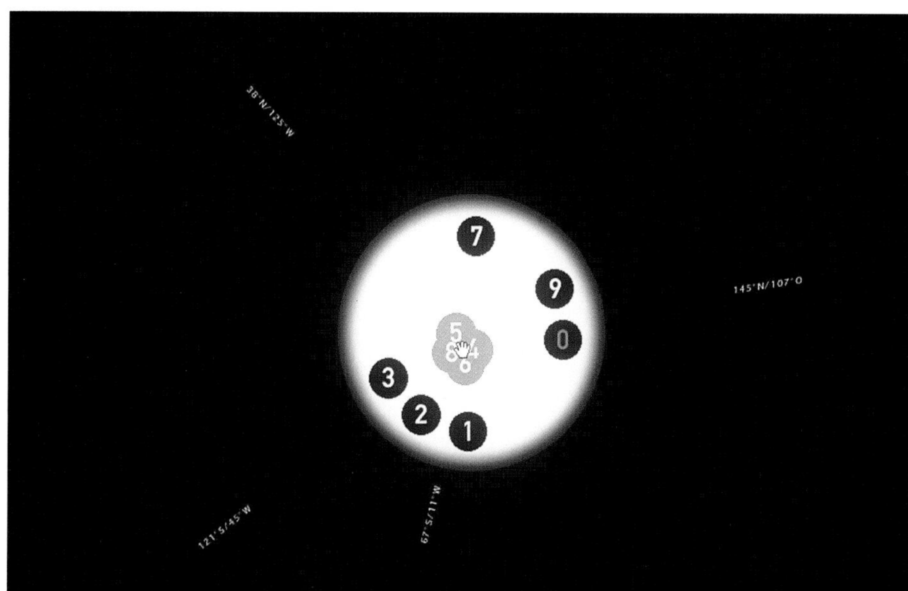

Design_Anuthin Wongsunkakon
Bangkok, Thailand
Art Direction_Anuthin Wongsunkakon

Studio_Graphic Behaviour

Principal Type_Son Gothic

Dimensions_8½ x 11 in.
(21.6 x 27.9 cm)

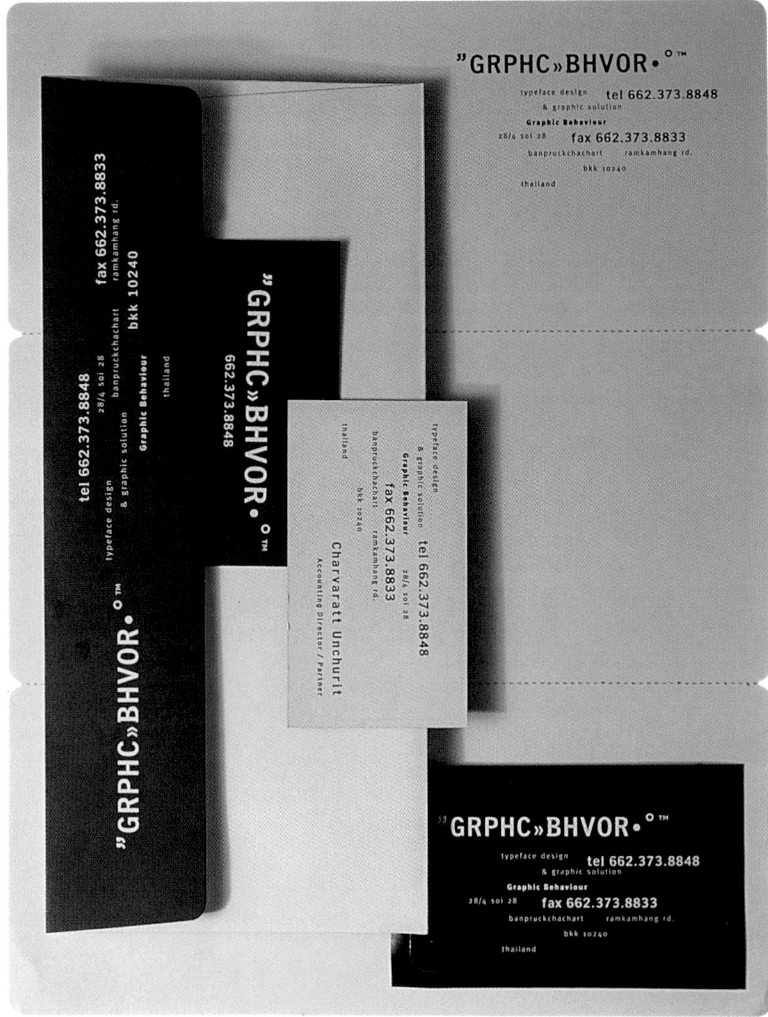

Stationery

Design_David Plunkert
Baltimore, Maryland
Art Direction_David Plunkert

Design Office_SPUR Design LLC

Principal Type_Akzidenz Grotesk

Dimensions_8 ½ x 11 in.

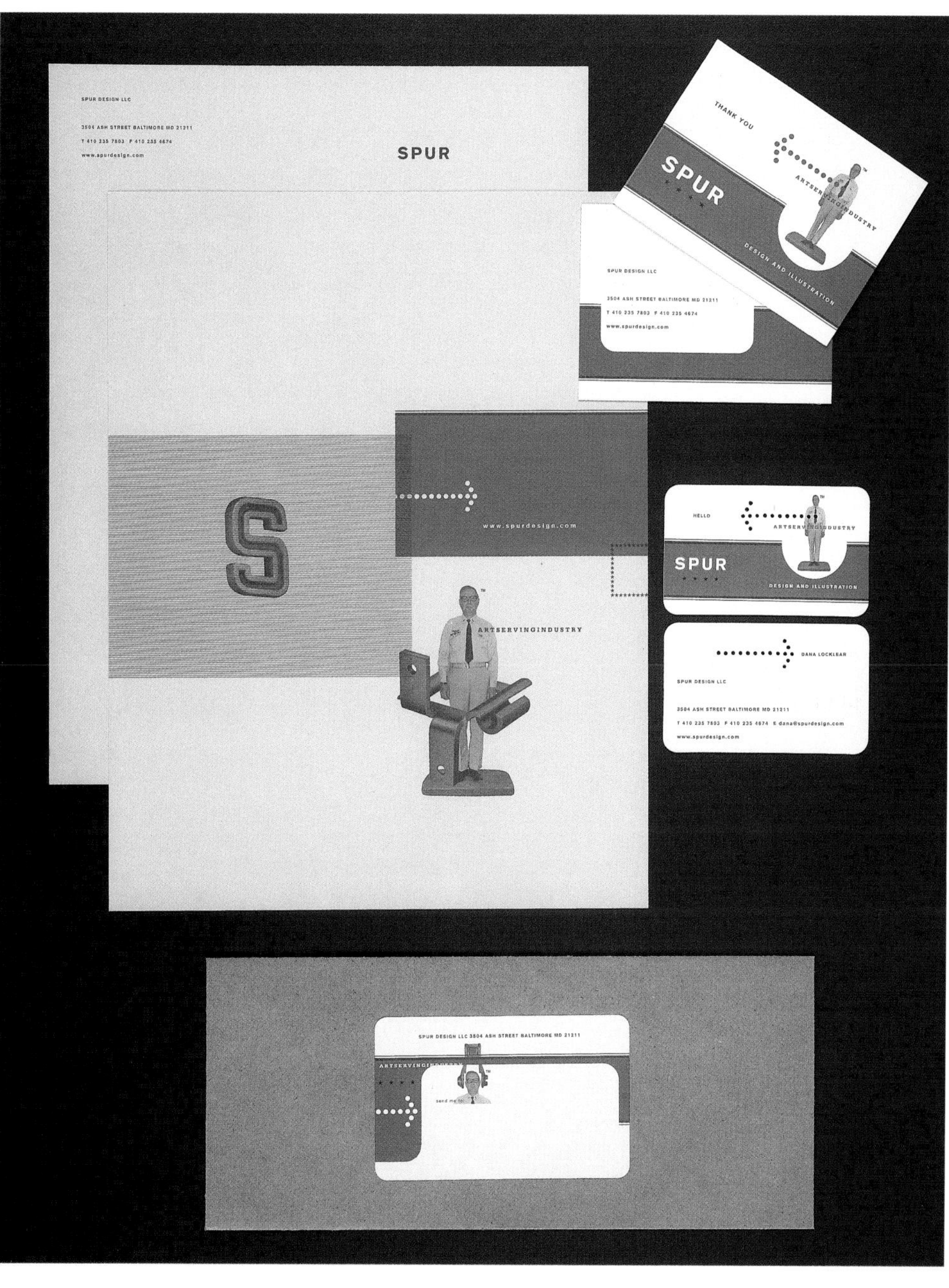

Design_Brian Dieckz
and Amanda Hayes
New York, New York
Creative Direction_Brian Dieckz
Animation_Dana Schecter
Editor_Chris O'Neil
Producer_Eve Ehrich

Agency_McCann Erickson, Detroit
Design Office_The Diecks Group, Inc.
Client_Buick

Principal Type_Beta Sans Oblique

1

Stationery

Design_Clive Piercy and Carol Kono
Santa Monica, California
Art Direction_Clive Piercy and Michael Hodgson

Design Office_Ph.D
Client_Foundation Press

Principal Type_Various

Dimensions_2 ⅛ x 3 ⅜ in. (5.4 x 8.6 cm)

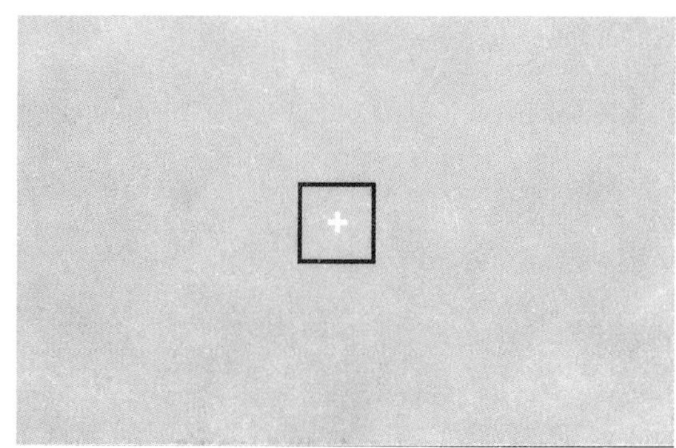

2050 SOUTH WESTGATE AVE.
West Los Angeles CA 90025
FOUNDATION PRESS
PRINTING COMPANY
TONY MANZELLA
phone 310.444.2014 fax 310.444.2013

FOUNDATION
PRESS
310.444.2014
2050 S. WESTGATE AVE.
W. L.A. CA 90025
TONY MANZELLA
fax 310.444.2013

FOUNDATION
PRESS
PRINTING
2050 SOUTH WESTGATE AVE. *west los angeles* CA 90025
TEL (310) 444 2014
FAX (310) 444 2013
TONY
MANZELLA

310 444 2014 FAX 310 444 2013
SCANNING IMAGE ASSEMBLY FILM OUTPUT COLOR PROOFING MULTI COLOR PRINTING EMBOSSING DIE CUTTING FOIL STAMPING EYELETTING SCORE DRILL PUNCH PERFORATE NUMBER PADDING SADDLE STITCH TABBING MOUNTING LAMINATION GUMMING PERFECT BIND HINGING WIRE-O SPIRAL BIND ENVELOPE CONVERTING HAND ASSEMBLY SOY INKS METALLIC INKS FLORESCENT INKS LASER INKS MATTE & GLOSS VARNISHING
TONY MANZELLA
2050 SOUTH WESTGATE AVE. WEST LOS ANGELES CA 90025
FOUNDATION
PRESS
PRINTING CO.

310.444-2014 *fax* 310.444-2013
FOUNDATION
PRINTING CO.
PRESS
Tony Manzella
2050 south westgate ave., west los angeles, ca. 90025

Design_Rishi Shourie
San Francisco, California
Art Direction_Rishi Shourie
and Mikon Van Gastel
Creative Direction_Brian Bacino,
Steve Fong, Dann Wilkens,
and Kyle Cooper
Writer_Dann Wilkens

Agency_Foote, Cone & Belding
Studio_Imaginary Forces
Client_Sega Dreamcast

Principal Type_DIN Mittelschrift
and Sackers Gothic

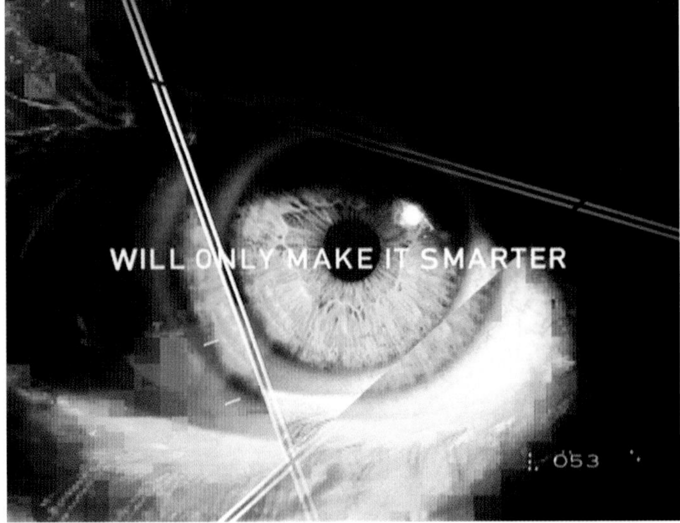

Stationery

Design_Richard Boynton
Minneapolis, Minnesota
Art Direction_Richard Boynton
Creative Direction_Richard Boynton

Design Office_Wink
Client_Push

Principal Type_Eurostile Extended and Bubbledot

Dimensions_8 ½ x 11 in. (21.6 x 27.9 cm)

Design_Nathan Durrant, Holly Holmquist, and Jennifer Tolo
San Francisco, California
Art Direction_Jennifer Jerde

Design Office_Elixir Design, Inc.

Principal Type_Mrs. Eaves and Interstate

Dimensions_2 x 3 ½ in. (5.1 x 8.9 cm)

ELXR:DSGN

2134 VAN NESS AVE. SAN FRANCISCO, CA 94109 TEL 415-834-0300 FAX 415-834-0101

DESIGNER: ND@ELIXIRDESIGN.COM

JENNIFER JERDE
DAVID CASO
NATHAN DURRANT
HOLLY HOLMQUIST
JENNIFER TOLO
MEREL KENNEDY
KYLE PIERCE
ERIC HEIMAN

CREATIVE DIRECTOR: JJ@ELIXIRDESIGN.COM

DAVID CASO
NATHAN DURRANT
JENNIFER TOLO
MEREL KENNEDY
HOLLY HOLMQUIST
JENNIFER JERDE
KYLE PIERCE
ERIC HEIMAN

GENERAL MANAGER: KP@ELIXIRDESIGN.COM

HOLLY HOLMQUIST
JENNIFER JERDE
DAVID CASO
NATHAN DURRANT
KYLE PIERCE
MEREL KENNEDY
JENNIFER TOLO
ERIC HEIMAN

DESIGNER: HH@ELIXIRDESIGN.COM

KYLE PIERCE
JENNIFER TOLO
JENNIFER JERDE
NATHAN DURRANT
HOLLY HOLMQUIST
DAVID CASO
MEREL KENNEDY
ERIC HEIMAN

DESIGNER: JT@ELIXIRDESIGN.COM

DAVID CASO
NATHAN DURRANT
MEREL KENNEDY
JENNIFER TOLO
HOLLY HOLMQUIST
KYLE PIERCE
JENNIFER JERDE
ERIC HEIMAN

DESIGNER: MK@ELIXIRDESIGN.COM

DAVID CASO
NATHAN DURRANT
JENNIFER TOLO
MEREL KENNEDY
HOLLY HOLMQUIST
JENNIFER JERDE
KYLE PIERCE
ERIC HEIMAN

P L U T O

www.plutodesign.com
1650 NW NAITO PARKWAY SUITE 301 PORTLAND, OR 97209
TEL 503.274.0944 FAX 503.226.1283

TIM LARSON
EXECUTIVE PRODUCER
TEL 503.274.0944
FAX 503.226.1283

P L U T O

1650 NW NAITO PARKWAY SUITE 301
PORTLAND, OR 97209
tlarson@plutodesign.com

Here are some catchy slogans we're working up;
Pluto. We're out there.
Pluto rhymes with Menudo.
Pluto. Has anyone seen my mittens?
Pluto. 4 million miles from Uranus.

I speak from experience when I say it does not help while
being shoved into the back of a police cruiser to yell
"You can't do this to me I'm from Pluto. Pluto, you hear!"
That would be Pluto environmental design.

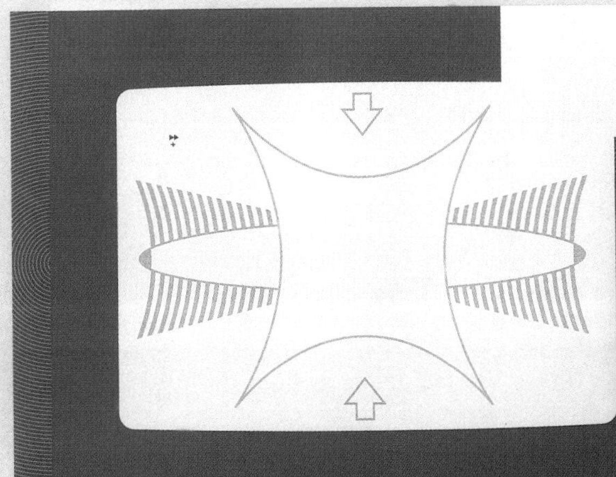

ANNI KUAN
242 W

Television Commercial

Design_Matt Cullen and Mikon van Gastel Hollywood, California
Executive Production_Saffron Kenny
Production_Lisa Laubhan (IF) and Jill Andresevic (Agency)
Art Direction_Mikon van Gastel and Alain Briere
Creative Direction_Peter Frankfurt
Editor_Adrian Kays
Inferno Artist_Marijose Auclair
Directon_Matt Cullen and Mikon van Gastel
2nd Animation_Matt Cullen
Coordinator_Keith Bryant
Voice-over_Henry Rollins
Agency_J. Walter Thompson
Design Office_Imaginary Forces
Client_Unicef and Merrill Lynch
Principal Type_FF DIN Alternate

Design_Joyce Nesnadny and Michelle Moehler Cleveland, Ohio
Art Direction_Mark Schwartz and Joyce Nesnadny
Photography_Stephen Frailey

Design Office_Nesnadny + Schwartz
Client_The Progressive Corporation

Principal Type_Interstate

Dimensions_8 ½ x 11 in. (21.6 x 27.9 cm)

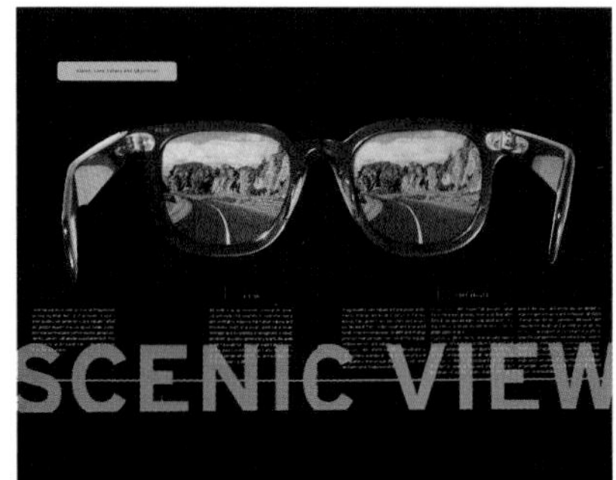

Annual Report

Design_Ted Bluey
San Francisco, California
Art Direction_David Salanitro
Creative Direction_David Salanitro
Photography_Hunter L. Wimmer

Design Office_Oh Boy,
A Design Company
Client_Robertson-Ceco Corporation

Principal Type_Helvetica Neue
Medium and Univers

Dimensions_11 x 17 in.
(27.9 x 43.2 cm)

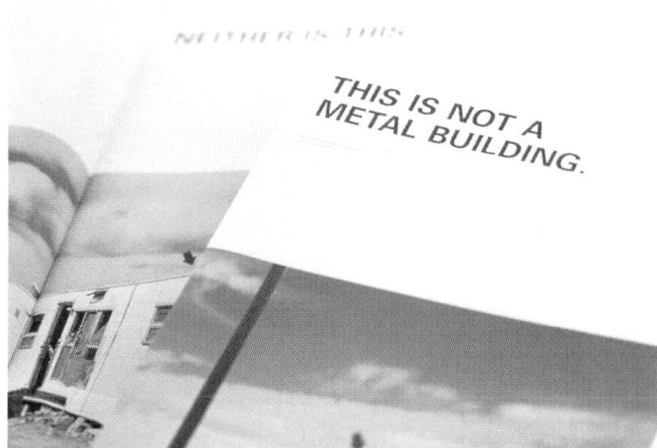

Design_Yasuyo Fukumoto
Osaka, Japan
Art Direction_Akio Okumura

Studio_Packaging Create Inc.
Client_Japan Bridge

Principal Type_Custom

Dimensions_11 $\frac{11}{16}$ x 8 $\frac{1}{4}$ in.
(29.7 x 21 cm)

Design_Akio Okumura
Osaka, Japan
Art Direction_Akio Okamura

Studio_Packaging Create Inc.
Client_Inter Medium Institute
Graduate School

Principal Type_Custom
Tomohiro Tokimoto

Dimensions_13 x 9 7/16 in.
(33.2 x 24 cm)

Design_Yasuyo Fukumoto
Osaka, Japan
Art Direction_Akio Okumura

Studio_Packaging Create Inc.
Client_Japan Bridge

Principal Type_Custom

Dimensions_11 11/16 x 8 1/4 in.
(29.7 x 21 cm)

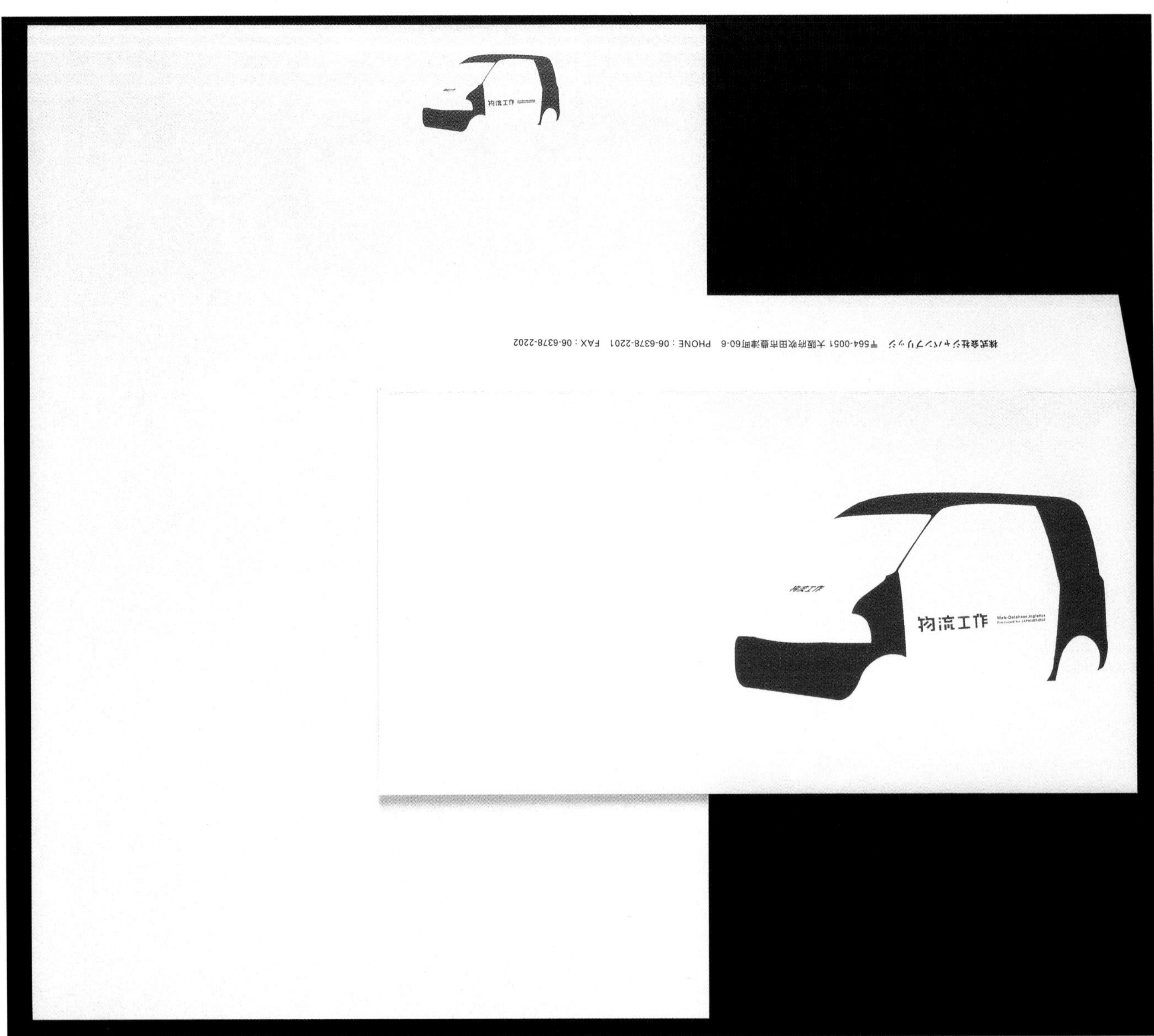

Television Commercial

Design_Kyle Cooper and Rafael Machó
Hollywood, California
Production_Lisa Laubhan
Editors_Jason Webb
and Lauren Giordano
Direction_Kyle Cooper
Agency Production_Robert Gondell
Art Director_Tom Rosenfield
Copywriter_Jeff Iorillo

Inferno Artist_Lori Freitag-Hild
2nd Animator_Rafael Machó
Coordination_Keith Bryant
and Chris Mantzaris

Agency_Foote, Cone & Belding
Design Office_Imaginary Forces
Client_Janus Mutual Funds

Principal Type_FF DIN (modified)

01

Design_John Bielenberg and Erik Cox San Francisco, California
Creative Direction_John Bielenberg
Sponsor_Appleton Papers
Contributors_Arthesia, Bob Aufuldish, Amy Franceschini, M.A.D., David Gaz, Michael Mabry, Adams Morioka, Jennifer Sterling, Michael Vanderbyl, and James Victore
Design Office_Bielenberg Design
Client_Virtual Telemetrix

Principal Type_Franklin Gothic Bold Condensed

Dimensions_5 x 6 in. (12.7 x 15.2 cm)

03

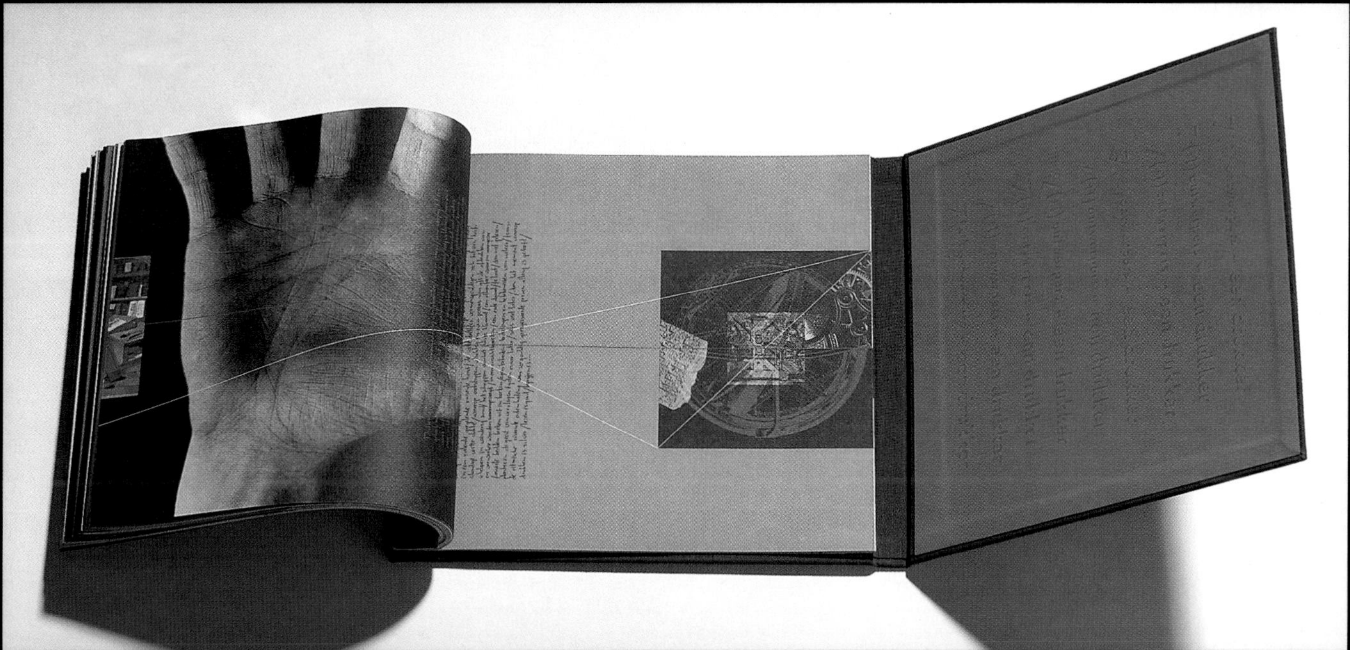

Design_Hideki Nakajima
Tokyo, Japan
Lettering_Hideki Nakajima
Art Direction_Hideki Nakajima
Creative Direction_Hideki Nakajima
Photography_Various

Design Office_Nakajima Design
Client_CUT magazine/Rockin'on Inc.

Dimensions_8 7/16 x 11 13/16 in.
(21.5 x 30 cm)

Design_Karin Fong, Grant Lau, and Chris Lopez
Hollywood, California
Producer_Anita Olan
Executive Producer_Saffron Kenny
Direction_Karin Fong
Creative Direction_Peter Frankfurt
Agency Producer_Kris Wong
Editor_Jeff Consiglio
Inferno Artist_Phil Man and Danny Yoon
2D Animator_Jeff Jankens
Art Director_Bobby Appleby
Agency_Fallon McElligott
Copywriter_Scott Vincent
Design Office_Imaginary Forces
Client_Qualcomm

Principal Type_T-26 Flux

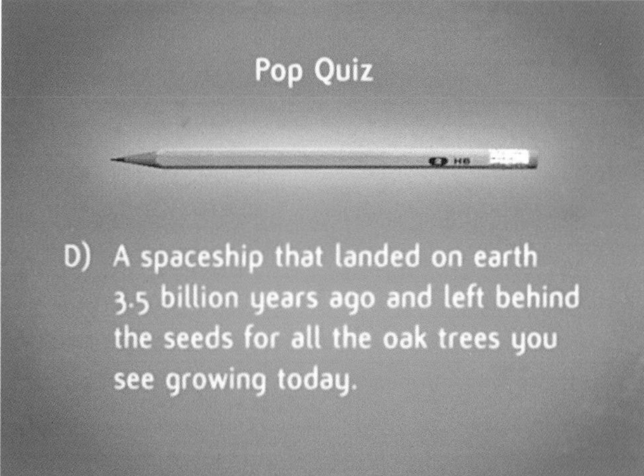

Design_Alex Scholing
Arnheim, The Netherlands
Lettering_Alex Scholing
Art Direction_Alex Scholing
Creative Direction_Alex Scholing

Design Office_Superstudios
Client_FontShop Benelux

Principal Type_FF Kipp (modified)
and FF DIN (modified)

Design_Uli Gürtler
Hamburg, Germany
Lettering_Uli Gürtler
Art Direction_Christina Petrich

Agency_Springer & Jacoby
Werbung GmbH
Client_Freie und Hansestadt
Hamburg

Principal Type_Handlettering

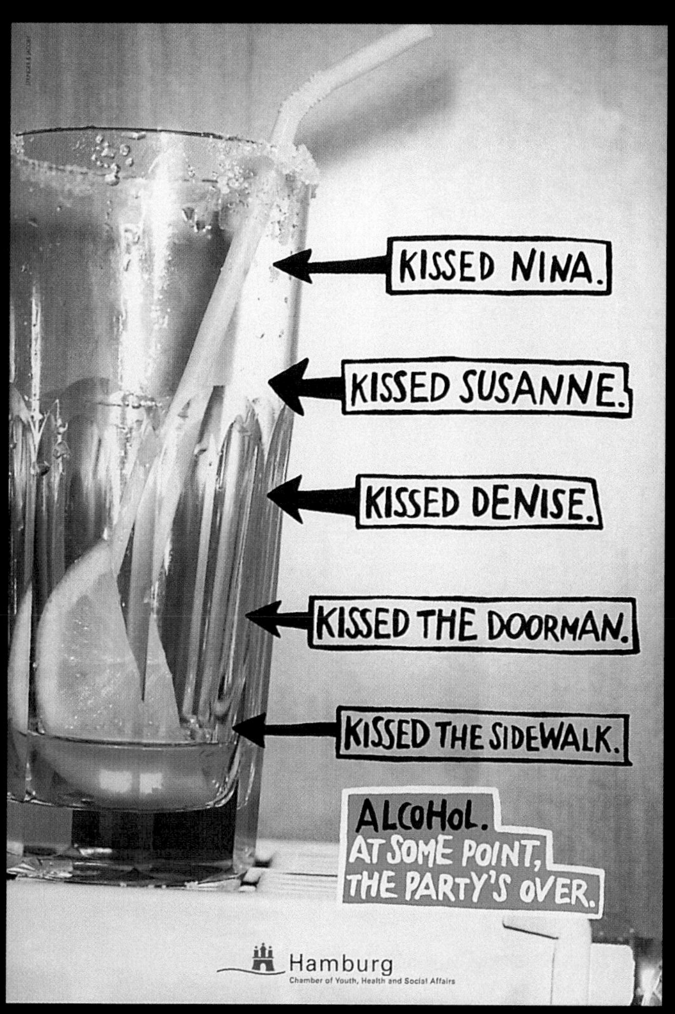

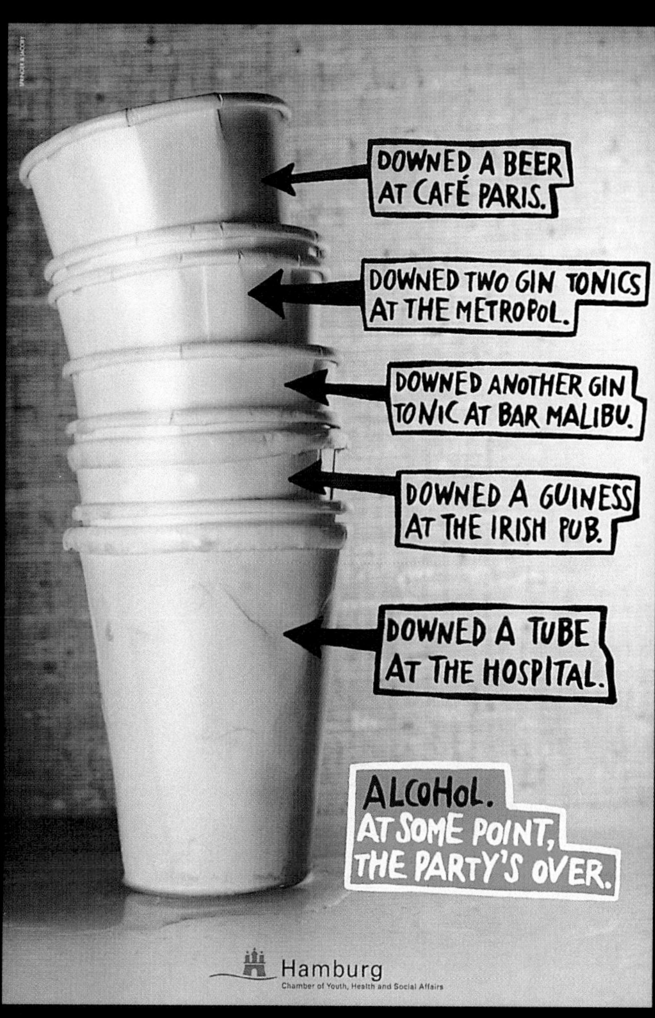

Design_Hal Wolverton
Portland, Oregon
Art Direction_Hal Wolverton and Jeff Williams
Creative Direction_Susan Hoffman
Photography_Mrs. Kathleen Williams, Mrs. Betty Bridges, Mrs. Melba Buttrem, Joe Peila, and Jeff Williams

Copywriter_Jeff Kling
Studio Artists_Sarah Starr and Alan Foster
Design Firm_Johnson & Wolverton
Client_Wieden & Kennedy

Principal Type_Geometric 415

Dimensions_130 x 60 in. (330.2 x 152.4 cm)

I like bacon.

The French can have the Mona Lisa.

How could a painting provide near the viewing satisfaction of a game trophy? For those who can't fend for themselves, and prefer to sip hot drinks from delicate cups, an oil painting might make a fine substitute for a proper wall hanging.

The visitor to the High Life household, however, can expect more discretion, decoratively. Wherever callused hands grip cold cans of Miller High Life, prize fish or game are suitable for wall display, as are pictures of family – both a testament to a man's virility.

Television Commercial

Design_Chris Lopez, Adam Bluming, Eric Cruz, Ben Lopez, and David Clayton
Executive Producer_Saffron Kenny
Producer_Alexander Dervin and Dani Stoller
Art Direction_Adam Bluming and Kara Verhoorn
Creative Direction_Peter Frankfurt
Editor_Scott Canning

Inferno Artist_Greg Paul Malone
2D Animators_Chris Lopez, Ben Lopez, Danny Yoon, and Rie Fukui
Coordinator_Christina Hwang
Copywriter_Jason Graff
Agency_Saatchi & Saatchi Advertising
Design Office_Imaginary Forces
Client_Tide

Principal Type_Franklin Gothic Extra Condensed

Design_Fons M. Hickmann
Berlin and Düsseldorf, Germany
Art Direction_Fons M. Hickmann
Editors_Siri Vorbeck,
Kristina Küompel, Nicole Koch,
and Stefan Lohmann
Publisher_Erwin Fey

Studio_Fons M. Hickmann
Client_zefa visual media

Principal Type_Corporate

Dimensions_11 13/16 x 18 1/8 in.
(30 x 46 cm)

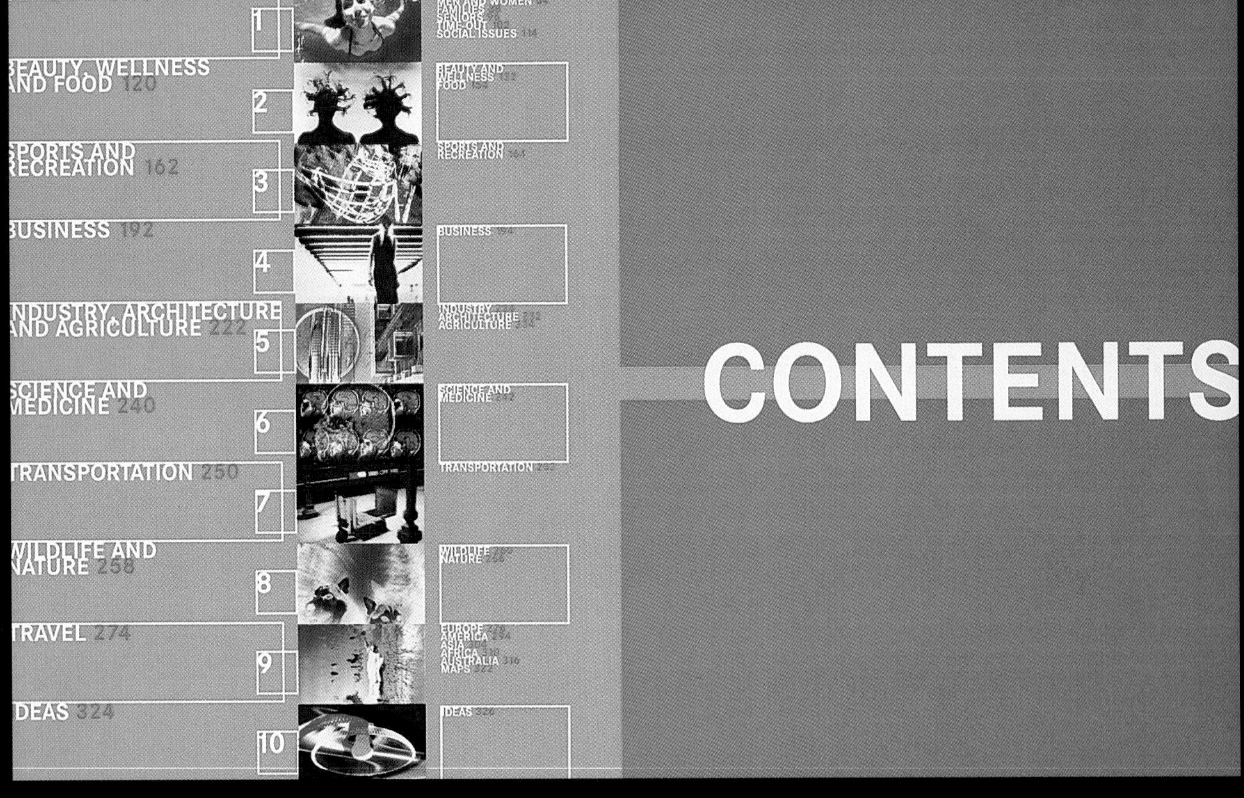

Design_Walter Bernard and Mirko Ilić
New York, New York
Art Direction_Walter Bernard and Mirko Ilić
Creative Direction_Walter Bernard and Mirko Ilić

Design Office_WBMG, Inc. and Mirko Ilić Design
Client_Neil Leifer

Principal Type_Bitstream Franklin Gothic Condensed

1

Cinema Advertisement

Design_Len Cheeseman, Hayden Doughty, Jason Bowden, David Colquhoun, Tom Eslinger, Brian Merrifield, and Tristam Sparks Wellington, New Zealand
Art Direction_Len Cheeseman
Creative Direction_Gavin Bradley
Copywriters_Nigel Richardson and Oliver Maisey
Producer_Tom Ackroyd

Agency_Saatchi & Saatchi Wellington
Client_New Zealand Symphony Orchestra

Principal Type_NZSO Non Regular

2

Design_Vanessa Marzaroli
Venice, California
Art Direction_Vanessa Marzaroli
Animator_Craig Tollifson
Producer_Casey Steele
Executive Producer_Matthew Marquis

Studio_Razorfish
Client_Travel Channel

Principal Type_Interstate
and Dot Mater Display

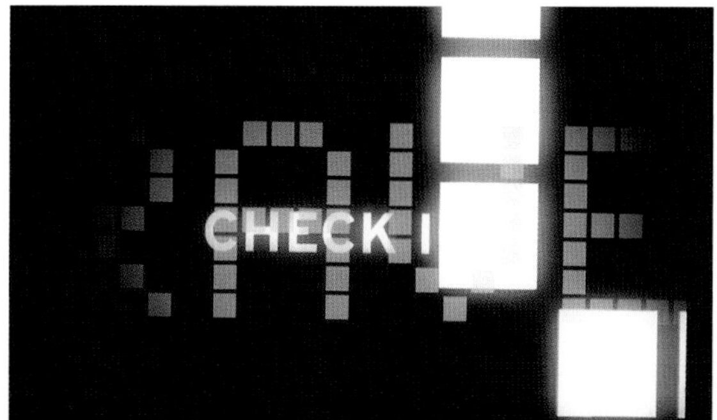

3

Design_Jun Takechi
Tokyo, Japan
Art Direction_Jun Takechi

Design Office_Jun Takechi
Client_Ruby in the Soda

Principal Type_Bank Gothic
Medium and Bolt Bold

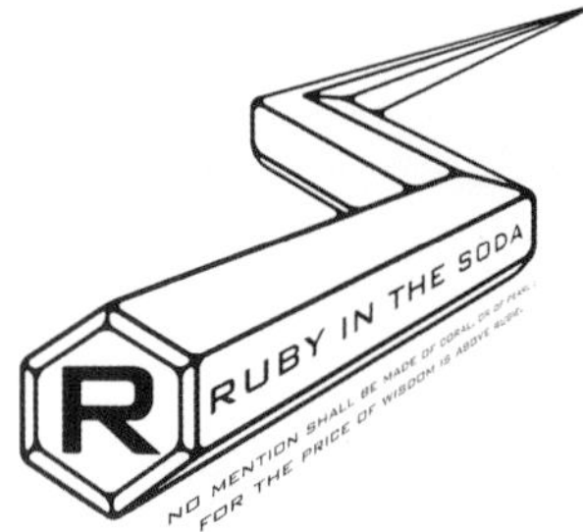

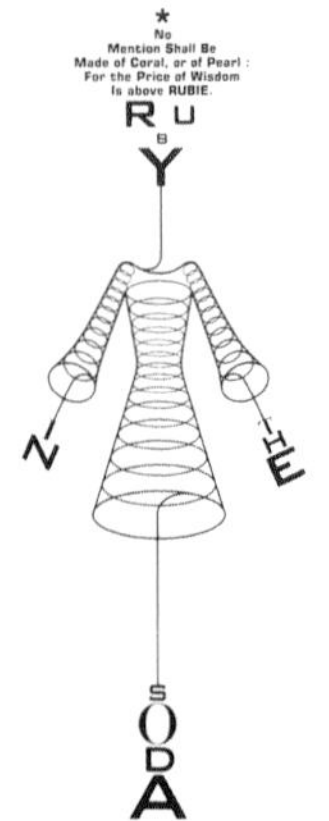

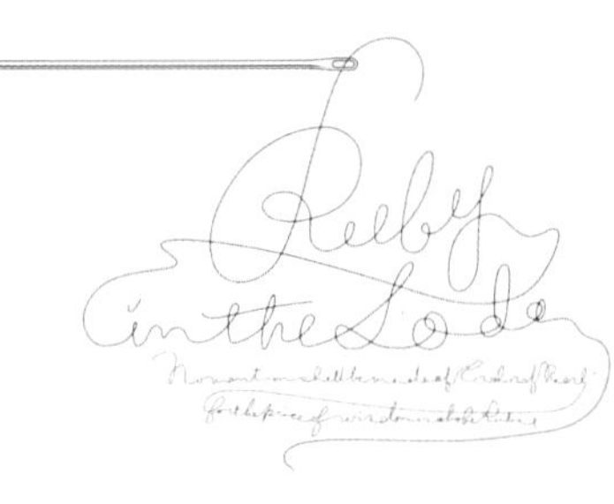

Corporate Identity

Design_Matt Eller and Topher Sinkinson
Portland, Oregon
Art Direction_Matt Eller
Creative Direction_Alicia Johnson
Production Team_Sarah Starr, Deborah Hyde, and Alan Foster
Creative Development_Alicia Johnson, Amie Champagne, Matt Eller, and Topher Sinkinson

Design Firm_Johnson & Wolverton
Client_Photonica USA

Principal Type_Univers

Dimensions_Various

15

Design_Teeranop Wangsillapakun
Chicago, Illinois
Lettering_Teeranop Wangsillapakun
Art Direction_Carlos Segura
Creative Direction_Carlos Segura

Studio_Segura Inc.
Client_yosho.com

Principal Type_Orator

Dimensions_Various

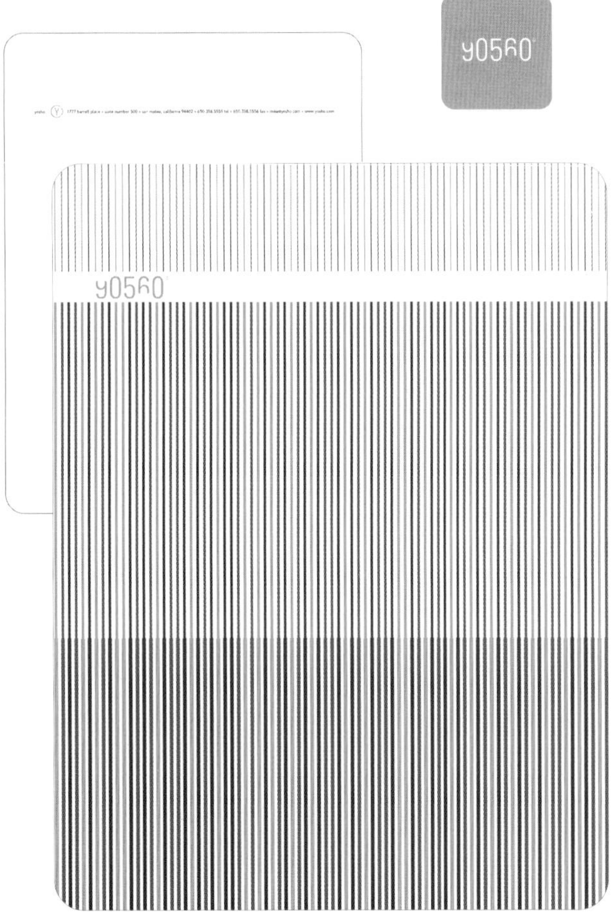

Design_Matt Checkowski and Mikon van Gastel Hollywood, California
Executive Producer_Saffron Kenny and Dan Kolsrud
Producers_Alexander Dervin, Chris Columbus, Mark Radcliffe, and Michael Barnathan
Art Direction_Mikon van Gastel
Creative Direction_Peter Frankfurt
Editor_Jason Webb and Nicholas DeToth
Inferno Artist_Nancy Hyland
2D Animators_Matt Checkowski and Jennifer Lee
Coordinator_Christina Hwang
Distributor_Touchstone/Columbia Pictures Entertainment
Post Production
Supervisor_Paula Dupre-Pesmen
Design Office_Imaginary Forces
Client_Chris Columbus

Principal Type_The Foundry Ballmer ArchiType and the Foundry Gridnik

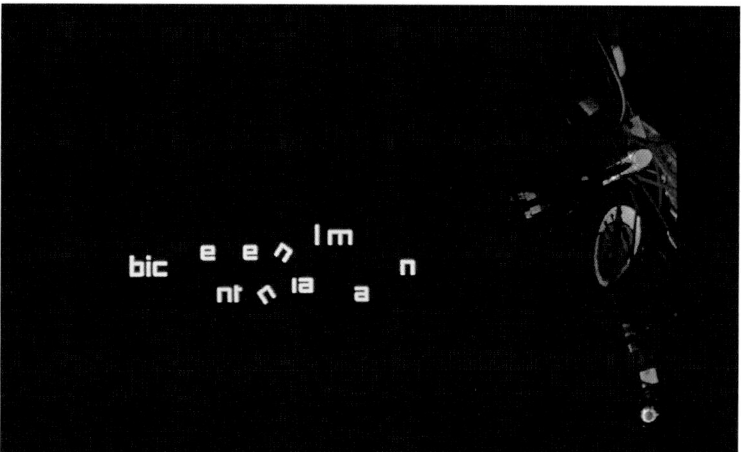

Design_Kirsten Dietz
Stuttgart, Germany
Art Direction_Kirsten Dietz
Creative Direction_Kirsten Dietz
and Jochen Rädeker

Agency_strichpunkt

Principal Type_FF TheSans

Dimensions_Various

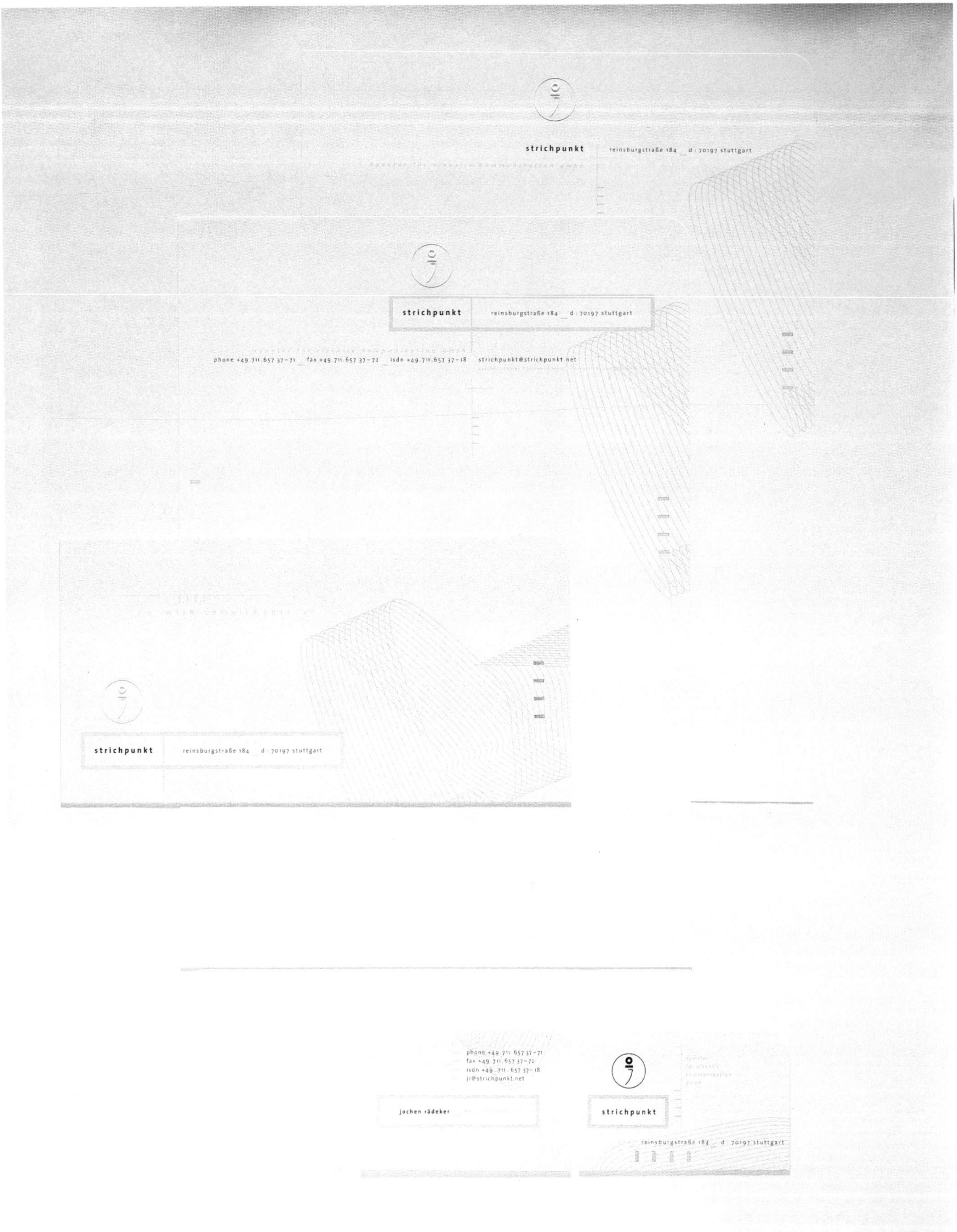

strichpunkt reinsburgstraße 184 _ d : 70197 stuttgart

strichpunkt reinsburgstraße 184 _ d : 70197 stuttgart

phone +49.711.657 37-71 _ fax +49.711.657 37-72 _ isdn +49.711.657 37-18 strichpunkt@strichpunkt.net

strichpunkt reinsburgstraße 184 _ d : 70197 stuttgart

phone +49.711.657 37-71
fax +49.711.657 37-72
isdn +49.711.657 37-18
jr@strichpunkt.net

jochen rädeker

Corporate Identity

Design_Mirko Ilić
New York, New York
Art Direction_Mirko Ilić

Studio_Mirko Ilić Corp.
Client_Adam D. Tihany International, Ltd., and the Time Hotel

Principal Type_Avenir

Dimensions_Various

19

Design_Mikon van Gastel
Hollywood, California
Coordinators_Jono Golding
and Paul Madeira
3D Animators_Sara Marandi
and Laurent Fauchere
Art Direction_Kurt Mattila,
Mikon van Gastel, and Debra Pregler
Creative Direction_John Parkinson
Executive Producer_Bob Swensen
Producers_Maureen Timpa,
Alexander Dervin, Denise Pouchet,
and Shelley Sink

Editor_Kurt Mattila and Jeff Consiglio
Inferno Artist_Danny Yoon and Phil Man
2D Animators_Matt Cullen
and Matt Checkowski
Copywriter_Jon Gustavson
Agency_DMB&B
Design Office_Imaginary Forces
Client_Cadillac EVOQ

Principal Type_FF DIN

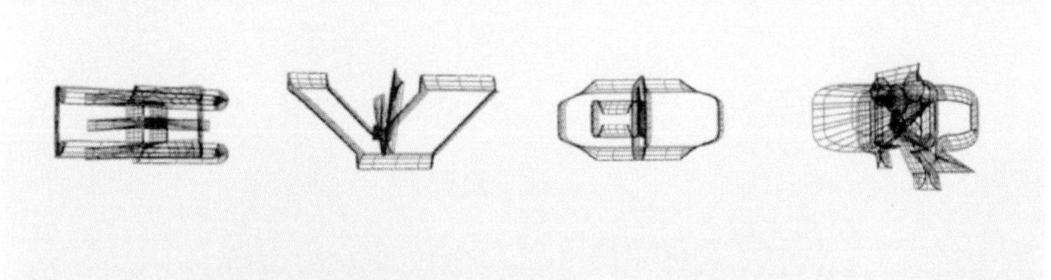

Campaign

Design_Jens Gehlhaar
Los Angeles, California
Lettering_Jens Gehlhaar
Creative Direction_Seth Epstein

Design Office_Fuel

Principal Type_CIA Oddjob

Dimensions_Various

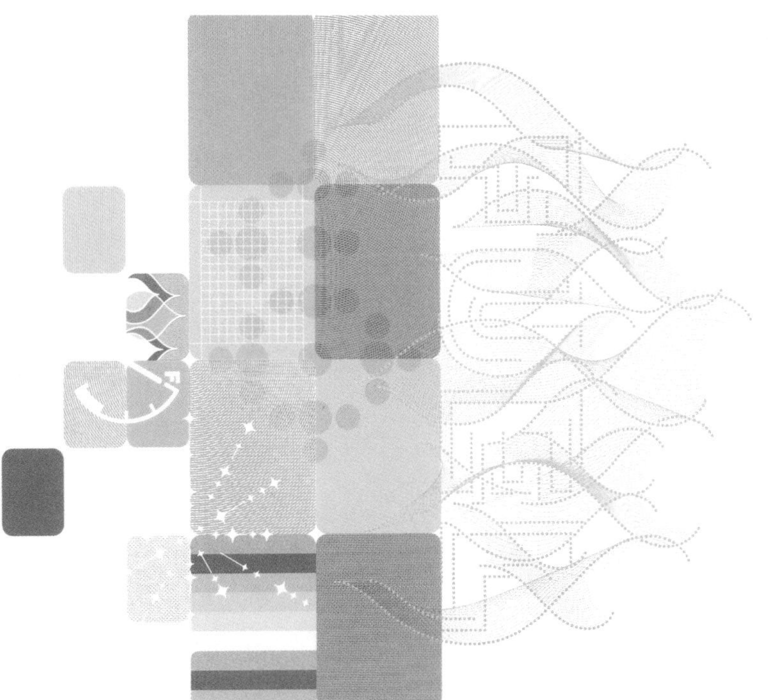

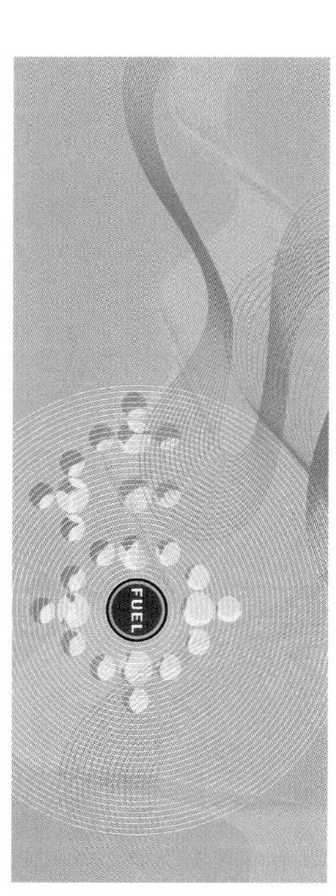

Design_Olivier Michel
Paris, France
Creative Direction_Tartière Brigitte
Photography_Gilles Bouchard

Author_Jean Pierre Luminet
Bookbinding_Atelier Paxion
Printer_RGP Paris

Principal Type_Times New Roman

Dimensions
(11 x 19 cm)

Design_Marion English Powers
Birmingham, Alabama
Art Direction_Marion English Powers
Creative Direction_Marion English Powers

Agency_Slaughter Hanson
Client_Friends of Rickwood

Principal Type_Alternate Gothic, Industrial 736, and Bell Centennial

Dimensions_5¾ x 8¾ in. (14.6 x 22.2 cm)

Design_Joerg Bauer
Stuttgart, Germany
Art Direction_Joerg Bauer
Creative Direction_Uli Weber
and Joerg Bauer

Studio_Joerg Bauer Design
Client_Leonhardt + Kern
Werbung GmbH

Principal Type_Filosofia,
Bell Gothic, and Trade Gothic

Dimensions_12 3/16 x 9 1/4 in.
(31 x 23.5 cm)

MICHAEL BILEK

Werbeagenturen ins Handelsregister eintragen, das können alle. Eine Werbeagentur als Geldmaschine betreiben, das tun viele. Eine Werbeagentur zum Markenzeichen machen, das gelingt wenigen.

Respekt!

Book

Design_Silja Götz, Floridan Koch, Rafael Koch, Peter Körner, Urs Lehni, and Marcus Wohlhüter Hamburg, Germany, London, England, and Lucerne, Switzerland
Art Direction_Katja Fössel, Ralf Herms, and Maurizio Poletto
Creative Direction_Ralf Herms
Photography_Johannes Paffrath, Iris Döring, and Konstanze Wagenhofer

Studio_+rosebud

Principal Type_Adobe Garamond and HTF Champion Gothic

Dimensions_7½ x 11 11/16 in. (19 x 29.7 cm)

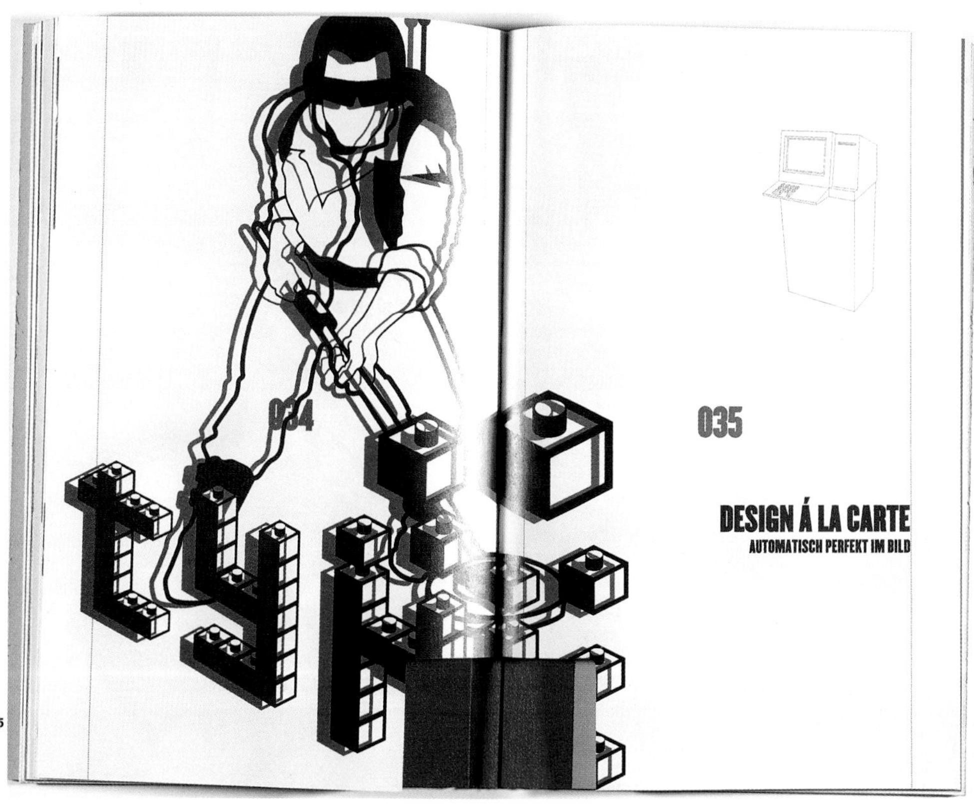

Teaser Trailer

Design_Matt Cullen
Hollywood, California
Executive Producer_Bob Swensen
Direction_Kurt Mattila
and Luc Besson
Live Action
Producer_Denise Pouchet
Creative Direction_Peter Frankfurt
Post Production
Producer_Anita Olan
Coordinator_Seri Bryant
Editors_Kurt Mattila
and Mark Hoffman
Inferno Artist_Phil Man
2D Animator_Matt Cullen
Director of Photography_Vilmos
Zsigmond, ASC
Producer_Patrice Ledoux
Copywriter_Tucker Parsons

Design Office_Imaginary Forces
Client_Columbia TriStar

Principal Type_Caslon Antique

Design_Kyle Cooper, Eric Cruz and Mike Jakab Hollywood, California
Executive Producer_Saffron Kenny and Kevin Jarre
Producers_Alexander Dervin, James Jacks, and Sean Daniel
Art Direction_Kyle Cooper
Direction_Stephen Sommers
Editors_Lauren Giordano and Bob Ducsay

Inferno Artist_Danny Yoon and Elton Garcia
Post Production Supervisor_Doreen Dixon
2D Animator_Ben Lopez
3D Animators_Emily Goodman and Jim Goodman
Coordinator_Jono Golding
Design Office_Imaginary Forces
Client_Universal

Principal Type_La Mummia

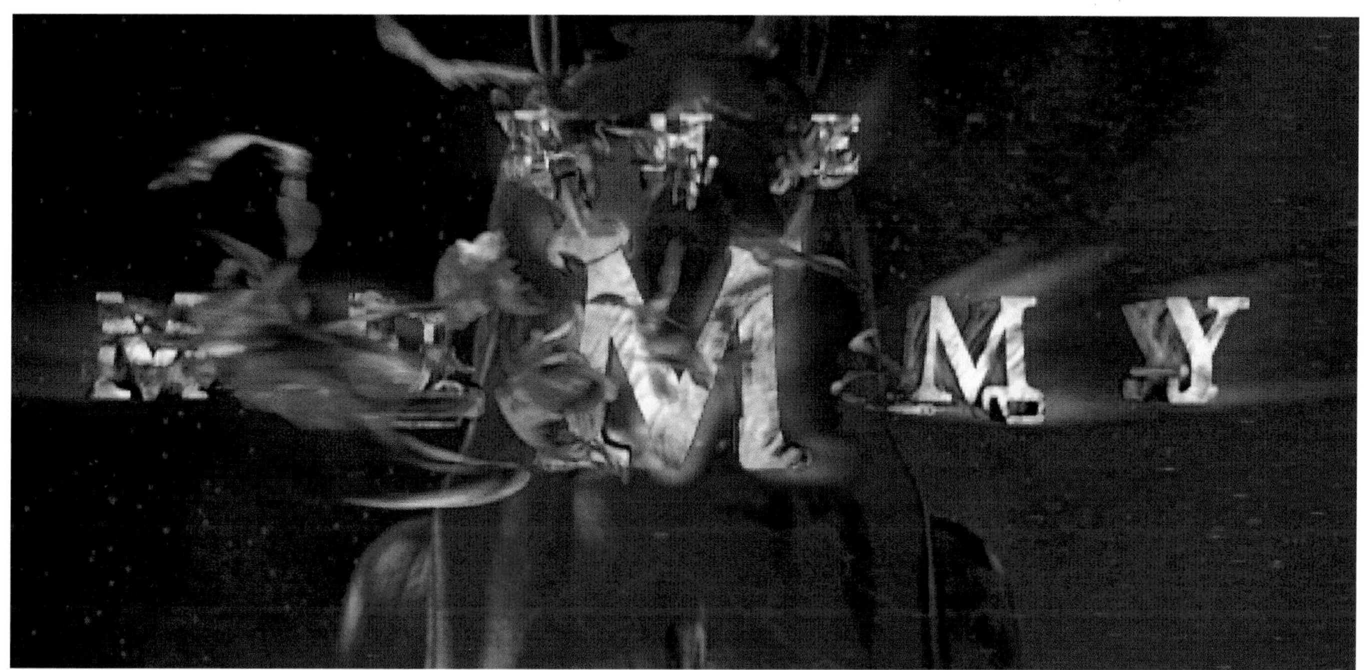

Design_Rymn Massand
New York, New York
Creative Direction_Michael Ian Kaye
Photography_Daniel Bibb

Studio_Little, Brown and Company

Principal Type_Univers Condensed

Dimensions_6 x 9¼ in.
(15.2 x 23.5 cm)

Book

Design_Gijs Sierman
Amsterdam, The Netherlands
Art Direction_van Lindonk Special Projects and Gijs Sierman
Creative Direction_van Lindonk Special Projects
Concept_Peter van Lindonk

Agency_van Lindoink Special Projects
Studio_Gijs Sierman
Client_Albert Heijn

Principal Type_ITC Century and Trade Gothic

Dimensions_10 11/16 x 9 7/8 in. (26 x 25 cm)

Design_Johannes Erler and Manus Fahrner
Hamburg, Germany
Art Direction_Johannes Erler
Creative Direction_Johannes Erler
Photography_Heribert Schindler and Ulrich Hoppe
Text_Jan Weiler

Design Office_Factor Design
Client_Römerturm Feinpapiere

Principal Type_Monotype Van Dijck, Univers, Akzidenz Grotesk, and Emigre Ten

Dimensions_9 ¼ x 12 $\frac{3}{16}$ in. (23.5 x 31 cm)

Student Work

Design_Oliver Henn
Düsseldorf, Germany

School_Fachhochschule
Düsseldorf
Instructors_Jean Ulysses Voelker
and Professor Roland Henss

Principal Type_Bell Gothic

Dimensions_8 3/16 x 7 in.
(20.8 x 17.8 cm)

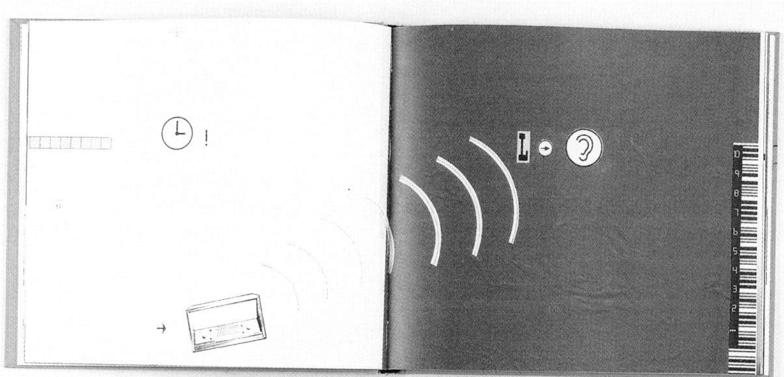

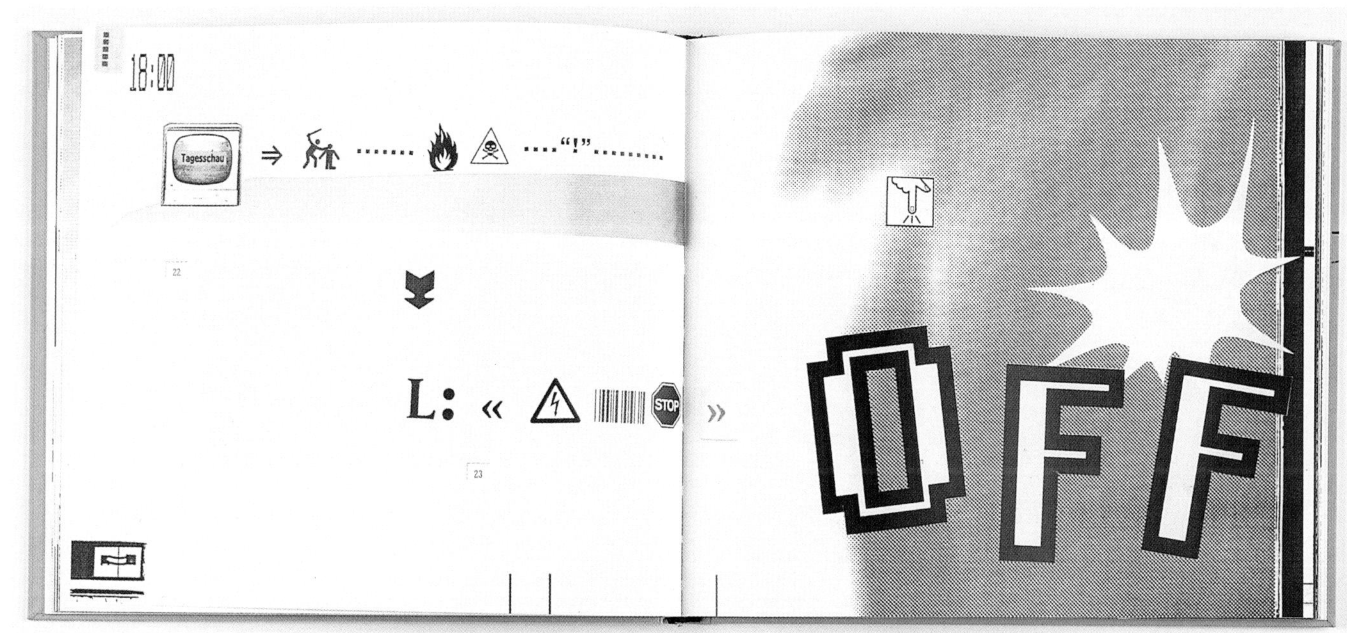

Design_Various Students
Pasadena, California
Art Direction_Vance Studley
Creative Direction_Vance Studley

School_Archetype Press at
Art Center College of Design
Client_Art Center College of Design

Principal Type_Various foundry types

Dimensions_8 x 12 in.
(20.3 x 30.5 cm)

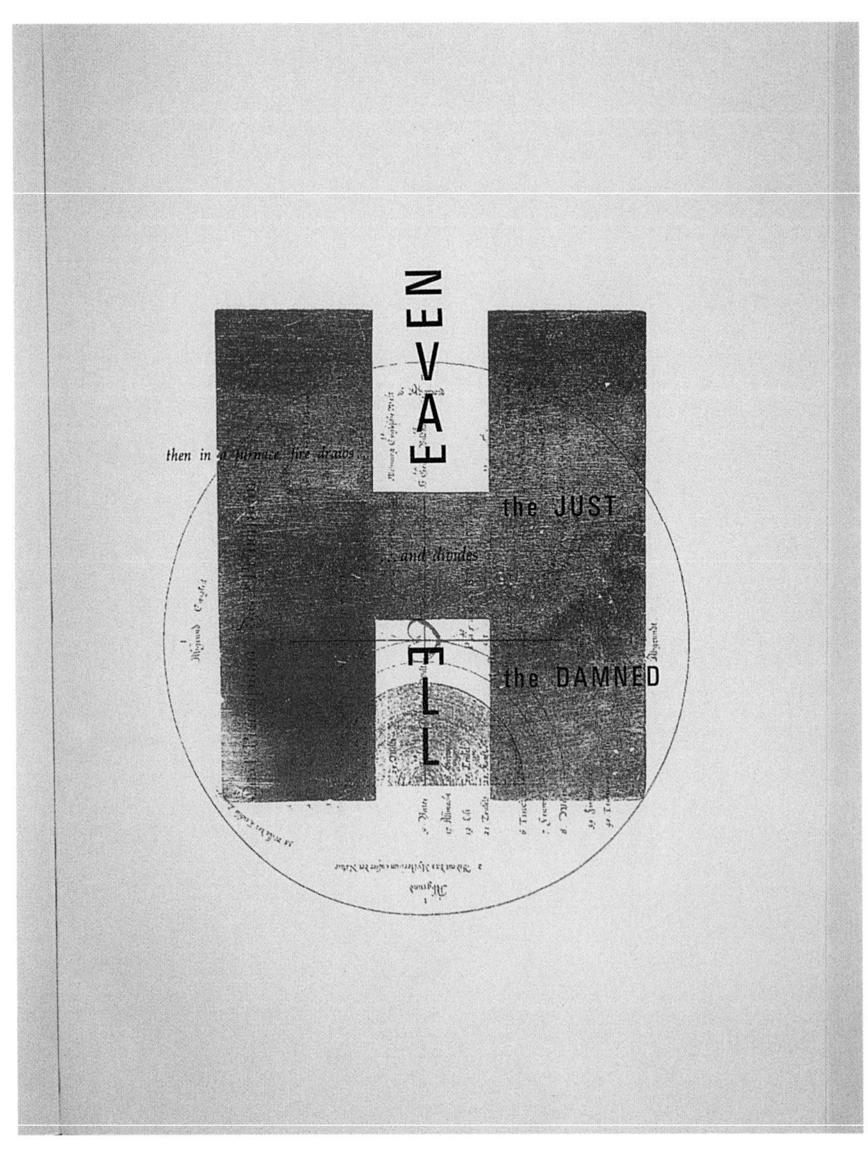

Book

Design_David Shields and Mark Todd
San Marcos, Texas

Studio_White Gas

Principal Type_ITC Franklin Gothic

Dimensions_9½ x 7 in. (24.1 x 17.8 cm)

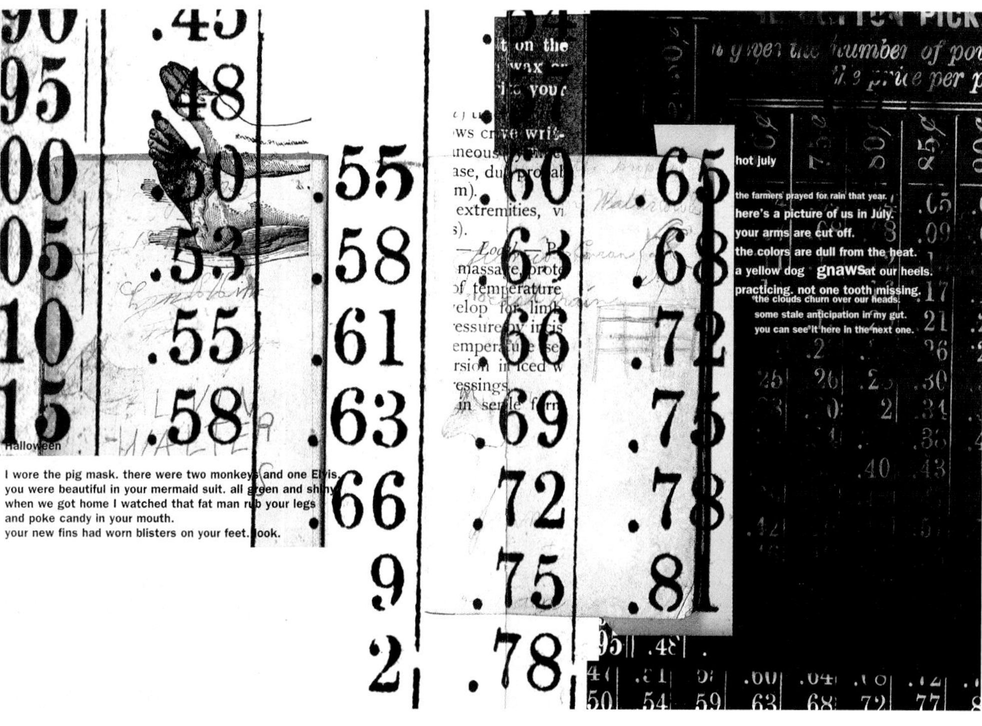

Television Commercial

Design_Christopher Wargin
Santa Monica, California
Art Direction_Gordon Melcher
Creative Direction_Christopher Wargin and Larry Kopald

Agency_Think New Ideas
Design Office_PRoGRESS bureau of design
Client_Oracle

Principal Type_Bawdy

Book

Design_Michael Bierut and Kerrie Powell
New York, New York
Art Direction_Michael Bierut

Design Office_Pentagram
Client_Yale School of Architecture

Principal Type_ITC Franklin Gothic and various

Dimensions_12 ½ x 9 in. (31.8 x 22.9 cm)

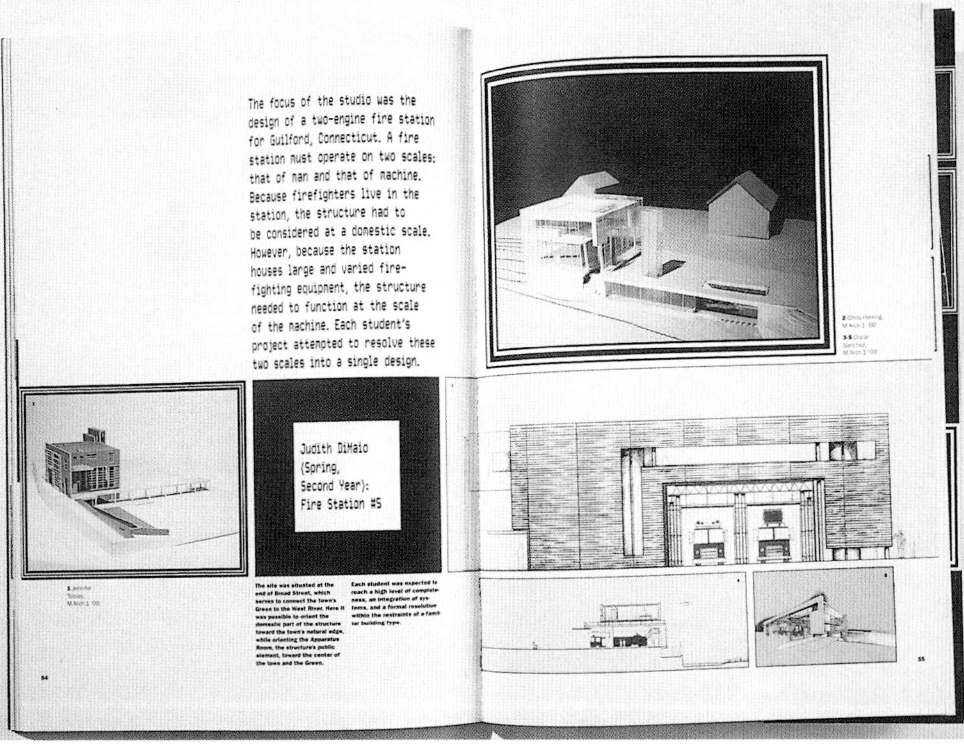

The focus of the studio was the design of a two-engine fire station for Guilford, Connecticut. A fire station must operate on two scales: that of man and that of machine. Because firefighters live in the station, the structure had to be considered at a domestic scale. However, because the station houses large and varied fire-fighting equipment, the structure needed to function at the scale of the machine. Each student's project attempted to resolve these two scales into a single design.

Judith DiMaio
(Spring,
Second Year):
Fire Station #5

The site was situated at the end of Broad Street, which serves to connect the town's Green to the West River. Here it was possible to orient the domestic part of the structure toward the town's natural edge, while orienting the Apparatus Room, the structure's public element, toward the center of the town and the Green.

Each student was expected to reach a high level of completeness, an integration of systems, and a formal resolution within the restraints of a familiar building type.

54

55

Design_Helmut Himmler
and Judith Treder
Frankfurt, Germany
Lettering_Judith Treder
Art Direction_Helmut Himmler
Creative Direction_Rolf Greulich
Copywriter_Dirk Galia

Agency_Michael Conrad
& Leo Burnett

Principal Type_Rechtmann Script,
ITC Franklin Gothic Compressed,
and Confidential

Dimensions_6 7/8 x 9 7/16 in.
(17.5 x 24 cm)

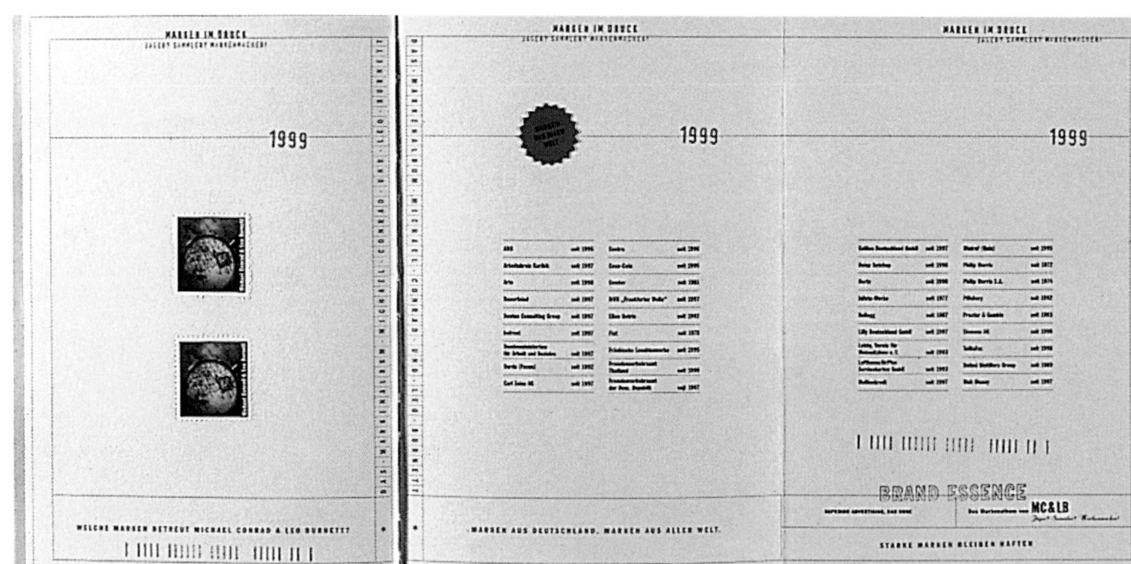

Book

Design_Stefan Sagmeister
New York, New York
Art Direction_Stefan Sagmeister
and David Byrne
Creative Direction_Stefan
Sagmeister and David Byrne
Photography_David Byrne

Design Office_Sagmeister Inc.
Client_David Byrne

Principal Type_Trade Gothic,
Helvetica, Frutiger, and handlettering

Dimensions_11 x 14 in.
(27.9 x 35.6 cm)

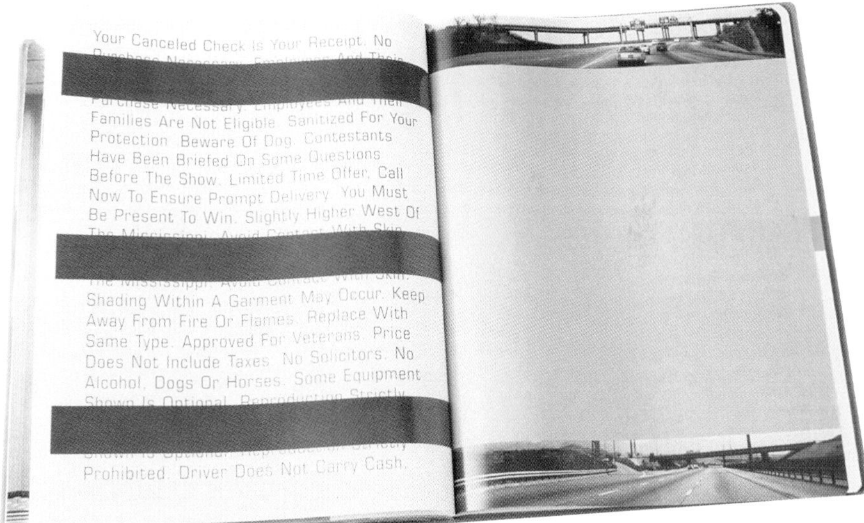

Design_Camille Utterback and Romy Achituv
New York, New York

School_Interactive Telecommunciations Program/ New York University

Principal Type_Windows OS System Fixed font

Stationery

Design_David Shrimpf
Minneapolis, Minnesota
Creative Direction_Bill Thorburn
Photography_Chuck Smith
Copywriter_Chuck Smith

Design Office_Carmichael Lynch Thorburn
Client_Poof

Principal Type_V.A.G Rounded

Dimensions_8 ½ x 11 in. (21.6 x 27.9 cm)

Karen Graham
Visual User
Interface Design
16 x 16
3270 Stoner Avenue
Los Angeles, CA
90066
310.398.3099 p
310.398.6100 f

WHEEL OF
FORTUNE
Live on Stage!

Stationery

Design_Douglas Dearden
Salt Lake City, Utah
Lettering_Douglas Dearden
and Dan Longhuest
Art Direction_Douglas Dearden

Design Office_AND

Principal Type_Adobe Garamond

Dimensions_8½ x 11 in.
(21.6 x 27.9 cm)

Magazine

Design_J. Abbott Miller, Scott Devendorf, and Roy Brooks
New York, New York
Art Direction_J. Abbott Miller

Design Office_Pentagram
Client_2wice Arts Foundation

Principal Type_FF Scala Sans

Dimensions_11½ x 8¼ in.
(29.2 x 21 cm)

Nutshell Study No. 1

LOG CABIN

ACTUAL CRIME REPORTED ON THURSDAY, OCTOBER 22, 1942

Arthur Roberts, a local insurance salesman, was found dead by police who responded to a call from a friend of the victim, Marian Chase. Mrs. Chase was questioned and gave the following statement. She met Arthur Roberts at the Log Cabin on Wednesday, October 21, 1942 at about 5:00 pm. They were having a meeting there. Roberts was married and was living with his wife. Mrs. Chase was also married but was not living with her husband. Roberts told her at this meeting that the affair between them was ended. There was no quarrel.

Mrs. Chase and Mr. Roberts were standing at the foot of the bunk. He turned toward the door, took a package of cigarettes from his outside pocket, selected a cigarette, but dropped it. As he stooped over to pick it up a shot was heard—he fell flat—a gun dropped beside him. Mrs. Chase said she picked up the gun then replaced it. It did not belong to her. She then ran out of the door, jumped into her car and drove to summon the police.

The gun was identified as belonging to Arthur Roberts. Mrs. Chase identified the handbag on the bunk as belonging to her. A single bullet had passed entirely through Mr. Roberts' chest from front to back and the powder around the entrance hole indicated that it had been fired at a fairly close range. The model showed the premises, just after Mrs. Chase left, and before her return with the police.

IN COLD BLOOD

THE NUTSHELL STUDIES OF UNEXPLAINED DEATH

PHOTOGRAPHY BY CORINNE MAY BOTZ

WHAT HAPPENED? THE PHOTOGRAPHS ON THE FOLLOWING PAGES BEGIN WITH THE END—A MURDER, A SUICIDE, A FIRE—AND ASK US TO PULL TOGETHER THE DETAILS THAT TELL THE WHOLE STORY. These lurid yet cozy scenes are one-inch-to-one foot scale models of actual crime scenes, dollhouses meticulously crafted to advance the understanding of forensic science. Called The Nutshell Studies of Unexplained Death, these miniature dioramas were created in the 1930's and 40's by Frances Glessner Lee, a New Hampshire woman of substantial wealth and a taste for detective work. Working with a carpenter assistant, Lee crafted about three scenes a year and ultimately produced 20 different case studies. Details such as bullet holes, blood stains, wallpaper, carpet, newspaper headlines, and calendars are rendered with unrelenting precision.

The Nutshell Studies grew out of Lee's concern that the vast number of unsolved crimes were due to lack of awareness of how to read the stories told by crime scenes. In the 30's and 40's the evidence of crime scenes was routinely ignored and sometimes accidentally destroyed by police who were untrained in the emerging science of forensics. The dioramas present the scenes as recorded in local police records and through eyewitness accounts. As training tools, police and detectives-in-training were asked to study the models and consider the statements provided by witnesses to arrive at a plausible hypothesis.

The dioramas were one aspect of work undertaken by Lee's Nutshell Laboratories. Her philanthropic support established the Department of Legal Medicine at Harvard University and a national forensics organization called the Harvard Associates in Police Science. Renowned internationally as a criminologist, Lee was named an honorary captain of the New Hampshire Police in 1943.

The Nutshell studies are now housed in the Chief Medical Examiner's Office in Baltimore, where they are still used in forensics seminars twice a year. Jerry Dziecichowicz, the chief administrator of the examiner's office, will not divulge the solutions to these riddles because each year dozens of detectives-in-training hone their skills by studying the dioramas. When pressed for details, Dziecichowicz offered two hints: First, if someone commits suicide in bed, they don't usually pull the blankets up over themselves afterward, and second, a housewife doesn't usually commit suicide in the midst of baking pies and ironing shirts.

53

Design_Hiroaki Nagai
and Hiroaki Seki
Tokyo, Japan
Art Direction_Hiroaki Nagai
Creative Direction_Kenichi Aki
Photography_Kazumi Kurigami
Copywriter_Masakazu Nifuji

Agency_Yomiko Advertising Inc.
Studio_N • G., Inc.
Client_Onward Kashiyama Co., Ltd.

Principal Type_Gothic MB101

Dimensions_57 5/16 x 40 9/16 in.
(145.6 x 103 cm)

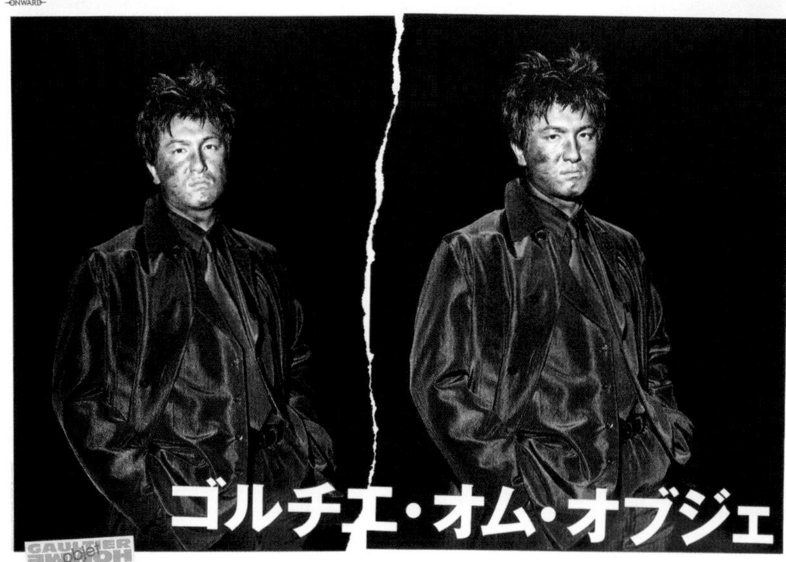

Poster

Design_Philippe Apeloig
Paris, France
Art Direction_Philippe Apeloig

Agency_Apeloig Design
Client_Cité du Livre, Aix-en-Provence

Principal Type_Univers Extra Black

Dimensions_47¼ x 67¾ in.
(120 x 172 cm)

Design_Brode Vosloo
Durban, South Africa
Lettering_Brode Vosloo
Art Direction_Brode Vosloo

Creative Direction_Brode Vosloo
Agency_Orange Juice Design (Pty) Ltd.
Client_Pro Helvetica,
Art Council of Switzerland

Principal Type_Various

Dimensions_16
(42 x 29.7 cm)

Design_Matthew Beckerle
Toronto, Canada
Creative Direction_Matthew Beckerle
Photography_Tim Morrison

Studio_Creative Activity Design Company
Client_Blonde Magazine

Principal Type_Melior and Univers Condensed

Dimensions_8 ⅜ x 11 in. (21.3 x 27.9 cm)

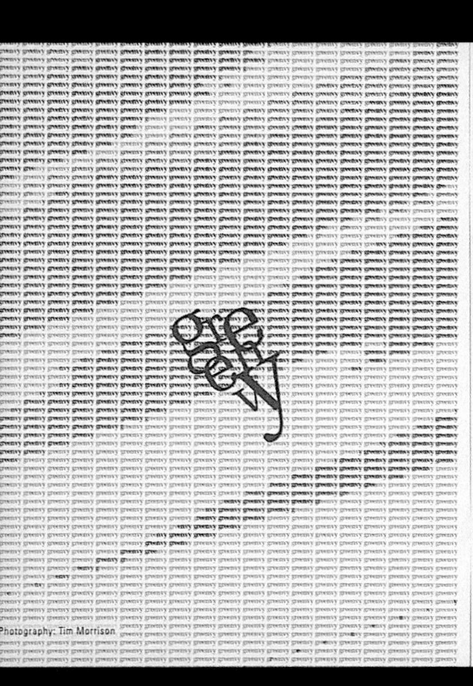

Magazine Spread

Design_Andrew Godfrey
Sydney, Australia
Art Direction_Andrew Godfrey

Client_The Masters

Principal Type_FF DIN

Dimensions_9 7/16 x 12 13/16 in.
(24 x 32.5 cm)

Magazine

Design_Garth Walker, Brode Vosloo, and Eben Keun
Durban, South Africa
Lettering_Garth Walker and Brode Vosloo
Art Direction_Garth Walker and Brode Vosloo
Creative Direction_Garth Walker and Brode Vosloo
Copywriter_Alex Sudheim and Steven Kotze

Agency_Orange Juice Design (Pty) Ltd.

Principal Type_Various

Dimensions_16 9/16 x 11 11/16 in. (42 x 29.7 cm)

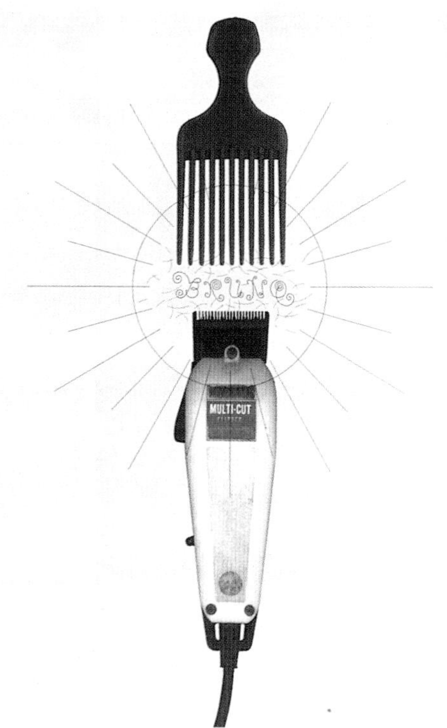

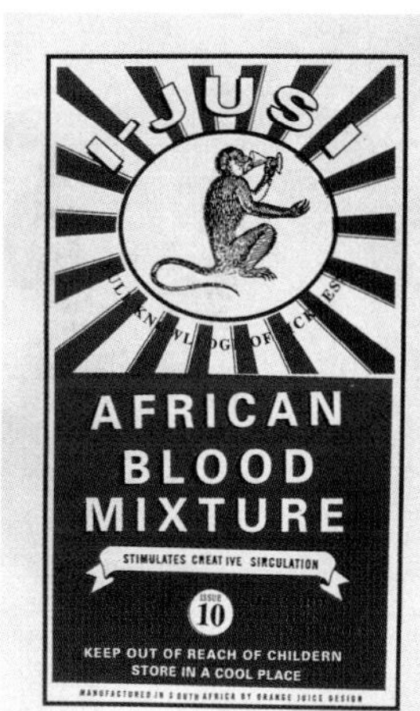

Angelina

Jolie

ADVANTAGE

Quarterly

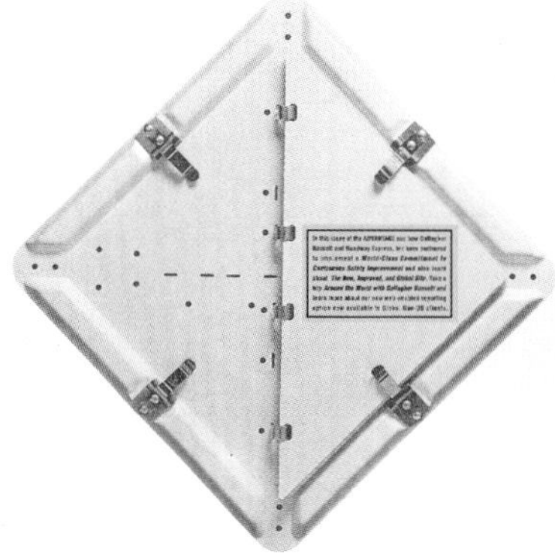

A safe, secure work environment is an expectation that most employees have of their employer. Most companies associate potential areas of risk with external factors, when in fact, a majority of their risk lies internally within their own policies and procedures. Gallagher Bassett Investigative Services recognizes the great loss potential inherent in these risks and offers effective services that companies can employ to help prevent the risk and the accompanying costs associated with security vulnerability. Using proven fact-finding techniques our Certified Protection Professionals (CPP) conduct security audits and assessments that provide employers with insight into potential threats that may hurt or interrupt business operations.

ASSESSING THE RISK Gallagher Bassett Investigative Services' certified professionals implement a thorough process that examines all elements of security, from perimeter control to the movement of products and people. This process begins with the establishment of the company's goals and needs. Once a client's goals and needs are determined, we coordinate a project that can range from 2 days to 6 weeks, depending upon the scope of the assessment. Interviews with the general employee population and key personnel are conducted to gather information. Once the interviewing process is complete, our staff conducts a physical security survey addressing internal and external elements including buildings, parking garages, fences, and access control systems. Once the physical security assessment is complete, Gallagher Bassett Investigative Services will analyze the findings and recommend controls, policies, and procedures. Our comprehensive services evaluate all existing security policies and procedures to determine if they have been appropriately applied.

Gallagher Bassett Investigative Services will then provide a thorough report detailing the potential vulnerabilities that affect the security of the workplace. Our professionals will work with you to implement the recommendations in three stages: procedures (written guidelines), technology (lock and key controls, card access, and intrusion alarms), and manpower (guard service or security personnel).

WE CAN HELP Employers recognize that reducing theft and potential violent acts in the workplace, from both internal and external sources, are benefits associated with identifying security risks. Gallagher Bassett Investigative Services offers security audits and assessments that are tailored to meet your company's specific needs. Our complete commitment to help our clients reduce security vulnerability is backed by our guarantee that you'll be completely satisfied with the timeliness, accuracy, and quality of our security audits and assessments. To learn more on how Gallagher Bassett Investigative Services can reduce your security vulnerability, please contact [illegible], Area Vice President Operations, Investigative Services at [illegible].

Poster

Design_Katsunori Nishi
Tokyo, Japan
Art Direction_Katsunori Nishi

Design Office_Brahman
company limited

Principal Type_Worm Hole

Dimensions_40 ⁹⁄₁₆ x 28 ⁵⁄₁₆ in.
(103 x 72.8 cm)

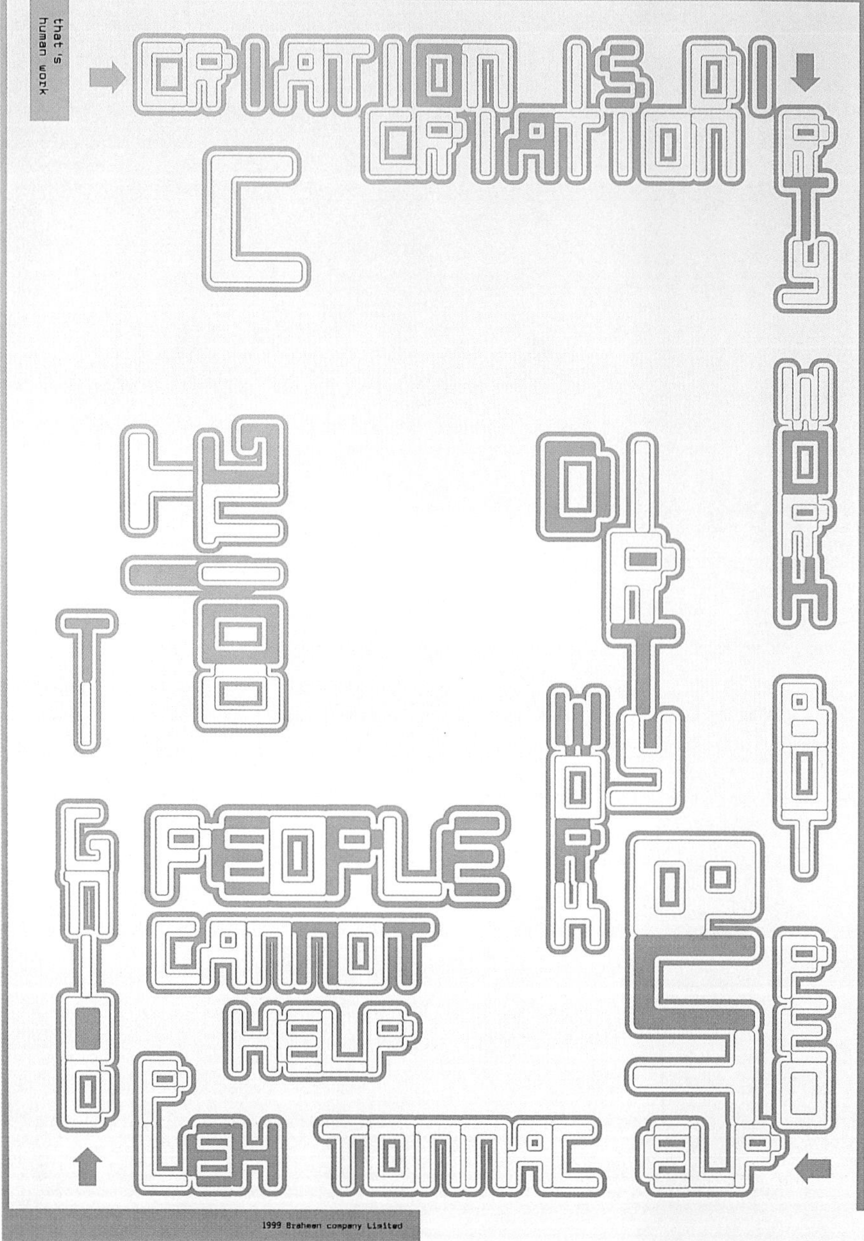

Book

Design_Susana Rodriguez, Hans Seeger, and Dave Ritter
Chicago, Illinois
Creative Direction_Curtis Schreiber
Editor_Mike Wang and Fred Guterl

Agency_VSA Partners
Client_IBM

Principal Type_Interstate

Dimensions_11 x 15 in. (27.9 x 38.1 cm)

Design_Benjamin Pham
San Francisco, California
Art Direction_Patricia Evangelista
Photography_Makota Kubota

Studio_Character
Client_Chronicle Books

Principal Type_Gill Sans and Futura BT Medium, and Futura BT Bold

Dimensions_10 1/16 x 13 1/2 in. (25.6 x 34.3 cm)

Magazine

Design_Domenic Lippa and Richard McGillan Twickenham, England
Art Direction_Domenic Lippa
Creative Direction_Domenic Lippa
Editor_Patrick Baglee
Assistant Editor_Clare Lundy

Studio_Lippa Pearce Design
Client_Typographic Circle

Principal Type_Zurich

Dimensions_11 x 14 in. (28 x 35.5 cm)

Design_Malcolm Brown and Carmen Dunjko
Toronto, Canada
Art Direction_Malcolm Brown
Creative Direction_Carmen Dunjko
Photography_Stephen Chung
Illustration_Christine Stephens

Client_Shift

Principal Type_Neue Helvetica 55 Roman

Dimensions_18 x 10¾ in. (45.7 x 27.3 cm)

"Antigua is ready for the computer age," PM Lester Bird intones on the local news. Then the screen blips to static, before the announcer returns. These interruptions occur almost nightly

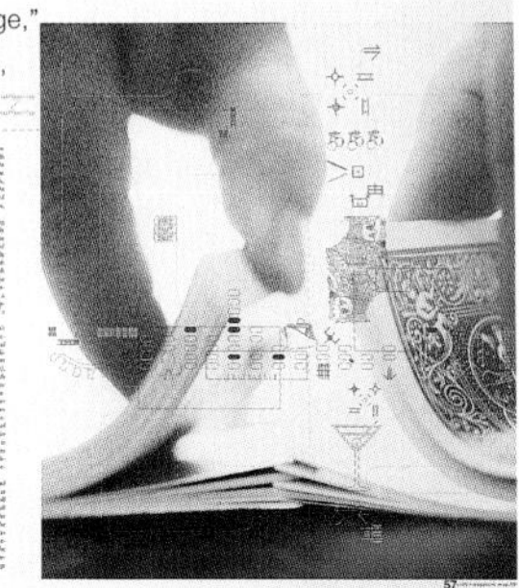

the tiny caribbean island of antigua has embraced online gambling with the zeal of a poker junkie holding a royal flush. and if meddling americans don't get in the way, it could bring in the big bucks of international e-commerce. can anyone lose?

flipflops, a desktop and one billion reasons never to leave

by chris turner / photographs by stephen chung / illustrations by christine stephens

52 shift magazine.may.1999

53 shift magazine.may.1999

Stationery

Design_Scott Thares
Minneapolis, Minnesota
Art Direction_Steven Sikora
Creative Direction_Steven Sikora

Design Office_Design Guys
Client_Hest & Kramer

Principal Type_Helvetica

Dimensions_8 ½ x 11 in.
(21.6 x 27.9 cm)

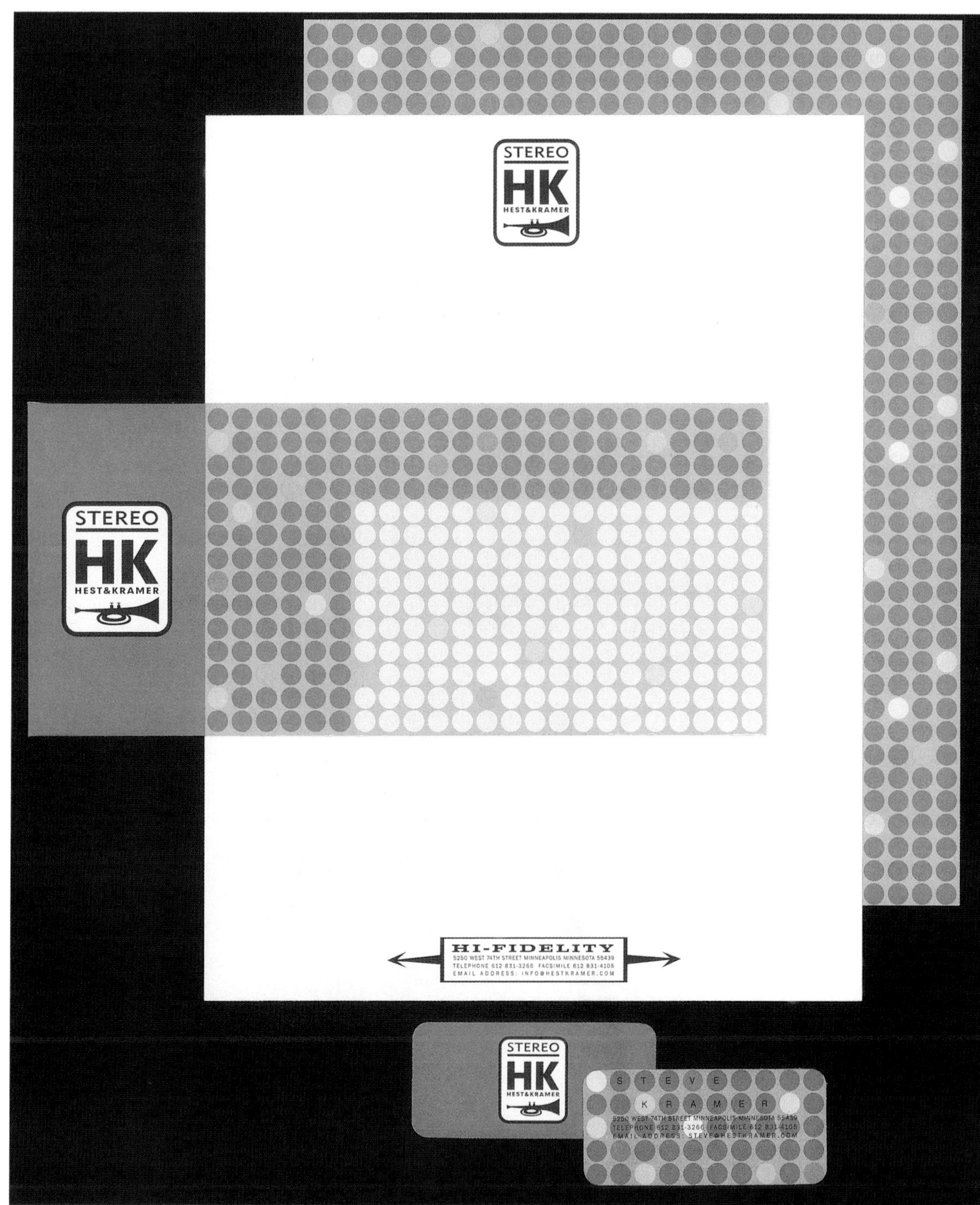

Design_Bill Douglas
Toronto, Canada

Studio_The Bang
Client_Coupe

Principal Type_Trade Gothic, Times New Roman, and Helvetica

Dimensions_9⅝ x 11½ in. (24.5 x 29. 2 cm)

Magazine

Design_Guy Pask, Aaron O'Donnel, and Alec Bathgate Christchurch, New Zealand
Art Direction_Guy Pask
Creative Direction_Guy Pask and Douglas Maclean

Design Office_Strategy Advertising & Design
Client_Robert McDougall Art Gallery

Principal Type_Adobe Jenson and Monotype Grotesque

Dimensions_11 ¹¹⁄₁₆ x 8 ¼ in. (29.7 x 21 cm)

Magazine Spread

Design_Bill Douglas
Toronto, Canada
Photography_Glenda Stuart

Studio_The Bang
Client_Coupe

Principal Type_Trade Gothic

Dimensions_19 ¼ x 11½ in.
(24.5 x 29.2 cm)

DREAMT IN **HEAVEN**. FORGED IN **HELL**. MADE IN **LAS VEGAS**.

TEXT BY STEPHEN BARRETT PHOTOGRAPHY BY GLENDA STUART

Throughout history great cities and civilizations have risen and fallen. Meccas like Babylon, ancient Egypt, Rome, Paris, and New York have shaped and defined the most dominant eras in the history of the world. The ideals and visions of these civilizations can be found in the art, architecture and ruins of their cities, with stories buried deep within their walls. But what of American civilization? The definitive American city must embody the American Dream — that concept which always seems to be just beyond the grasp of definition. God only knows what the American Dream is. It has not been defined, but it has been pursued. The American Dream, perhaps no longer deemed enough, seems to be ever expanding, taking on global proportions. There is one city, one American city that seems up to the task of offering its citizens and visitors the world and everything in it — even if this city's vision of the world is a bit skewed. Only one city can deliver all the world has to offer, be it Rome in the guise of Caesar's palace; New York's Empire State Building and Statue of Liberty; Paris's Eiffel Tower; or the great pyramids of Egypt cleverly camouflaged as the Luxor Hotel and Casino. It is the world brought to your feet. Plastic. Prefab. American. Las Vegas.

The American Dream is exactly that: a dream. It is both a vision and a quest. The Las Vegas version of that dream began in the mind of Ben Siegal with the planning and opening of the Flamingo in 1946 on a desolate stretch of Highway 91 in the Nevada desert. Writer Nick Tosches said in *Dino* his biography of Dean Martin, that "It was Siegal who believed that the desert town in the middle of nowhere could become the air-conditioned Eden of every dirty dream." This was it. To hell with the idea of owning a little bungalow in middletown America; that's no dream. The real fantasy is fast women and fast money cruising the Vegas strip. And by the 1960s Las Vegas was the mecca for a decadent American lifestyle.

Magazine Spread

Design_Frank Gehrke
Munich, Germany
Art Direction_Horst Moser

Studio_Independent Medien – Design
Client_Computerwoche – Verlag I.D.G.

Principal Type_ITC Officina Sans

Dimensions_21 7/16 x 15 in.
(54.5 x 38 cm)

Visionen

TITEL

Hinterbliebene nach Suizid

Der doppelte Tod

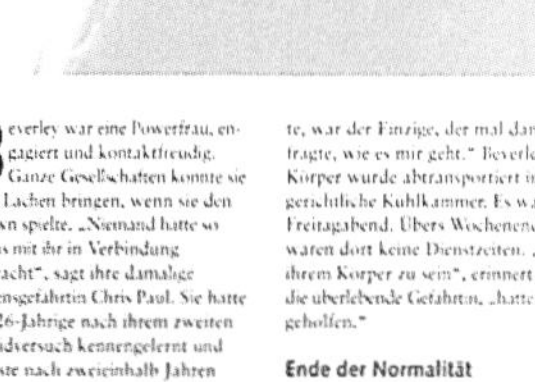

Tod

Wenn er dem Leben mit uns den Tod vorgezogen hat: Wie soll mich auf der Welt irgendjemand sonst wertschätzen?

Beverley war eine Powerfrau, engagiert und kontaktfreudig. Ganze Gesellschaften konnte sie zum Lachen bringen, wenn sie den Clown spielte. „Niemand hatte so etwas mit ihr in Verbindung gebracht", sagt ihre damalige Lebensgefährtin Chris Paul. Sie hatte die 26-Jährige nach ihrem zweiten Suizidversuch kennengelernt und musste nach zweieinhalb Jahren miteinander geteilten Lebens die „fürchterliche Erfahrung" machen, dass „Liebe kein Allheilmittel ist". Als abends spät ein Polizist an ihrer Tür klingelte, wusste Chris schon Bescheid. „In Ihrem Keller hängt eine junge Frau", sagte er, einfühlsam wie ein Stadtwerker, der zum Stromablesen kommt. Ein polizeiliches Rollkommando fegte durch die Wohnung, beschlagnahmte Beverleys Kalender und ein Gedicht, das über ihrem Schreibtisch hing. Als Chris sich weigerte, die Leiche zu identifizieren, wurden die Polizisten wütend. „Der Sanitäter, der sie abholte, war der Einzige, der mal danach fragte, wie es mir geht." Beverleys Körper wurde abtransportiert in die gerichtliche Kühlkammer. Es war Freitagabend. Übers Wochenende waren dort keine Dienstzeiten. „Bei ihrem Körper zu sein", erinnert sich die überlebende Gefährtin, „hätte sehr geholfen."

Ende der Normalität

1997 setzten in Deutschland 12 201 Menschen ihrem Leben selbst ein Ende. Zurück blieben schätzungsweise 40 000 fassungslose Angehörige: Lebenspartner, Kinder, Mütter, Väter, Geschwister, Großeltern, Freunde. Sie erleben den Verlust ihrer Angehörigen, wie es eine zurückgelassene Ehefrau formuliert, als einen „doppelten Tod". Denn sie haben nicht nur die Trauer zu bewältigen, sondern auch die Scham und die Schuldgefühle für dieses Ende. Denn Suizid ist kein „normaler" Tod.

„Es ist, als ob ich mit einem Kainsmahl behaftet bin", klagt eine junge Frau aus Karlsruhe. Vor acht Monaten wurde sie mit ihren beiden acht und zehn Jahre alten Kindern allein im Leben zurückgelassen. „Ich konnte nicht einmal mehr mit aufrechtem Gang den Müll wegbringen." Den Satz: „Mein Mann hat sich das Leben genommen" hat sie erst mühsam aussprechen lernen müssen. Als ein Versicherungsvertreter bei ihr anrief, gab sie spontan die falsche Auskunft, ihr Mann sei bei einem Unfall gestorben.

Dabei gab es den Suizid zu allen Zeiten und in allen Gesellschaften. Dennoch fragen sich die Zurückgelassenen: „Was haben wir falsch gemacht?" Als ob ein Mensch einen anderen retten könnte, wenn der es selber gar nicht will. „Wir müssen dem anderen auch die Würde und Verantwortung für sein Leben lassen", beschreibt Chris Paul die Gratwanderung der Freunde und Angehörigen suizidgefährdeter Menschen. „Wir können doch nicht alle Freunde, die in eine Krise geraten, in die Psychiatrie einweisen lassen."

Manchmal passiert die Katastrophe nach langen Depressionen, manchmal wie aus heiterem Himmel. Barbara Sillack wurde, nach 25-jährigem Zusammenleben, plötzlich von ihrem Mann verlassen. „Waren unsere neunjährige Tochter und ich ihm nichts wert gewesen?", fragt sie verzweifelt. Das nagt am Selbstwertgefühl. „Wenn schon mein Mann den Tod einem Leben mit mir vorgezogen hatte, wie sollte dann irgendjemand sonst auf der Welt mich wertschätzen?" Sie fühlt sich nicht nur um die gemeinsame Zukunft betrogen, sondern auch um die Vergangenheit. War sie gar nicht so glücklich gewesen, wie sie es erlebt hatte?

„Angehörige von Suizidtoten", weiß Ellen Wittke, Sprecherin der Arbeitskreise Leben in Baden-Württemberg (AKL), „sind selbst in hohem Maß suizidgefährdet. Sie gelten als ausgewiesene Risikogruppe." In diesem Jahr fand die bundesweit erste Tagung für Trauernde nach einem Suizid und ihre Helfer(innen) – die häufig selbst Betroffene sind – statt. Betroffene aus ganz Deutschland und der Schweiz waren gekommen, um „Menschen zu treffen, die das Gleiche erlebt haben wie ich".

Trauer nach Suizid ist anders

Trauergruppen, die dem Tod seine soziale Dimension wieder abgewinnen wollen, gibt es schon viele in Deutschland. Trauernde nach einem Suizid fühlen sich in diesen Gruppen nicht aufgehoben. Sie bleiben meist isoliert mit ihrer Trauer, Schuld und Scham. Eine Tochter, deren Mutter im Januar in den Tod gegangen ist, hat die Teilnahme an der Tagung ihrem Vater zum Geburtstag geschenkt. „Zu Hause habe ich niemanden kennengelernt, der so etwas aus eigener Erfahrung kennt." Er ist der einzige Mann in einer Runde aus etwa 20 Betroffenen. Das spiegelt die Statistik. Zu zwei Dritteln sind es Männer, die sich das Leben nehmen. In der Gruppe kommen Frauen zusammen, die ihre Männer oder Söhne betrauern, manche auch beide. Einige haben beide Eltern und weitere Familienangehörige durch Suizid verloren.

Eine Frau aus Nordrhein-Westfalen musste vor zwölf Jahren den plötzlichen Herztod ihres Ehemannes hinnehmen. Nun hat sich ihr neuer Partner das Leben genommen. Nach drei Wochen ließen sich die meisten Freunde nicht mehr blicken. „Er wurde totgeschwiegen, als hätte es die sechs Jahre mit ihm nie gegeben. Das tut weh." Von ihrer Umgebung

LITERATUR

Chris Paul
Warum hast du uns das angetan?
Ein Begleitbuch für Trauernde, wenn sich jemand das Leben genommen hat.
Gütersloh 1998, 24,80 DM

TRAUER SCHULD UND

Design_Massimiliano Patrignani
Urbania, Italy
Art Direction_Leonardo Sonnoli
Creative Direction_Leonardo Sonnoli

Studio_Dolcini Associati
Client_Municipality of Pesaro

Principal Type_ITC Franklin Gothic Condensed and Jurriaan Square Leonardo Sonnoli

Dimensions_6⁵⁄₁₆ x 7⁷⁄₁₆ in. (16 x 19 cm)

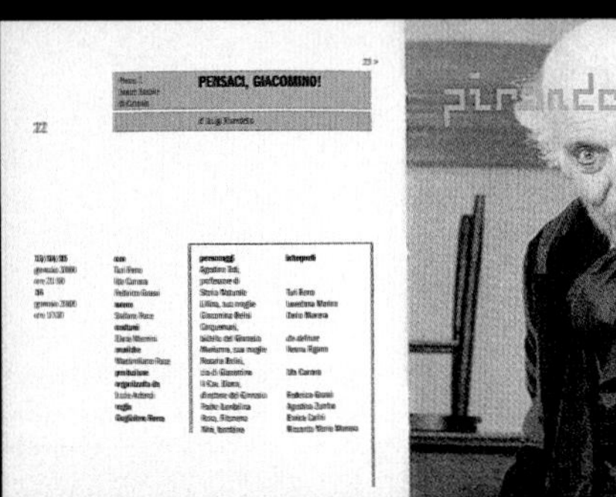

3 >

Indice

2

Avvertenze per il pubblico

!

Gli abbonati sono tenuti a rispettare date e turni di abbonamento secondo il calendario pubblicato a pagina 4/5 del presente libretto. Si precisa che durante la stagione non sarà in alcun caso possibile cambiare turno. Non è previsto alcun rimborso per gli spettacoli non fruiti. Gli abbonamenti non sono nominativi e possono essere ceduti ad altre persone; quelli a tariffa ridotta possono essere ceduti solo a persone aventi diritto alla medesima agevolazione. Lo spettatore deve essere sempre munito di biglietto, tessera d'abbonamento o d'ingresso, da esibire al personale di sala addetto al controllo su semplice richiesta. Nel corso delle rappresentazioni, ad eccezione di specifiche autorizzazioni della Direzione del Teatro e della Compagnia ospitata, è vietato l'uso di apparecchi fotografici o di registrazione audio e video. **Gli spettatori sono pregati di spegnere i telefoni cellulari prima di entrare in Teatro. Attenzione:** le date degli spettacoli possono subire variazioni per cause di forza maggiore. Si raccomanda agli spettatori di verificare le date degli stessi sul materiale informativo (locandine e manifesti) che viene esposto in Teatro, e di prestare attenzione a eventuali annunci dello speaker. In caso di annullamento dello spettacolo il relativo biglietto verrà rimborsato nei giorni successivi. Qualora non fosse possibile il recupero o la sostituzione dello spettacolo annullato, verranno rimborsate anche le rispettive quote agli abbonati. **Salvo diversa indicazione gli spettacoli avranno inizio alle ore 21.00 nei giorni feriali e alle ore 17.00 la domenica e i giorni festivi.**

Si raccomanda la massima puntualità, **a spettacolo iniziato è vietato l'accesso alla platea e ai posti numerati di galleria.**

Magazine Spread

Design_Bill Douglas
Toronto, Canada
Photography_Johnny Chavez

Studio_The Bang

Principal Type_Times New Roman

Dimensions_19 ¼ x 11 ½ in.
(24.5 x 29.2 cm)

Magazine Spread

Design_Bill Douglas
Toronto, Canada

Studio_The Bang

Principal Type_Times New Roman

Dimensions_19 ¼ x 11 ½ in.
(24.5 x 29.2 cm)

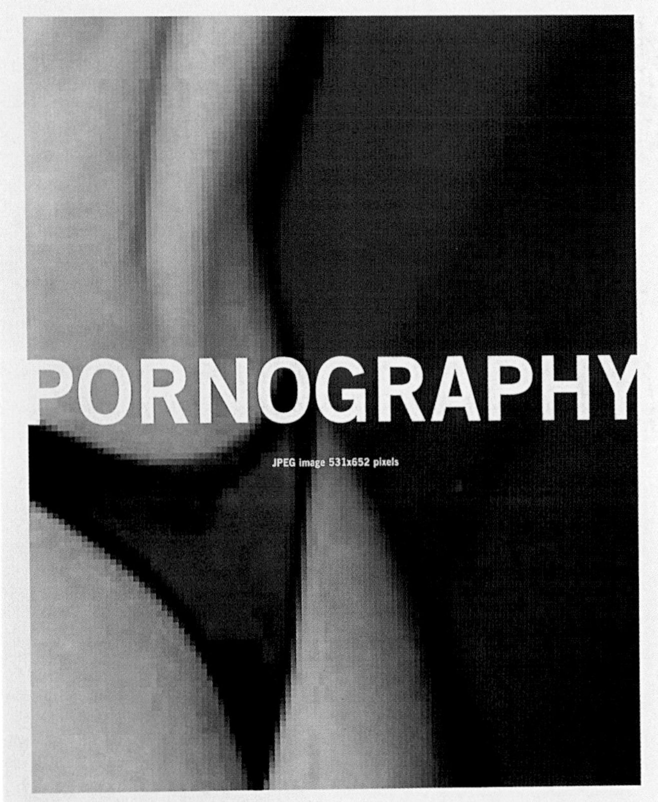

Poster

Design_Stefan Sagmeister and Martin Woodtli
New York, New York
Lettering_Stefan Sagmeister and Martin Woodtli
Art Direction_Stefan Sagmeister
Creative Direction_Stefan Sagmeister
Photography_Tom Schierlitz

Design Office_Sagmeister Inc.
Client_American Institute of Graphic Arts, Detroit

Principal Type_Handlettering

Dimensions_27 x 39 in.
(68.6 x 99.1 cm)

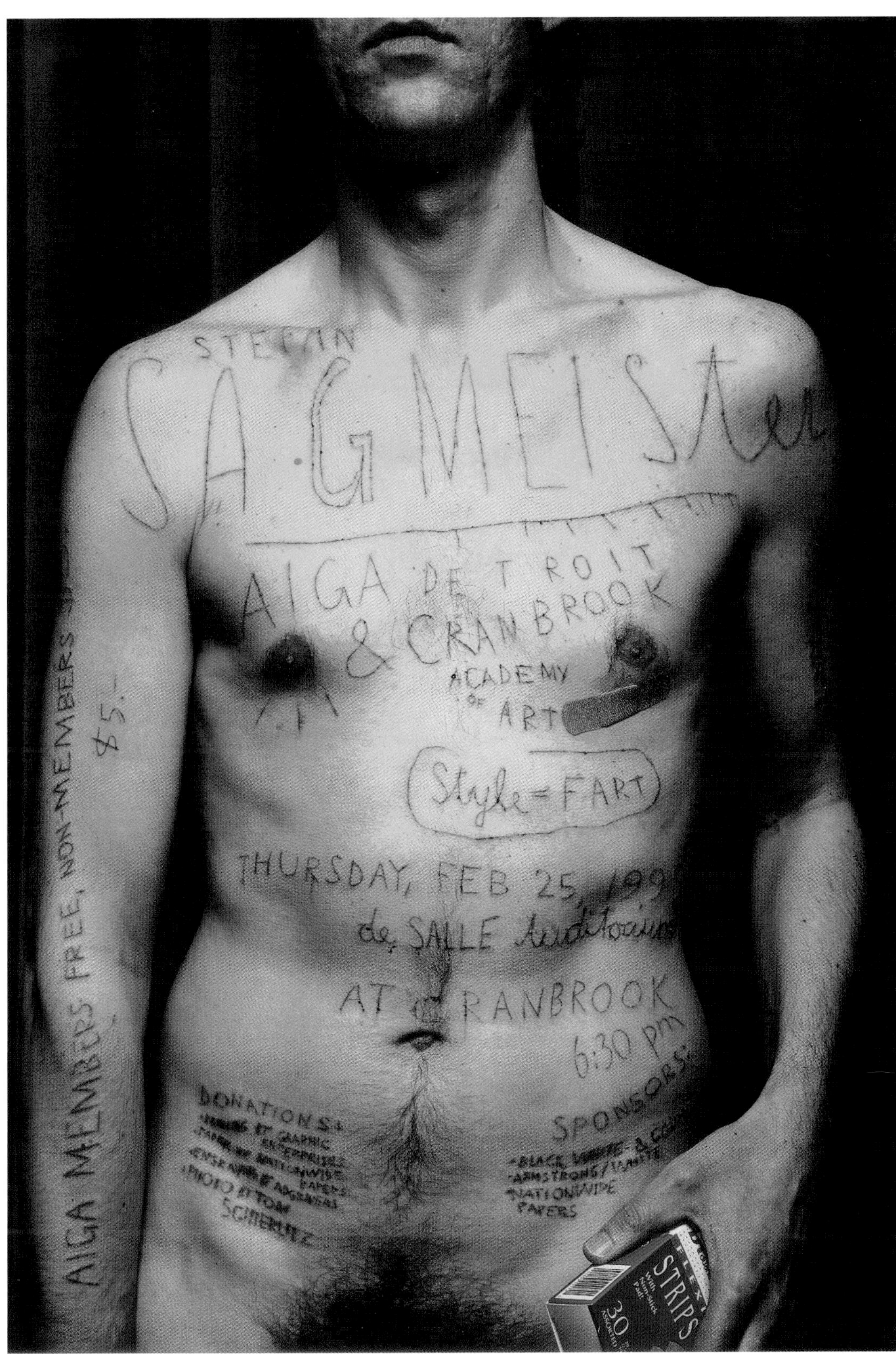

Design_Iwao Miura, Rikiya Tanaka, and Mizuho Hayashi
Tokyo, Japan
Art Direction_Iwao Miura
Creative Direction_Atsushi Shikano
Editor-in-Chief_Atsushi Shikano
Editors_Shinji Hyogo and Koremasa Uno

Studio_rockin'on inc. design department
Client_rockin'on, Buzz Magazine

Dimensions_10 ¼ x 16 ⁹⁄₁₆ in. (26 x 42 cm)

Poster

Design_Leonardo Sonnoli, Rimini, Italy
Art Direction_Leonardo Sonnoli

Studio_Dolcini Associati

Principal Type_Walker and Bell Centennial

Dimensions_27 9⁄16 x 39 3⁄8 in. (70 x 100 cm)

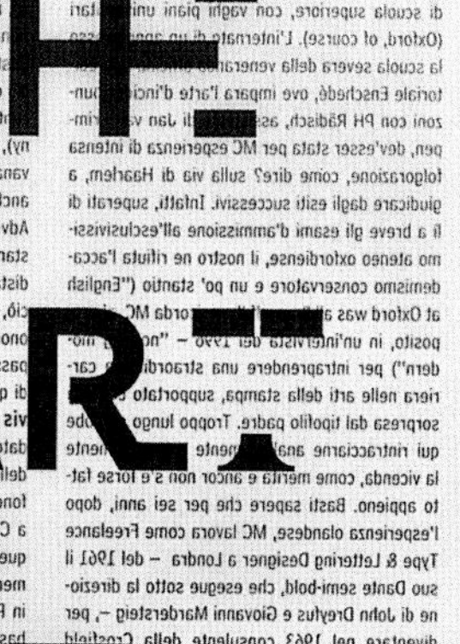

THE ART OF TYPE

Lecturer	→	MATTHEW CARTER
Date	→	24-04-1999
Place	→	DOLCINI ASSOCIATI

City	→	PESARO>ITALY
Design	→	LEONARDO SONNOLI
Type	→	WALKER + BELL CENTENNIAL

Design_Marion English Powers, Jeanne Renneker
Birmingham, AL
Art Direction_Marion English Powers
Creative Direction_Marion English Powers
Illustrator_David Webb
Photographer_Don Harbor

Agency_Slaughter Hanson
Client_Plain Clothes

Principal Type_Centaur

Dimensions_6 ⅛ x 7 in.
(15.6 x 17.8 cm)

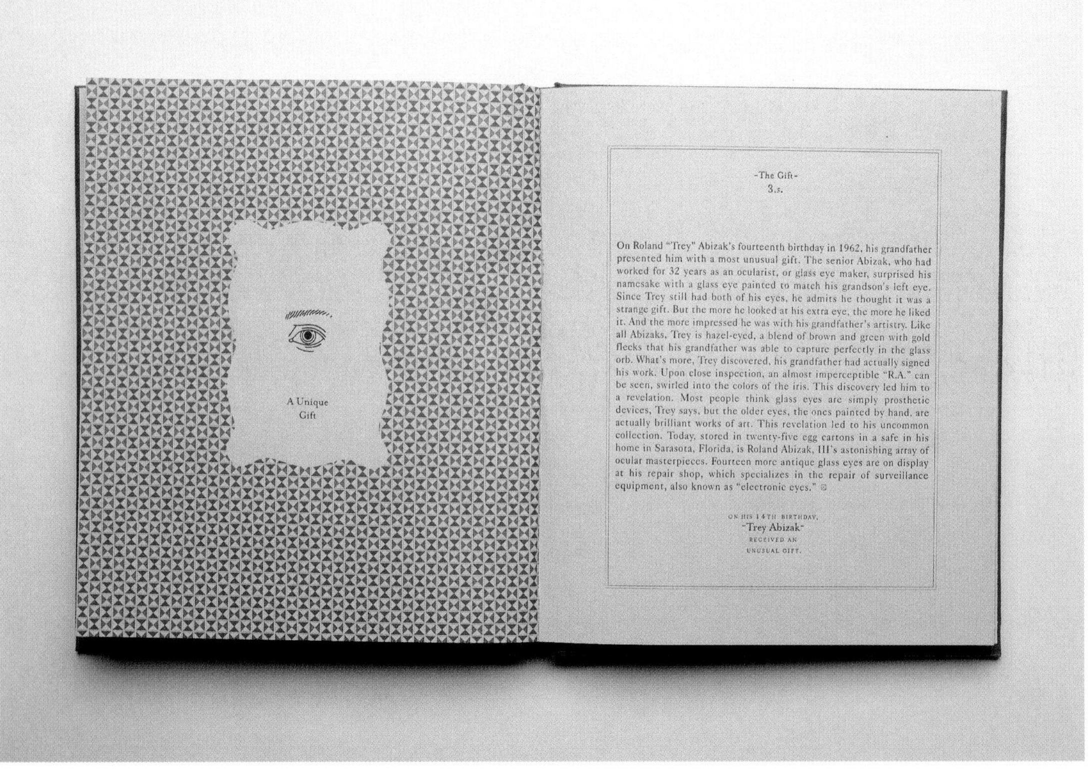

OLD STYLE . MD . REGULAR . ITALIC . MD ITALIC . BOLD . BOLD ITALIC . SUPER
abcdefghijklmnopqrstuvwxyz
ABCDEFGHIJKLMNOPQRST
DON'T BELIEVE THE TYPE
TypeDirectorsClub
TDC² 2000
TDC 46+ P.271

00 Maxim Zhukov

TypeDirectorsClub
TDC^2 2000 Chairman's Statement

TDC 46+ P.272

Type A

Type B

Type AB

Type O

Name

TDC[2] chairman Maxim Zhukov, the Typographic Coordinator for the United Nations, has a broad background in typographic communications. His main occupation is multilingual typography. Maxim is one of the leading experts on Cyrillic type design in America. Half of his professional life he spent in the USSR, designing art and science books, and other print. For a few years he taught typographic design at his alma mater, Moscow Printing Institute. Maxim writes on typography and type design. He is a member of ATypI, and a country delegate for Russia.

TDC[2]: Types & Times

"Hey, you, what century is it out there?" Boris Pasternak

What makes the TDC competitions different, or even unique? Type design contests are often managed by the font manufacturers. But not ours: the TDC[2]s are held by the designers for the designers; they are completely self-funded. The rules of our competitions are quite simple and straightforward, and most of the decisions on the presentation of entries are left to the participants. There are no provisions of exclusivity or confidentiality to the participation.

Winning in a TDC competition offers no [immediate] material gain. All there is to it is an opportunity to show off one's work, to have it noticed and, perhaps, appreciated by fellow designers, industry experts, and typographic enthusiasts at large. Amazingly, such a prospect appears to be attractive enough to ensure impressive participation in our annual contests.

102 designers from twenty-four countries sent in their works to the TDC competition. Nine alphabets/writing systems have been represented by these entries: Arabic, Armenian, Cyrillic, Glagolitic, Greek, Hebrew, Japanese, Latin, and Morse code. That last one made even the most qualified and competent jurors of TDC[2] 2000 feel kind of humble. (Now that was ironic, for two out of four jurors are among the top ten expert in non-Latin scripts world-wide.) The level of graphic quality in the submissions was remarkably high, which made the task of selecting the winners both easy and difficult.

The wide array of styles, the variety of approaches, the scope of design objectives, the diversity of scripts and writing systems, etc., displayed by the entries, plus the unique frequency of the TDC[2]s (they are held annually, more frequently than any other recurrent type design competition in the world), make them representative of the industry's trends, and thus provide for interesting observations, speculations, hypotheses, and conclusions.

Chairing TDC[2] 2000 was both a privilege and a challenge. Timing is everything, they say, and it just so happened that the third typeface competition of the Type Directors Club fell on the first year of the new millennium. There was a sense of history to it: our competition, together with two more contests–Linotype's and Morisawa's–which preceded it by a couple of months, happened to close the books on type design in the 20th century. How is that for a challenge?!

The past century witnessed breathtaking developments in typographic communications. Type folks measure time in their very own way (well, chronology is nothing but convention anyway)–1900: Century; 1913: Imprint; 1928: Futura; 1932: Times; 1940: Corona; 1957: Univers; 1966: Sabon; 1970: Avant Garde Gothic; 1988: Variex; 1991: Trixie; 1996: Verdana, etc. I kept thinking to myself, what face will 1999 be remembered for, if any? What will we find at the end of that long and winding road that was the typographic history of our times? And, sure enough... there were no great surprises.

Predictably, many designs submitted to TDC[2] 2000 offered elaborations–often sensitive and sophisticated–on the trends of yore, and of late, that are well known to type people. A few entries featured attempts–some daring and ambitious–at pushing the limits, and exploring uncharted territories. The whole thing turned out to be the usual mix of the comfortable old and the unsettling new.

Let's face it: there is no solid line one can draw between the millennia. Moreover, those in the know insist that, technically speaking, we are still living in the twentieth century. So much for the sense of history... Millennium schmillennium.

SECTION CONTAINS: 4 Judges Biographies and Sample Work.
Judges: Matthew Carter Barry Deck John Hudson Kathleen Tinkel

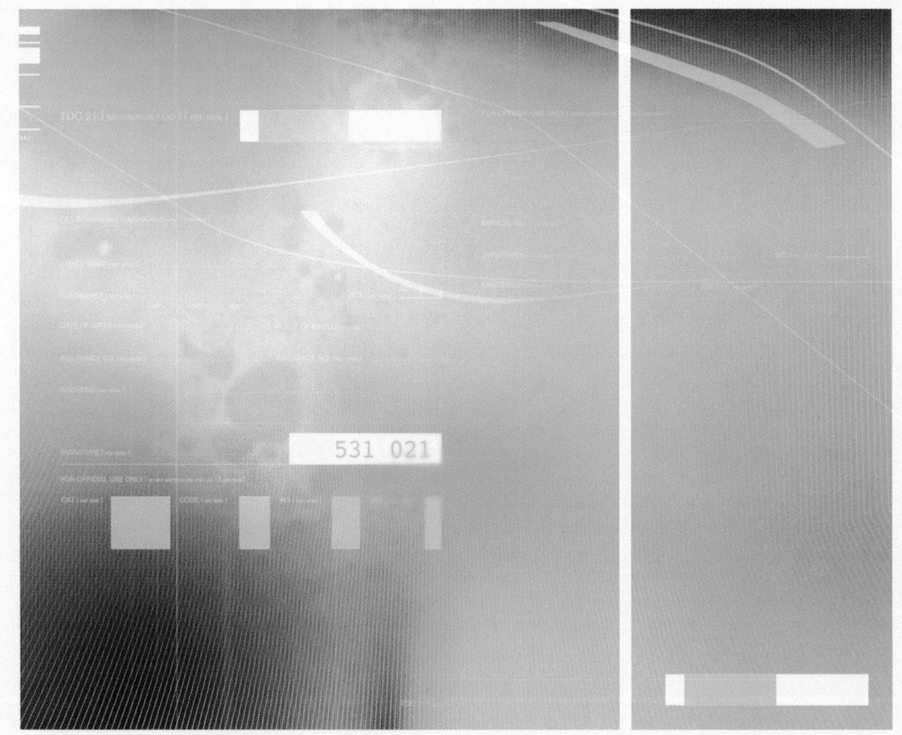

TypeDirectorsClub

TDC² 2000 The Judges

TDC 46+ P.274

J.01 Matthew Carter

J.02 Barry Deck

J.03 John Hudson

J.04 Kathleen Tinkel

Matthew Carter is a type designer with forty years' experience of typographic technologies ranging from hand-cut punches to computer fonts. He designed the typefaces ITC Galliard, Snell Roundhand, Shelley Script, Bell Centennial (for the US telephone directories), ITC Charter, Mantinia, Sophia, Big Caslon, Miller, Miller News (for newspaper text), and types commissioned by Apple, Microsoft (the screen fonts Verdana and Georgia), *Time* magazine, *Newsweek, Wired, U.S. News & World Report, Sports Illustrated, The Washington Post, The Philadelphia Inquirer* and the Walker Art Center. He is a principal of Carter & Cone Type Inc. in Cambridge, Massachusetts, designers and makers of original typefaces.

Barry Deck is a graphic designer for whom typefaces created by experts were simply not distinctive enough. In an arrogant attempt to control every aspect of his work, he began to design his own. The resulting aesthetic of ineptitude was gobbled up by the design world and now everybody says he's a type designer. His typefaces include Arbitrary, Barry Sans Serif, Canicopulis, Caustic Biomorph, Cyberotica, Eunuverse, Faux CRA, Orgasm Heavy, Repressed, Template Gothic, Traitor, Truth, Washout Light, and typefaces commissioned by MTV Networks, Conde Nast Publishing, MCI Communications, and *Ray Gun* magazine. After an unsuccessful, ten-year-long search for a full time job, he has opened his New York studio this fall.

John Hudson is a full-time professional type designer and co-founder of Tiro Typeworks in Vancouver, Canada. He specializes in providing custom font solutions to design firms, software developers, and information technologists, and is regularly consulted as an expert on multilingual typography. His clients to date include Microsoft, Linotype Library, Agfa, and many smaller companies. John received an award of excellence in the Kyrillitsa '99 competition, for his typeface Sylfaen Cyrillic (commissioned by Microsoft Corp.), and special recognition from the Moscow Golden Bee Association for his "outstanding contribution to the development of Cyrillic typography and international typographic communications."

Writer/designer Kathleen Tinkel first set type on a pre-WWII VariTyper machine while in high school in Anchorage, Alaska. She established Tinkel Design in 1968 and has spent most of the intervening years as a graphic designer. She studied type and typography by spec'ing it, moonlighting on cold-typesetting systems in the 1970s, occasionally setting foundry type for a small letterpress, and, for the past ten years, writing about design and typography. Her articles have appeared in *U&lc*, *Aldus* and *Adobe* magazines, *Step-by-Step* magazine and *Electronic Design* newsletter, *x-Height, MacWeek, MacWorld, MacUser*, and others.

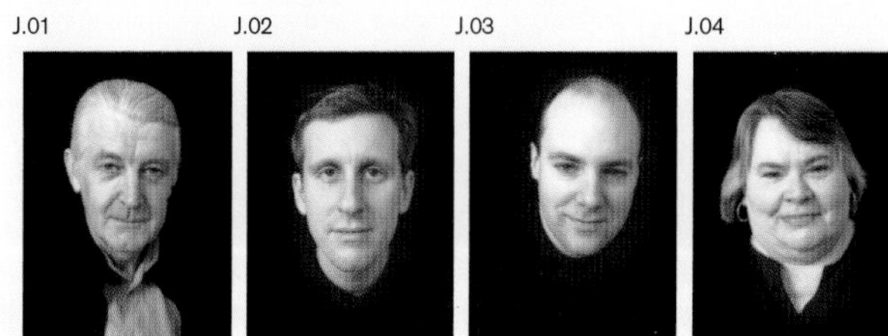
J.01 J.02 J.03 J.04

#	Name
J.01	Matthew Carter
J.02	Barry Deck

J.01

MATTHEW·CARER'S
MANTINIA
A·NEW·DESIGN
WITH·CAPITALS
TALL·CAPITALS
ALTERNATIVES
SUPERIORS·&
LIGATURES

J.02

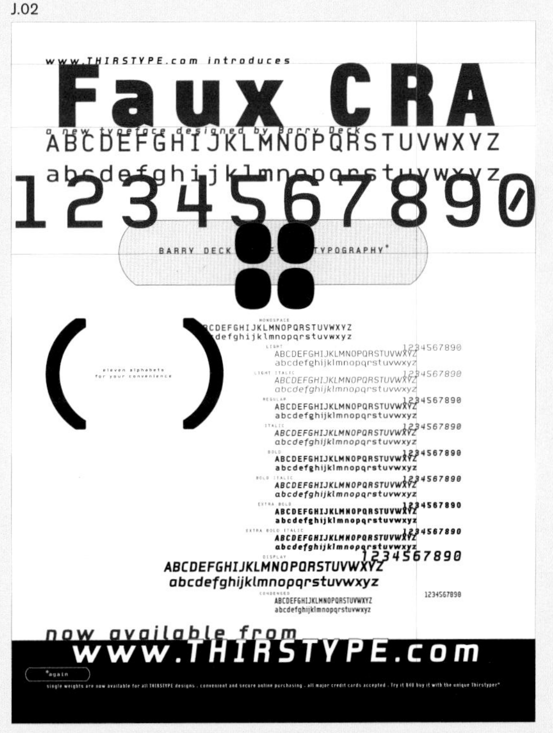

J.03 John Hudson
J.04 Kathleen Tinkel

TDC 46+ P.280

Name

J.03

Heidelberg Gothic, a corporate identity typeface de signed by Tiro Typeworks in association with Linotype Library GmbH for Heidelberger Druckmaschinen AG…
AaBbCcDdEeFfG **a** gHhIiJiKkLlMmNnOoPpQ
qRrSsTtUuVvWw XxYyZzAaБбВвГгДдЕеЁё
ЖжЗзИиЙйКкЛл МмНнОоПпРрСсТтУуФф
ХхЦцЧчШшЩщЪъЫыЬьЭэЮюЯя **к** ЃѓЌќЄєЌ
ќЉљЊњЋћЂђΑαΒβΓγΔδΕεΖζΗη ΘθΙιΚκΛ
λΜμΝνΞξΟοΠπΡρΣσςΤτΥυΦφΧχ ΨψΩωΆ
άΈέΉήΊ **в** ίΐΌόΎύΰΏώ*AaBbCcDdEeFfGgHhIi*
JjKkLlM *mNnOoPpQqRrSsTtUuVvWwXxYy*
ZzAaБбВ *вГгДдЕеЁёЖжЗзИиЙйКкЛлМмН*
нОоПпРрСсТтУуФфХхЦ **σ** *цЧчШшЩщЪъЫ*
ЯяЃѓЃѓЌќЉљЊњЋћЂђA *αΒϐΓγΔδΕεΖζΗη*
ΘϑΙιΚκΛλΜμΝνΞξΟοΠπΡ *ρΣσςΤτΥυΦφΧχΨ*
*ψΩωΆάΈέΉήΊίΐΌόΎύΰΏώ*ÀàÁáÂâÃãÄäÅåĀāĂăĄąÆ
æĆćČčÇçĎďĐđÈèÉéÊêËëĘęĚěĒēĖėĞğĢģÌìÍíÎîÏïĮįĶķŁł
ĹĺĽľĻļŃńÑñŇňŅņÑñÒòÓóŐőØø **Heidelberg Gothic**

J.04

TypeDirectorsClub
TDC² 2000 The Judges' Choices
and Designers' Statements
TDC 46+ P.283

J.01 Matthew Carter

D.01.5 František Štorm

Design_František Štorm, Czech Republic

Biblon

Type Foundry_Štorm Type Foundry

Family_Regular, Bold: Roman, Italic (each in Normal and SC character sets)

ABCDEFGHIJKLMNOPQ RSTUVWXYZ1234567890

ABCDEFGHIJKLMNOPQRSTUVWXYZ

abcdefghijklmnopqrstuvwxyz 1234567890

Two terms, Baroque and Rococo, are used by František Štorm in his description of Biblon, and perhaps both are needed to do justice to its sheer exuberance. Hardly a period piece, this splendid typeface, but somewhere in it a historical style is either waving or drowning. There may be a clue in the text used to show the face to the TDC jury, in archaic French complete with long esses, taken from the 1621 specimen of Jean Jannon, that impertinent and ever-so-slightly cack-handed invigorator of Garamond's stately legacy. Wherever František Štorm got his inspiration, he took nothing for granted. No convention is safe: the Roman and Italic are condensed; the small caps are wider (they are also smaller than the lowercase, while they're at it, and float nonchalantly above the baseline in the Italic). Horizontal serifs in the Roman lowercase, where they exist at all, are turned inward to give the letterforms a pigeon-toed stance that adds to the general jauntiness. No two strokes in the Italic are in parallel, whence its syncopated rhythm–and its legibility. A couple of the swashest Italic capitals have gone over the top in the direction of whimsy, but this seems a small price to pay for the overall vigor of this wonderfully uninhibited design. Great stuff.

In our modern times people print ever more futile ideas and intersperse them with many blank pages. There is no need to economize on paper and to look out for optically narrowed type faces. An opposite situation is in every biblical society where the editors must cram a text containing some 2000 pages into a single volume. That is where there is a need for type faces which are economizing, legible and spiritually cultivated. The new Biblon type face, therefore, does not need to rely on a wide range of sizes; it is sufficient if it looks well from approximately five to eighteen points. Its elegance decreases commensurately with its increasing size. In poster sizes the speculative construction of the letter form is already revealed–the points of gravity of the strokes are shifted as much as possible in the horizontal directions and the crotches–the spaces between the rounded stroke and the shaft–are emphasized. In small-size letters we hardly notice that almost all horizontal serifs (if they have not disappeared entirely) have been pushed inside the letter form so that they should not hamper the adjacent letters. To quieten the lines, the accents have been miniaturized as well. The figures have uniform width and avow the lower case principle. The italics of Biblon have been stylized more daringly, with the use of long-forsaken Rococo elements. The slanted designs of the small capitals have upper case letters slightly submerged under the capital line, in order to enhance the decorative character of titles and headings. Biblon has a large x-height of lower-case letters and one can get used to its compressed proportions. Many condensed type faces leave a feeling of distress after longer reading. Here, however, this has been sophisticatedly eliminated. We have availed ourselves in this type face design also of several optical tricks dating from fairly recent period, but our main source of inspiration was the daringness of type designers of the 18th century. Underneath the contemporary-looking design of Biblon one can conjecture a Baroque play with the shifting of shadows, intentional overstatement or absolute simplification of forms. Even though Biblon probably will not be used for its purpose in the near future, it represents a very sound body type.

Summa Gambit

Design_Damir Gamulin,
Zagreb, Croatia

Family_Regular

J.02 Barry Deck

D.02.5 Damir Gamulin

Name

Σ beton three

100% concrete

. a b c d e f g h i j k l m n o p q r s t u v w x y z

. A B C D E F G H I J K L M N O P Q R S T U V W X Y Z

. 0 1 2 3 4 5 6 7 8 9 . ; : ! " # $ % & ' (ø) = ? * / + -

. { ‡ } ≤ ± ≥ ¶ bonez @ < µ Δ ≠ ¢ ∑ > ∏ ¯ ß ø ® © ‰

summa gambit

I enjoyed the references to chain-link fencing, coat hangers, OCR computer type and the automatic smoothing function of early bitmap fonts. It reminds me of what I got when I printed Geneva from MacDraw in 1987. Sort of like a pseudo-futuristic version of Zuzana Licko's Citizen with these eastern block gulag references thrown in. But, I really chose it because I want the designer to work on it some more. I would like to see some of these bent wire references articulated more solidly. Some of the shapes seem a little tentative to me; the stem on the h, for instance. They're not deliberately curved, nor geometric, neither here nor there. The broken characters don't work for me. This move seems unrelated to the other ideas in the face.
I enjoy the shapes in the o, six, seven, nine, dollar sign, percent sign and ampersand, characters which come closest to what the face should be.

Working on Summa Gambit I had light, architectonic aesthetics in mind.
I wanted to reveal joints that would normally stay hidden under the 'bold' cover. As a result you get an 'imperfect' font. Summa is first in the line of the typefaces created using a single principle–accumulating details on uniform centerlines that serve as basic construction elements. And yes, it also reflects my desire to lose weight.

Kis Cyrillic

Design_Vladimir Yefimov, Russia

Type Foundry_ParaType

Family_Roman, Italic

Script_ Cyrillic

J.03 John Hudson

D.03.5 Vladimir Yefimov

#	Name

АБВГДЕЁЖЗИЙ
АБВГДЕЁЖЗИЙ
КЛМНОПРСТУФ
КЛМНОПРСТУФ
ХЦЧШЩЪЫЬЭЮЯ
ХЦЧШЩЪЫЬЭЮЯ
абвгдеёжзийклмнопр
абвгдеёжзийклмнопр
стуфхцчшщъыьэюя
стуфхцчшщъыьэюя

This typeface is my personal favourite among the many excellent entries in the competition, not only because it is a fine example of Cyrillic type design and of the often tricky business of 'cyrillising' an existing Latin design, but because it seems to me a wonderful re-imagining of an important moment in typographic history. The design is based on the letterforms of the early 18th century alphabet reform of Peter the Great, which recast the mediaeval Cyrillic script in the mould of some fairly basic contemporary Dutch types. The new fonts provide a physical–and eminently useable–answer to the question: What if the Tsar's reform had been modeled on the very best Dutch typefaces of the day, the designs of the Hungarian emigre punchcutter Miklos Kis?

I always loved the types of Miklos Kis: I happen to prefer them to all other Old Styles, and for sure, they are my first choice among all Dutch Old Styles. I always wanted to develop a Cyrillic version of Kis (Janson). I first tried it, just for myself, about ten years ago. Lately, the licensing agreement between ParaType and Bitstream offered me a perfect opportunity to do a production-quality PT/BT Kis Cyrillic. There was a hidden agenda to this project: to put myself in Peter the Great's Hessian boots, and to apply the principles used in his devising Civil Type to the best design model that existed in his times: Kis roman.

Chêneau/Lyons

Design_Daniel Carr, USA

Type Foundry_Golgonooza Letter Foundry & Press

Family_Roman (Chêneau), Italic (Lyons)

Chêneau

Roman, *Italic* & Small Capitals with *Lyons Italic*

To be vital and permanent a work of art (it seems to me) must, to begin with, bear evidence that its author possessed each of three things, intellect, passion, and skill. Intellect and skill, without passion, give us only cold academicism; passion and skill, without intellect, fail to appeal to our intelligence; intellect and passion without skill, are inarticulate. In a work of art we must therefore look for these qualities, the absence of any one which means that a painting or a piece of sculpture is merely a futile exercise. This is only a primary test, but it is to this test that works of art must first of all be put, in order that their primary significance may be measured. Who among painters and sculptors, past and present, will, in *your opinion*, pass this test? That is the question.

Porter Garnett
What is it?
An Aesthetical Investigation

With Chêneau and Lyons display italic, type designer Dan Carr does an interesting job of exploiting digital technology to simulate letterforms of hundreds of years ago. But the result is a hybrid that fails both as a museum piece and as a useful digital font for today. Photo-offset printing can never replicate the look and feel of 16th-century pages. We miss the subtle 3D effect and subtle shadowing of pages printed in relief, and are compelled to notice the contrived irregularities of the digital font for what they are.

Like many other fonts based on designs of the past, Chêneau also suffers from lack of what is arguably the most important technique used for ancient typefaces, a separate design for each size. Instead of trying to recreate the past, I'd echo the concerns of type designers Hermann Zapf, Warren Chappell, and others when they ask not only whether we can faithfully simulate ancient typefaces, but should we even try.

Chêneau Roman, Italic and Small Capitals with Lyons Italic is a small type family with a display italic font included, they are my first digital typefaces. Simultaneously I cut a metal typeface called Regulus using traditional hand punchcutting. My purpose for both was the same; I wanted to have typefaces in both mediums that would express visible forms of my voice as a writer and typographer. The design of Chêneau preserves the space of each letterform and does not use kerning. For a sense of immediacy Lyons Italic was drawn quickly in one sitting with little editing. There are four Italic ampersands, three in Lyons, and one in Chêneau Italic. Chêneau has ligatures and text figures and the small capital font includes titling figures.

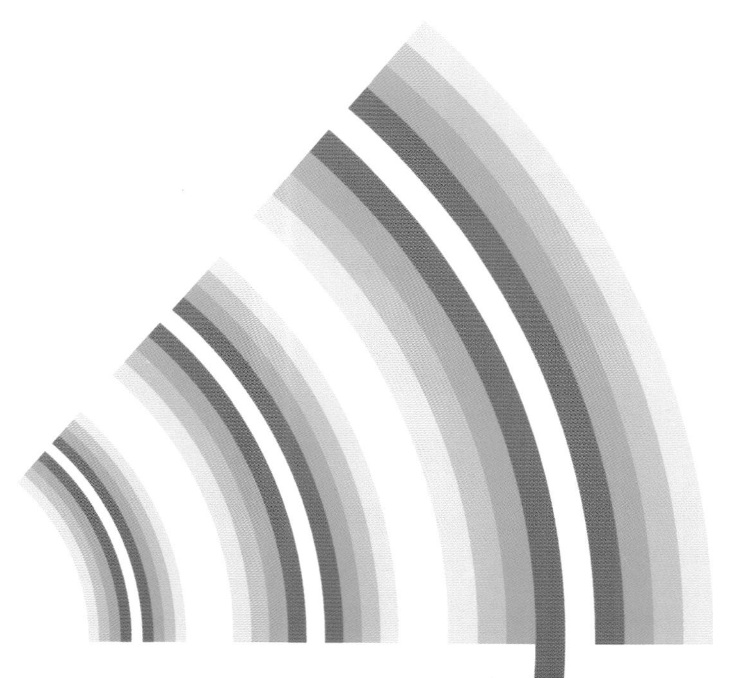

TypeDirectorsClub
TDC² 2000 Winners
TDC 46+ P.293

Arcana Manuscript

Design_Gabriel Martínez Meave
Mexico

Type Foundry_Adobe Systems

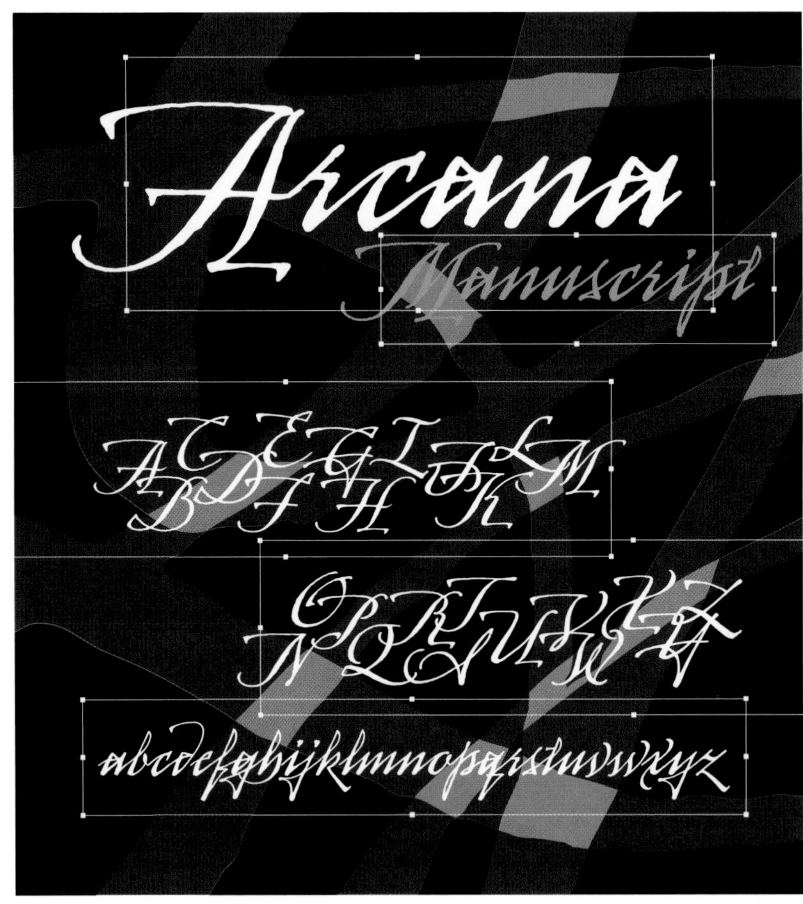

Blue Island

Design_Jeremy Tankard, United Kingdom

Type Foundry_Adobe Systems

ABCDÐEFGHIJKLŁMNOPQRSTUVWXYZÞ
abcdðefghijklłmnopqrstuvwxyzþß&@ªº
1234567890Ø¹²³¼½¾£$¢¥€ƒ¤%‰
ŒÆÁÀÄÂÃÅÇÉÈËÊÍÌÏÎÑÓÒÖÔÕØŠÚÙÜÛÝŸŽ
œæáàäâãåçéèëêfiflıíìïîñóòöôõøßšúùüûµýÿž
?!¿¡([{}]):;.,'‘“”‚„…‹›«»§¶†‡*±÷×+−=<>^/\|¦#•¯˘˙˚¸˝˛ˇ~^©®™

Es eS cages

Southeasterly veering southwesterly 6 to gale 8, becoming cycl

Viking. Southerly 3 increasing 5 or 6. Fair.

Thames. Westerly backing southwesterly

fog patches

Cholla Sans

Design_Sibylle Hagmann, USA

Type Foundry_Emigre

Family_Thin, Regular, Italic, Bold

TRADE CHOLLA MARK

CHOLLA SANS REGULAR

ABCDEFGHIJKLMNOPQRSTUVWXYZa
bcdefghijklmnopqrstuvwxyzﬁﬂßæ
œÀÁÂÄÃÅÇÈÉÊËÌÍÏÎÑÒÓÖØÙÚÛÜŸà
áâäãåçèéêëıìíïîñòóôöõøùúûüÿ012
3456789{([*/,....:;¿?¡!&$¢£¥€%‰+
÷=±|¶§†‡ƒÆŒ@®©™ªº^#_'"''""',„\
-–—·•‹›«»~])}

CHOLLA SANS ITALIC

ABCDEFGHIJKLMNOPQRSTUVWXYZa
bcdefghijklmnopqrstuvwxyzﬁﬂßæ
œÀÁÂÄÃÅÇÈÉÊËÌÍÏÎÑÒÓÖØÙÚÛÜŸà
áâäãåçèéêëıìíïîñòóôöõøùúûüÿ012
3456789{([/,....:;¿?¡!&$¢£¥€%‰+*
÷=±|¶§†‡ƒÆŒ@®©™ªº^#_'"''""',„
-–—·•‹›«»~])}

CHOLLA SANS THIN

ABCDEFGHIJKLMNOPQRSTUVWXYZabc
defghijklmnopqrstuvwxyzﬁﬂßæœÀÁ
ÂÄÃÅÇÈÉÊËÌÍÏÎÑÒÓÖØÙÚÛÜŸàáâäãåç
èéêëıìíïîñòóôöõøùúûüÿ0123456789
{([*/,....:;¿?¡!&$¢£¥€%‰+÷=±|¶§†‡ƒ
ÆŒ@®©™ªº^#_'"''""',„\-–—·•‹›«»~])}

CHOLLA SANS BOLD

ABCDEFGHIJKLMNOPQRSTUVWXYZ
abcdefghijklmnopqrstuvwxyzﬁﬂß
æœÀÁÂÄÃÅÇÈÉÊËÌÍÏÎÑÒÓÖØÙÚÛÜ
Ÿàáâäãåçèéêëıìíïîñòóôöõøùúûüÿ
0123456789{([*/,....:;¿?¡!&$¢£¥€
%‰+÷=±|¶§†‡ƒÆŒ@®©™ªº^#
'"''""',„\-–—·•‹›«»~])}

Certain **ideas** DON'T CHANGE THAT QUICKLY...they don't go out of **FASHION** *with the same speed that colors do. So this* ***notion of the hybrid—*** of interconnection, of **human machine** **growing together—are ideas** **that AREN'T GOING TO GO AWAY SOON.**

FF Clifford

Design_Akira Kobayashi, Japan

Type Foundry_FSI FontShop International

Family_Six, Nine, Eighteen_Roman (Normal, SC and LF character sets), Italic (Normal and Alt. LF character sets), Borders

Design_Jean-François Porchez, France

Type Foundry_Porchez Typofonderie for Costa Crociere_Landor Associates, Paris

Family_Light, Regular, Italic, Bold, Logotype

Costa
Costa
Costa
Costa

COSTA IS A CORPORATE TYPEFACE DESIgned for Costa Crociere. The new typeface, developed in conjunction with Landor Associates is used by Costa Crociere for all their publications, from website, catalogs, corporate leaflets to annual reports, etc. The typeface is developed in four styles. Available for the retail market through Porchez Typofonderie in 2003. Costa est un caractère *typographique d'identité visuelle conçu* pour Costa Crociere. Ce nouveau caractère, développé en conjonction avec Landor Associates, **est utilisé par Costa Crociere pour l'ensemble de leurs publications, de leur**

abcdefghijklmnop
qrstuvwxyzgðłþæ
œfiflßABCDEFGHI
JKLMNOPQRSTUV
WXYZŁÐPÆŒ&01
23456789$¥¢£€f@
!?([{/%½¼«",.#¶§†‡*

Erica Sans

Design_Yanek Iontef
Israel

Type Foundry_Iontef Type Foundry

Script_Hebrew

אבגדהוזחטיכלמנסעפצקר
שתךםןףץ 1234567890
(%₪#$✡;:!?)

אבגדהוזחטיכלמנסעפצק
רשתךםןףץ 1234567890
(%₪#$✡;:!?)

אבגדהוזחטיכלמנסע
פצקרשתךםןףץ
(%₪$✡;:!?)1234567890

Homemade

Design_Takaya Goto, USA
Takashi Konuma, Japan

Type Foundry_Oxygen Design

Family_Regular, Rough

Script_Japanese

カスタード
ピーナツバター
シークレットレシピ
スウィートホイップクリーム
フレッシュベイクトチョコレートチップクッキー

ホームメイド

アイウエオカキクケコサシスセソタチツテトナニヌネノハヒフヘホ
マミムメモヤユヨラリルレロワヲンガギグゲゴザジズゼゾヴダヂ
ヅデドバビブベボパピプペポァィゥェォャュョッー/、。・'()「」!?

ホームメイド・ラフ

アイウエオカキクケコサシスセソタチツテトナニヌネノハヒフヘホ
マミムメモヤユヨラリルレロワヲンガギグゲゴザジズゼゾヴダヂ
ヅデドバビブベボパピプペポァィゥェォャュョッー/、。・'()「」!?

Klin

Design_Gayaneh Bagdasaryan, Russia

Type Foundry_ParaType

Scripts_Cyrillic, Latin

Design_Gabriel Martinez Meave
Mexico

Family_Roman, Italic

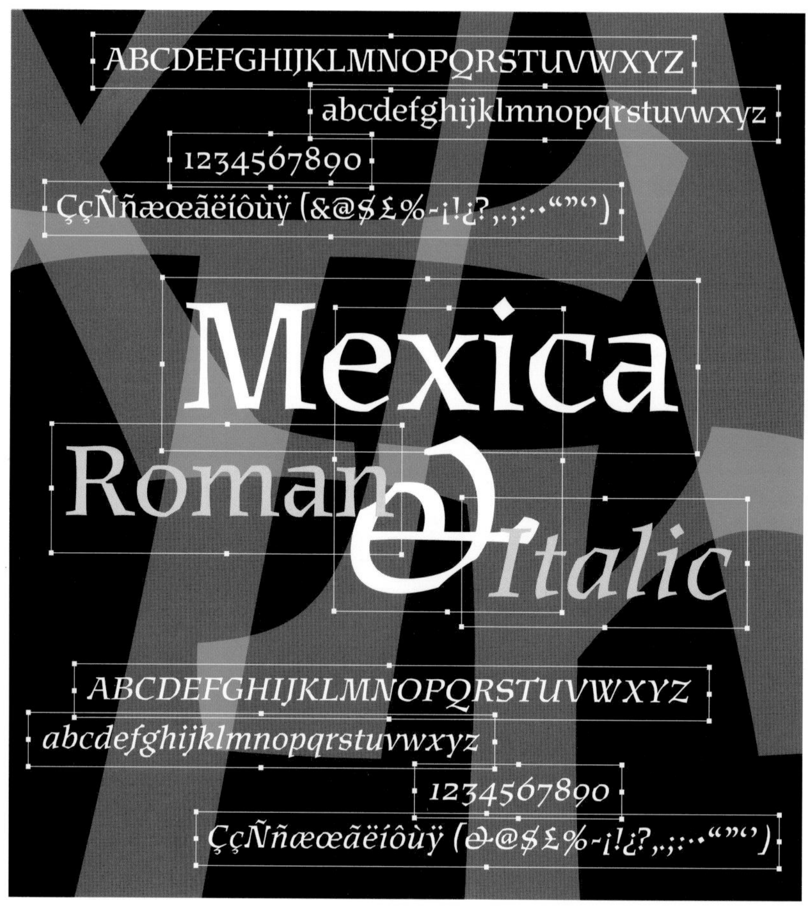

Mirra

Design_Tagir Safayev, Russia

Type Foundry_Paratype

Family_Light, Bold

Scripts_Cyrillic, Latin

ABCDEFGHIJKLMNOPQRSTUVWXYZ
abcdefghijklmnopqrstuvwxyz
АБВГДЕЁЖЗИЙКЛМНОПРСТУФХЦЧШ
ЩЪЫЬЭЮЯабвгдеёжзийклмнопрст
уфхцчшщъыьюэя(1234567890).,:;!?
{№.$¢£¥¶}-„‘’”†&ÇçŒÆœæ•«®§©»*

ABCDEFGHIJKLMNOPQRSTUVWXYZ
abcdefghijklmnopqrstuvwxyz
АБВГДЕЁЖЗИЙКЛМНОПРСТУФХЦЧШ
ЩЪЫЬЭЮЯабвгдеёжзийклмнопрст
уфхцчшщъыьюэя(1234567890).,:;!?
{№.$¢£¥¶}*-„‘’”†&ÇçŒÆœæ•«®§©»

قال الله جل جلاله في كتابه العزيز في الآيات الأخيرة من سورة يونس عليه السلام :

بِسْمِ ٱللَّهِ ٱلرَّحْمَٰنِ ٱلرَّحِيمِ

وَإِن يَمْسَسْكَ ٱللَّهُ بِضُرٍّ فَلَا كَاشِفَ لَهُۥٓ إِلَّا هُوَ ۖ وَإِن يُرِدْكَ بِخَيْرٍ
فَلَا رَآدَّ لِفَضْلِهِۦ ۚ يُصِيبُ بِهِۦ مَن يَشَآءُ مِنْ عِبَادِهِۦ ۚ وَهُوَ ٱلْغَفُورُ
ٱلرَّحِيمُ ١٠٧ قُلْ يَٰٓأَيُّهَا ٱلنَّاسُ قَدْ جَآءَكُمُ ٱلْحَقُّ مِن رَّبِّكُمْ ۖ
فَمَنِ ٱهْتَدَىٰ فَإِنَّمَا يَهْتَدِى لِنَفْسِهِۦ ۖ وَمَن ضَلَّ فَإِنَّمَا يَضِلُّ
عَلَيْهَا ۖ وَمَآ أَنَا۠ عَلَيْكُم بِوَكِيلٍ ١٠٨ وَٱتَّبِعْ مَا يُوحَىٰٓ إِلَيْكَ وَٱصْبِرْ
حَتَّىٰ يَحْكُمَ ٱللَّهُ ۚ وَهُوَ خَيْرُ ٱلْحَٰكِمِينَ ١٠٩

صدق الله العظيم

Myriad Greek

Design_Carol Twombly and Robert Slimbach, USA

Type Foundry_Adobe Systems

Style_Light, Regular, Semibold, Bold, Black_Roman, Italic (each in Condensed, Normal and Semi-extended widths)

Script_Greek

Νομίζω ότι είναι ιδιαίτερα δύσκολο να δημιουργηθεί μια καινούργια *γραματοσειρά όπως είναι δύσκολο* **να δημιουργηθεί ένα καινούργιο *ο, τιδήποτε που χρησιμοποιείται* καθημερινα. Η δημιουργία μιας *νέα γραματοσειράς αντιστοιχεί σε* ενα καινούργιο *κομάτι* μουσικής.**

26/33 LIGHT, REGULAR, SEMIBOLD, BOLD BLACK AND ITALICS

ΑΛΦΆΒΗΤΟΥ

87PT BLACK CONDENSED

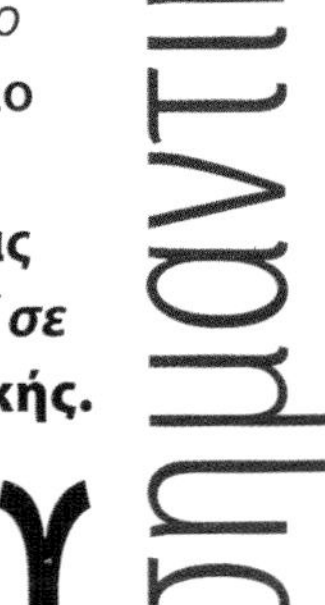

122PT LIGHT CONDENSED

Νομίζω ότι είναι ιδιαίτερα δύσκολο να δημιουργηθεί μια καινούργια γραματοσειρά όπως είναι δύσκολο να δημιουργηθεί ένα καινούργιο ο, τιδήποτε που *χρησιμοποιείται καθημερινα. Η δημιουργία μιας νέα γραματοσειράς αντιστοιχεί σε ενα καινούργιο κομάτι*

10/12 LIGHT SEMI-EXTENDED, LIGHT SEMI-EXTENDED ITALIC

Νομίζω ότι είναι ιδιαίτερα δύσκολο να δημιουργηθεί μια καινούργια γραματοσειρά όπως είναι δύσκολο να δημιουργηθεί ένα καινούργιο ο, τιδήποτε *που χρησιμοποιείται καθημερινα. Η δημιουργία μιας νέα γραματοσειράς αντιστοιχεί σε ενα καινούργιο κομάτι*

10/12 SEMI-EXTENDED, SEMI-EXTENDED ITALIC

Νομίζω ότι είναι ιδιαίτερα δύσκολο να δημιουργηθεί μια καινούργια γραματοσειρά όπως είναι δύσκολο να δημιουργηθεί ένα καινούργιο ο, *τιδήποτε που χρησιμοποιείται καθημερινα. Η δημιουργία μιας νέα γραματοσειράς αντιστοιχεί σε*

10/12 SEMIBOLD SEMI-EXTENDED, SEMIBOLD SEMI-EXT ITALIC

Νομίζω ότι είναι ιδιαίτερα δύσκολο να δημιουργηθεί μια καινούργια γραματοσειρά όπως *είναι δύσκολο να δημιουργηθεί ένα καινούργιο ο, τιδήποτε που χρησιμοποιείται καθημερινα. Η*

10/12 BOLD SEMI-EXTENDED, BOLD SEMI-EXTENDED ITALIC

Νομίζω ότι είναι ιδιαίτερα δύσκολο να δημιουργηθεί μια καινούργια γραματοσειρά όπως *είναι δύσκολο να δημιουργηθεί ένα καινούργιο ο, τιδήποτε που χρησιμοποιείται καθημερινα. Η*

10/12 BLACK SEMI-EXTENDED, BLACK SEMI-EXTENDED ITALIC

Nani

Design_Charles Nix, USA
(ornaments by Stefano Arcella)

Type Foundry_New Fonts

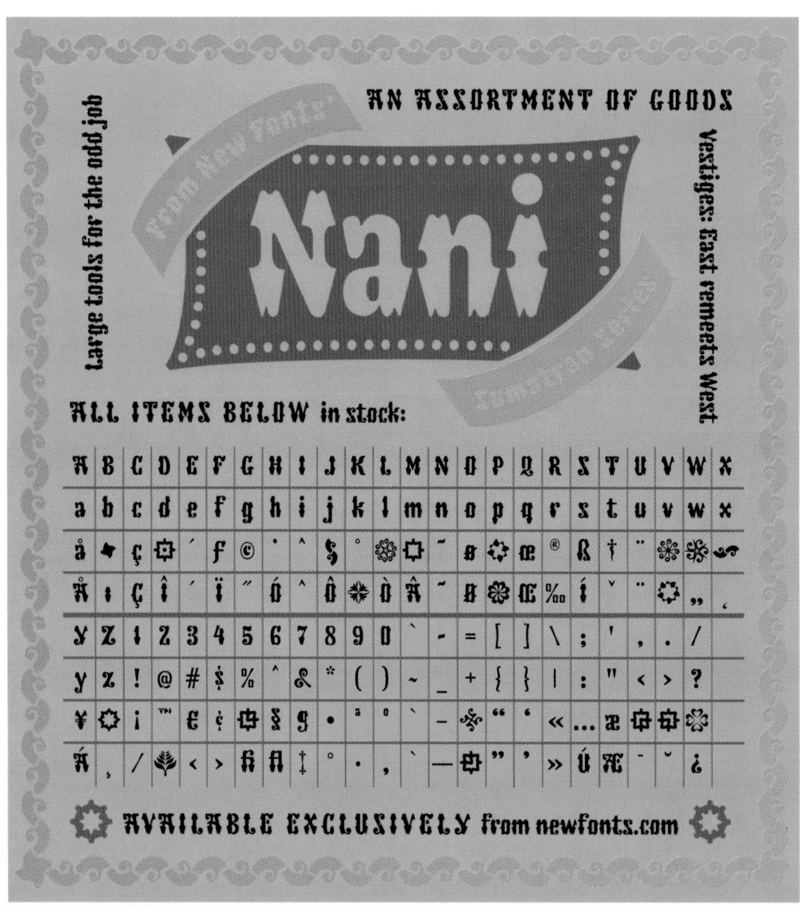

FF Profile

Design_Martin Wenzel, The Netherlands

Type Foundry_FSI FontShop International

Style_Light, Regular, Medium, Bold, Black_ Roman, Italic

(each in Normal, SC, No and Xp character sets)

WOMEN COME AND GO talking of Xxx. *Yearning* toward Zero. **ALTHOUGH thy hand and faith By *children's* births, and death, Could make me any summer's story tell. *DEATH is like the insect*, Exhuberant, restless,** Flesh of his excavated flesh. Glory is that *bright tragic thing*, **HOLY the groaning saxophone!** I have nourish'd the wounded Journeyers with their own sublime Knowing. Let us go then, you and Me. No coward soul is mine. OH, LET ME OUT! Prison and palace and reverberation, Quoth the Raven, nevermore. *Some say good-night at night*, The riddle we can guess, Unto me? Violence leaped and appeared in the room the *WOMEN COME AND GO* talking of Xxx.

aɑAA
aɑAA
aɑAA
aɑAA
aɑAA

a b c d e f g h i j k l m n o p
q r s t u v w x y z 0 1 2 3 4 5
6 7 8 9 A B C D E F G H I J K L
M N O P Q R S T U V W X Y Z *0 1*
2 3 4 5 6 7 8 9 a b c d e f g h
i j k l m n o p q r s t u v w x y
z ą @ á à â ä ã å 0 1 2 3 4 5 6
7 8 9 $^{1}{}_{1}{}^{2}{}_{3}{}^{4}{}_{5}{}^{6}{}_{7}{}^{8}{}_{9}{}^{0}$ ¢ € € ƒ £ £
$ $ ¥ ¥ ¶ & & ?? !! § # ©)] } ← *

[Ypsilon kam hier noch gar nicht vor...]

MONTAG NACHT: 2.36 Uhr. Typografen schlafen nicht? (Nicht bei £140,–/h) Doch, aber nur selten wenn es dunkel ist *("Schazile, es is schoh gans negadiv drœse.")*. Der Enthusiasmus hält sie wach und aufmerksam. Der Inhalt von Geschriebenem verschwindet hinter der Form, dem Bild einzelner Buchstaben oder dem ganzer typografischer Landschaften.

Die Euphorie, sich STUNDENLANG in Welten von allerkleinsten Einheiten zu bewegen, ist für *andere* meist nicht nachvollziehbar. **Selbst bei *"Dißäner"*-** Kollegen **ist *DIESE Lust* am Wort leider *nicht* so etc.**

Silentium Pro

Design_ Jovica Veljović, Yugoslavia/Germany

Type Foundry_Adobe Systems

Style_Roman I, Roman II

KNAPSACK

ADDITIONAL CHARACTERS–ROMAN I

A B C D E E F G G H I J K L M N O P Q R R S T T U V W X Y Z ABCDEFGHIJKLMNOPQRSTUVWXYZ&01234567890 !?¡¿ $£¥€ ÆŒÞFIFLSS AEGMMPQRTaaeegiiorrſttvw !?¡¿

æœ ß þ ð

(¼½¾%‰/°) [#$¢£€ƒ¥¤] {¥} ao1234 1234 ℓ ∂∏∑µπ√∞∫^=÷×+−¬

±<>~≈≠≤≥◊§†‡¶* .,:;‘’“” ,„…•·«»‹›-–—_\/|¦@©®™

ACCENTED CHARACTERS–ROMAN I

ăāąáâäàåãćçďđěėēęéêëèğģīįíîïìķĺľļłñńňņőōóôöòõøŕřŗśşșšťţűūųůúûüùýÿźżž

ĀĂĄÁÂÄÀÅÃĆČÇĎĚĖĒĘÉÊËÈĞĢĪĮÍÎÏÌİĶĹĽĻŁŃŇŅÑŐŌÓÔÖÒÕØŔŘŖŚŞȘŠŤŢŰŪŲŮÚÛÜÙÝŸŹŻŽ

ORNAMENTS

Here is sanctity which shames our religions, & reality which discredits our heroes. Here we find nature to be the circumstance which dwarfs every other circumstance, and judges like a god all men that come to her. We have crept out of our close and crowded houses into the night and morning, and we see what majestic beauties daily wrap us in their bosom. How willingly we would escape the barriers which render them comparatively impotent, escape the sophistication and second thought, and suffer nature to entrance us. The tempered light of the woods is like a perpetual morning, and is stimulating and heroic. The anciently reported spells of these places creep on us. The stems of

Linotype Syntax

Design_Hans Eduard Meier, Switzerland

Type Foundry_Linotype Library GmbH

Style_Light, Regular, Medium_Roman, Italic (each in Normal, SC and OsF character sets) Bold, Heavy, Black_Roman, Italic (each in Normal and OsF character sets)

TypeDirectorsClub
Board Members / Typographic Index
General Index

TDC 48+ P.308

Board of Directors 1999/2000

Officers
President — Mark Solsburg, DsgnHaus, Inc.
Vice President — Gerard Huerta, Gerard Huerta Design, Inc.
Secretary/Treasurer — Daniel Pelavin

Directors-at-Large
Syndi Becker, Money Magazine
John Berry
Ronn Campisi, Ronn Campisi Design
Susan Cotler-Block, Fashion Institute of Technology
David Cundy, Design Trust, Inc.
James Montalbano, Terminal Design
Ina Saltz, Golf Magazine
Maxim Zhukov, The United Nations

Executive Director — Carol Wahler

Board of Directors 2000/2001

Officers
President — Daniel Pelavin
Secretary/Treasurer — James Montalbano, Terminal Design, Inc.

Directors-at-Large
John Berry
Ronn Campisi, Ronn Campisi Design
Matthew Carter, Carter & Cone
Allan Haley, Resolution
Gary Munch, MunchFonts
Louise Fili, Louise Fili Ltd.
Ina Saltz, Golf Magazine
Maxim Zhukov, United Nations

Chairman — Mark Solsburg, DsgnHaus, Inc.
Executive Director — Carol Wahler

Committee for TDC46

Chairperson — Susan Cotler-Block
Design — ATTIK
Coordinator — Carol Wahler
Assistant Coordinator — Klaus Schmidt

Assistants to Judges
Abigail Arafeli
Peter Bain
John Berry
Deborah Gonet
Gerard Huerta
Nathalie Kirsheh
Nana Kobayashi
Rosemary Markowsky
Lawrence Mirsky
James Montalbano
Eric Neuner
Alexa Nosal
Daniel Pelavin
Agatha Sohn
Martin Solomon
Mark Solsburg
Allan R. Wahler
Samantha Wahler
Matt Weber

Type Directors Club Presidents

Frank Powers, 1946, 1947
Milton Zudeck, 1948
Alfred Dickman, 1949
Joseph Weiler, 1950
James Secrest, 1951, 1952, 1953
Gustave Saelens, 1954, 1955
Arthur Lee, 1956, 1957
Martin Connell, 1958
James Secrest, 1959, 1960
Frank Powers, 1961, 1962
Milton Zudeck, 1963, 1964
Gene Ettenberg, 1965, 1966
Edward Gottschall, 1967, 1968
Saadyah Maximon, 1969
Louis Lepis, 1970, 1971
Gerard O'Neill, 1972, 1973
Zoltan Kiss, 1974, 1975
Roy Zucca, 1976, 1977
William Streever, 1978, 1979
Bonnie Hazelton, 1980, 1981
Jack George Tauss, 1982, 1983
Klaus F. Schmidt, 1984, 1985
John Luke, 1986, 1987
Jack Odette, 1988, 1989
Ed Benguiat, 1990, 1991
Allan Haley, 1992, 1993
B. Martin Pedersen, 1994, 1995
Mara Kurtz, 1996, 1997
Mark Solsburg, 1998, 1999
Daniel Pelavin, 2000

TDC Medal Recipients

Hermann Zapf, 1967
R. Hunter Middleton, 1968
Frank Powers, 1971
Dr. Robert Leslie, 1972
Edward Rondthaler, 1975
Arnold Bank, 1979
Georg Trump, 1982
Paul Standard, 1983
Herb Lubalin, 1984 (posthumously)
Paul Rand, 1984
Aaron Burns, 1985
Bradbury Thompson, 1986
Adrian Frutiger, 1987
Freeman Craw, 1988
Ed Benguiat, 1989
Gene Federico, 1991
Lou Dorfsman, 1995
Matthew Carter, 1997
Rolling Stone magazine, 1997
Colin Brignall, 2000
Günter Gerhard Lange, 2000

Special Citations to TDC Members

Edward Gottschall, 1955
Freeman Craw, 1968
James Secrest, 1974
Olaf Leu, 1984, 1990
William Streever, 1984
Klaus F. Schmidt, 1985
John Luke, 1987
Jack Odette, 1989

2000 Scholarship Recipients

Brian J. Hoffer, *The Cooper Union School of Art*
Pei Wen Sharon Goh, *Pratt Institute*
Beom Seok Kim, *School of Visual Arts*
Paul T. Reid, *Art Center College of Design*
Eugene Rogovitz, *Fashion Institute of Technology*
Alejandra Santos, *Parsons School of Design*
Philipp Arnold, *Hochschule für Grafik und Buckkunst Leipzig*

International Liaison Chairpersons

AUSTRALIA
Mark Simkins
Simkins & Smart
Suite 3, 6-7 Gurrigal Street
Mosman, Sydney 2088

ENGLAND
David Farey
HouseStyle Graphics
31 Clerkenwell Close
London EC1R 0AT

FRANCE
Christopher Dubber
Signum Art
94, Avenue Victor Hugo
94100 Saint Maur Des Fosses

GERMANY
Bertram Schmidt-Friderichs
Universitatsdruckerei und Verlag
H. Schmidt GmbH & Co.
Robert Koch Strasse 8
Postfach 42 07 28
55129 Mainz Hechtsheim

JAPAN
Zempaku Suzuki
Japan Typography Association
Sanukin Bldg. 5 Fl.
1-7-10 Nihonbashi-honcho
Chuo-ku, Toyko 104-0041

MEXICO
Prof. Felix Beltran
Apartado de Correos
M 10733 Mexico 06000

SOUTH AMERICA
Diego Vainesman
Punto Sur, Inc.
420 East 79 Street, #4B
New York, New York 10021

SWEDEN
Ernst Dernehl
Dernehl & Son Designers
Box 8073
S-10420 Stockholm

SWITZERLAND
Eric Alb
Syndor Press
Lindenbühl 33
CH 6330 Cham

VIETNAM
Richard Moore
21 Bond Street
New York, NY 10012

Type Directors Club
60 East 42nd Street
Suite 721
New York, NY 10165
212-983-6042 FAX: 212-983-6043
E-mail: director@tdc.org
www.tdc.org

Carol Wahler, Executive Director
For membership information, please contact the Type Directors Club office.

MEMBERS INDEX

A Marcelle Accardi '98s
Debbie Adams '98
Jim Aitchison '93
Eric Alb '96
Jack Anderson '96
Martyn Anstice '92
Don Ariev '98s
Jenna Ashley '97
Jeffrey Austin '98
B Jaques Bagios '95
Peter Bain '86
Boris Balant '99
Bruce Balkin '93
Kevin Balluf '99
Stephen Banham '95
Maria Helena Ferreira Braga Barbosa '93s
David Barrineau '96
Lucy Bartholomay '96
Barbara Baumann '96
Gerd Baumann '95
Clarence Baylis '74
Chris Bean '00
Lisa Beaudoin '96s
Daniel Garcia Becerril '98s
Syndi Becker '96
Felix Beltran '88
Ed Benguiat '64
Anna Berkenbusch '89
John Berry '96
Peter Bertolami '69
Davide Bevilacqua '99
Klaus Bietz '93
Henrik Birvig '96
Roger Black '80
Alan Boarts '96
Barbara A. Boccio '99
Karlheinz Boelling '86
Garrett Boge '83
Matteo Bologna '00
John Bonadies '95
Marguerita Bornstein-Fahrer '96
Gianni Bortolotti '98
Jamie Boyle '99
Patricia Bradbury '93
Fred Brady '97
Bud Braman '90
Ulrike Brenner '99
Ed Brodsky '80
Andreas Brunlinghaus '97s
Bill Bundzak '64
Ulrich Burgdorf '96
Queenie Burns '94
Sara Burris '97
Thomas F. Burroughs '00
Steve Byers '98
C Lynn Cabot-Puris '99
Joanne Cadovius '99s
Casandra Calo '98s
Ronn Campisi '88
Diane Carrier '98
Matthew Carter '88
Steve Cassar '96
Tony Castellano '97
Ken Cato '88
Paul Caullettt '98s
Amy H. N. Chan '96s
Eric Chan '97
Theseus Chan '94
Jennie Chano '99
David Chaves '96
Len Cheeseman '93
David Cheung, Jr. '98
Heung-Heung Chin '98s
Kai-Yan Choi '90
Kyong Choi '96s
Stanley Church '97
Traci Churchill '95
Sheri Cifaldi '97s
John V. Clarke '99
Travis Cliett '53
Graham Clifford '98
Mahlon A. Cline* '48
Tom Cocozza '76
Lisa Cohen '93
Stuart Cohen '96
Angelo Colella '90
Ed Colker '83
Kyle Cooper '97
Rodrigo Corral '98
Madeleine Corson '96
Lynette Cortez '99
Susan Cotler-Block '89
Freeman Craw* '47
Laura Crookston '00
Bart Crosby '95
Ray Cruz '99
Jeff Culver '97s
David Cundy '85
Brian Cunningham '96
Rick Cusick '89
D Michael Damare '98
Ziya Danishmend '00
Susan Darbyshire '87
Richard Dawson '93
Einat Lisa Day '97s
Matej Decko '93
Paige De Leo '98
Josanne De Natale '86
Phil Delbourgo '98
Margi Denton '99
Ernst Dernehl '87
Meir Deutsch '00s
Roberto de Vicq de Cumptich '97
W. Brian Diecks '98
Claude A. Dieterich '84
Joseph DiGioia '96
Jeanette Wilkinson Dill '99
Tom Dolle '95
Jonathan Doney '96
Lou Dorfsman '54
Pascale Dovic '97
Stephen Doyle '98
John Dreyfus** '68
Christopher Dubber '85
Rod Durso '98
Simon Dwelly '98
Lutz Dziarnowski '92
Lasko Dzurovski '00
E Friedrich Eisenmenger '93
Jeani Eismont '96
Lise Ellingson '98s
Dr. Elsi Vassdal Ellis '93
Garry Emery '93
Elke Erschfeld '99
Rafael Esquer '00
Joseph Michael Essex '78
Leslie Evans '92
Florence Everett '89
F John Fahey '98s
Peter Fahrni '93
Joihn Fairley '00
Dug Falby '99
John R. Falker '00
David Farey '93
Michael Farmer '94
Erik Faulhaber '97s
Sean Fermoyle '00
Antero Ferreira '97
Louise Fili '00
Simon Fitton '94
Kristine Fitzgerald '90
Gonçalo Fonseca '93
Wayne Ford '96
Margaret Kane Forgosh '99
Thomas Fowler '93
Alessandro Franchini '96
George Frederick '00
Carol Freed '87
Tobias Frere-Jones '00
Adrian Frutiger ** '67
Mario Fuhr '97
G Christopher Galvin '99s
Christof Gassner '90
Martina Gates '96s
David Gatti '81
Matthew Gaynor '00s
Jeremy Gee '92
Kai Gehrmann '96s
Robyn Gill-Attaway '93
Lou Glassheim * '47
Howard Glener '77
Rüdiger Goetz '95
Carin Goldberg '97
Lorenz Goldnagl '99s
Ronnen Goren '97
Holly Goscinsky '98s
Edward Gottschall '52
Norman Graber '69
Diana Graham '85
Austin Grandjean '59
Stefanie Grashoff '99s
Stephen Green '97
Karen Greenberg '95
Adam Greiss '89
Ariel Grey '00
James Grieshaber '96
Jeff Griffith '91
Frank E.E. Grubich '96
Rosanne Guararra '92
Grace Guarte '00s
Christiane Gude '97
Stefan Guggenbichler '97
Sandra Gulla '00
Olga Gutierrez de la Roza '95s
Einar Gylfason '95
Peter Gyllan '97
H Doug Haden '97
William Hafeman '96
Allan Haley '78
Crystal Hall '97
Debra Hall '96
Egil Haraldsen '00
Keith Harris '98
Theodore Harrison '96
Knut Hartmann '85
Helen Hayes '98
Bonnie Hazelton '75
Jeri Heiden '94
Frank Heine '96
Wild Heinz '96
Earl M. Herrick '96
Klaus Hesse '95
Michael Heu '00s
Eric Heupel '00s
Fons M. Hickmann '96
Jay Higgins '88
Helmut Himmler '96
Norihiko Hirata '96
J. Drew Hodges '95
Michael Hodgson '89
Jonathan Hoefler '00
Fritz Hofrichter '80
Troy Holder '99
Catherine Hollenbeck '93
Roman Holt '99
Kevin Horvath '87
Tonya Hudson '99
Gerard Huerta '85
David Hukari '95
Harvey Hunt '92
I Yanek Iontef '00
Terry Irwin '96
J Donald Jackson ** '78
Michael Jager '94
Mark Jamra '99
Andy Johnson '99
Iskra Johnson '94
Margo Johnson '99
K Otso Kallinen '00
John Kallio '96
Rosanne Kang '98
Kelly Kao '98
Maryann Karr Saggese '96
Carolyn Kaufman '99
Ronan Keane '99
Nan Keeton '97
Brunnette Kenan '99
Kay Khoo '99
Jang Hoon Kim '97s
Linda S. Kim '98
Rick King '93
Richard King '00
Brandie Kirkman '98s
Alexander Knowlton '96
Cynthia Knox '95
Nana Kobayashi '94
Akira Kobayashi '99
Claus Koch '96
Jesse Taylor Koechling '98s
Daniel Kolcinsky '99s
Steve Kopec '74
Matthias Kott '96s
Katharina Kramer '99s
Andrej Krátky '93
Marcus Kraus '97
Philip Krayna '97
Bernhard J. Kress '63

Peter Kruty '99
Christian Kunnert '97
Ralf Kunz '93
Kuang Chun Kuo '97s
Yoshiko Kusaka '97s
L Gerry L'Orange '91
Raymond F. Laccetti '87
Angela Lai '99
John Langdon '93
Günter Gerhard Lange '83
Terje Laneggen '98
Amanda Lawrence '99s
David W. Lecours '99
Susan Jeehoon Lee '97s
David Lemon '95
Herbert Lenzner '99
Olaf Leu '65
Adam Levite '97
Renee Levitt '98s
Richard S. Levy '99
Katherine Leyton '00
Miles Markum Linklater '98
Monica Little '98
Wally Littman '60
Esther Liu '98
Lorena Llaneza '98s
Doug Lockyer '99
Uwe Loesch '96
John Howland Lord ** '47
Alexander Luckow '94
Frank Luedicke '99
Gregg Lukasiewicz '90
Linnea Lundquist '99
M Burns Magruder '00
Monib Mahdavi '96s
Sol Malkoff '63
Marilyn Marcus '79
Ari Mardewi '97s
Marie Mariucci '98
Rosemary Markowsky '98s
David Marshall '98
Frank Martinez '99
Rogério Martins '91
Igor Masnjak '98
Les Mason '85
Michelle Mason '97
Andreas Maxbauer '95
Caroline McAlpine '99
Eileen McCarren '00s
Rod McDonald '95
Marc A. Meadows '96
Donna Meadows Manier '00
Roland Mehler '92
Friederika Meissner '00
Uwe Melichar '00
Dr. Frieder Mellinghoff '99
Jeff Merrells '99
Frédéric Metz '85
David Michaelides '97
Tony Mikolajczyk '97
John Milligan '78
Elena Miranda '97s
Michael Miranda '84
Oswaldo Miranda (Miran) '78
Ralf Mischnick '98s
Dean Mitchell '00
Susan L. Mitchell '96
Michael Moesslang '99
Sakol Mongkolkasetarin '95
James Montalbano '93
Joseph Montebello '96
Christine Moog '99s
Richard Earl Moore '82
Minoru Morita '75
John Michael Morris '98
Tobias Moss * '47
Lars Müller '97
Joachim Müller-Lancé '95
Gary Munch '97
Jerry King Musser '88
Alexander Musson '93
Louis A. Musto '65
Norikazu Nakamura '99s
N Cristiana Neri-Downey '97
Helmut Ness '99
Robert Newman '96
Lillian Ng '00s
Shuichi Nogami '97
Gillian R. Norrie '97a
Robert Norton '92
Alexa Nosal '87
O Richard O'Connell '99
Nicole B. O'Connor '99
Oisin O'Malley '98s
Jack Odette '77
Nina v. Oertzen '99
Akio Okumara '96
Scott Olason '99
Mark Oldach '96
Michel Olivier '94
Hui Ming Ong '00s
Petra Cerne Oren'94
Nancy Ovedovitz '96
Robert Overholtzer '94
P Frank Paganucci '85
Robert Palmer '96
Deborah Pang '99
A. Samantha Panzier '97s
Aubree Pappas '98s
Enrique Pardo '99
Sam Park '98s
Jim Parkinson '94
Guy Pask '97
Babita Patel '99s
Jayesh Patel '97
Jane Patterson '98
Gudrun Pawelke '96
Melanie Paykos '96
Christi Payne '96
B. Martin Pedersen '85
Daniel Pelavin '92
Robert Peters '86
Oanh Pham-Phu '96
Ken Phillips '99
Max Phillips '00
Clive Piercy '96
Ian Pilbeam '99
Margaret Piscitelli '00s
Lisa Powers '96s
Will Powers '89
Vaneerat Pramongkit '99s
Vittorio Prina '88
Richard Price '00
James Propp '97
Richard Puder '85
Q David Quay '80
R Erwin Raith '67
Zeljko Rajacic '99
Renee Ramsey-Passmore '99
Marcus Ratliff '99
Bob Rauchman '97
Marco Ravanetti '99
Jo Anne Redwood '88
Hans Dieter Reichert '92
Liz Reitman '97
James T. Rhoades '99
Erik Ries '00s
Robert Rindler '95
Phillip Ritzenberg '97
Rick Roat '99
Nadine Robbins '95
Eva Roberts '95
Frank Rochell '99
Tim Rolands '96
Salvadore Romero '94
Hoet Ronane '99
Edward Rondthaler* '47
Wendy Ronga '96
Kurt Roscoe '93
Gabriela Rotaru '00s
Gil Rukenstein '00
Paul Rustand '99
Erkki Ruuhinen '86
Timothy J. Ryan '96
Michael Rylander '93
S Gus Saelens '50
Ilja Sallacz '99
David Saltman '66
Ina Saltz '96
Anthony Salvo '96
Diana Salzburg '98
Aleya Anil Samji '98s
Rodrigo Sanchez '96
Susan Sanderson '96
Stephanie Sassola-Struse '97
Frank Sax '94
John Sayles '95
David Saylor '96
Hermann J. Schlieper '87
Holger Schmidhuber '99
Hermann Schmidt '83
Klaus Schmidt '59
Markus Schmidt '93
Bertram Schmidt-Friderichs '89
Michaela Schmied '00s
Helmut Schmitt-Siegel '97
Werner Schneider '87
Geraldine Schoeller '96
Curtis Schreiber '97
Eileen Hedy Schultz '85
Lauren Schultz '98s
Eckehart Schumacher-Gebler '85
Jo Scraba '97s
James Sebastian '95
Enrico Sempi '97
Kathryn Shagas '97
Jessica Shatan '95
Mark E. Shaw '99
Paul Shaw '87
Leslie Sherr '96a
Jieun Shin '99s
Kim Shkapich '97
Philip Shore, Jr. '92
Susan Silton '96
Mark Simkins '92
Scott Simmons '94
Todd Simmons '97
Mae Skidmore '98
Finn Sködt '00
Martha Rice Skogen '99
Pat Sloan '97
James C. Smith '99
Silvestre Segarra Soler '95
Martin Solomon '55
Jan Solpera '85
Mark Solsburg '89
Ronnie Tan Soo Chye '88
Brian Sooy '98
Prof. Erik Spiekermann '88
Rolf Staudt '84
Thomas Stecko '94
Olaf Stein '96
Jennifer Sterling '96
Charles Stewart '92
Sumner Stone '88
William Streever '50
Ilene Strizver '88
Matthew J. Strong '98s
Vance Studley '95
Katja Stuke '97
Hansjorg Stulle '87
Gregor Stute '98s
Melissa Sunjaya '99
Zempaku Suzuki '92
Paul Sych '93
Laurie Szujewska '95
Alicia Szwec '99
T Kan Tai-Keung '97
Douglas Tait '98
Yukichi Takada '95
Hirohiko Takahashi '98
Yoshimaru Takahashi '96
Jack Tauss '75
Lisa Marie Taylor '97
Pat Taylor '85
Anthony J. Teano '62
Ana Teixeira '98s
Regine Thienhaus '96
George H. Thomas '98
Wayne Tidswell '96
Fred Tieken '95
Eric Tilley '95
Colin Tillyer '97
Anton Tilo '98
Eugene Timerman '99
Laura Tolkow '96
Minao Tsukada '00
Klaus Trommer '97
James Tung '97
François Turcotte '99
Michael Tutino '96
V Diego Vainesman '91
Patrick Valleé '99
Christine Van Bree '98
Mark Van Bronkhorst '93
Kevin Van Der Leek '97
Jan Van Der Ploeg '52
Ryan Van Meter '99
Yuri Vargas '99
Ané Vecchione '97s
Anna Villano '99s
Annette Von Brandis '96
Thilo Von Debschitz '95
Alex Voss '98
W Scott Wadler '95
Frank Wagner '94
Allan R. Wahler '98
Jurek Wajdowicz '80
Sergio Waksman '96
Susan Waksmonski '96
Garth Walker '92
Xu Wang '93
Jane Ward '98s
Kurt Watson '99
Jessica Watts '99
Janet Webb '91
Harald Weber '99
Matt Weber '98s
Joy Weeeng '93s
Prof. Kurt Weidemann '66
Claus F. Weidmueller '97
Patrick Weir '99
Judy Wert '96a
Paul Wharton '96
Alex White '93
Scott White '99
Albert L. Whitley, Jr. '98s
Bambang Widodo '98
Richard Wilde '93
James Williams '88
Joseph R. Williams '98s
Tom Williams '00s
Caroline Winata '00s
Carol Winer '94
Conny J.Winter '85
Penina Wissner '96
Delve Withrington '97
Peter C. Wong '96
Anuthin Wongsunkakon '98s
Peter Wood '97
Jon Woodhams '00
Fred Woodward '95
Laura Coe Wright '99
Y Chien Hui Yang '98s
Lynn Yeo '98s
Ronald Yeung '00
Doyald Young '96
Z Hermann Zapf ** '52
Maxim Zhukov '96
Roy Zucca '69
Jeff Zwerner '97

Sustaining Members

Adobe Systems, Inc. '90
Agfa/Monotype '96
Galapagos Design Group, Inc. '96

* Charter member
** Honorary member
s Student member
a Associate member

Membership as of May 22, 2000

TYPE INDEX

GENERAL INDEX

TDC 46
TDC² 2000

Exhibition
June 21 –
September 8

Parsons School of Design

SUSAN COTLER-BLOCK
FASHION INSTITUTE OF TECHNOLOGY

MAXIM ZHUKOV
UNITED NATIONS

Parsons School of Design

TDC 46
TDC² 2000

Exhibition
June 21 –
September 8

TDC 46
TDC² 2000

Exhibition
June 21 –
September 8